STYLE AND STRUCTURE

IN

BIBLICAL HEBREW NARRATIVE

STYLE AND STRUCTURE

IN

BIBLICAL HEBREW NARRATIVE

Jerome T. Walsh

A Michael Glazier Book
THE LITURGICAL PRESS
Collegeville, Minnesota

www.litpress.org

A Michael Glazier Book published by The Liturgical Press

Cover design by Ann Blattner. Photo: Corbis Digital Stock.

1   2   3   4   5   6   7   8

Library of Congress Cataloging-in-Publication Data

Walsh, Jerome T., 1942–
    Style and structure in Biblical Hebrew narrative / Jerome T. Walsh.
      p. cm.
    "A Michael Glazier book."
    Includes bibliographical references and index.
    ISBN 0-8146-5897-0 (alk. paper)
    1. Bible. O.T.—Criticism, Narrative. 2. Narration in the Bible. 3. Hebrew
language—Style. 4. Bible as literature. I. Title.

BS1182.3 .W35 2001
221.6'6—dc21

00-057469

In memory of
J.-P. A.
1962–1995
"like a pearl on dark brown velvet"

CONTENTS

List of Abbreviations   xiii

Introduction   1

Part I: Structures of Organization

Symmetry and asymmetry   7
Repeated elements   8
Organizing elements and organized units   10
Balance of subunits   11
Interpretation   11

1. Reverse Symmetry   13

A. Concentric symmetry   15
1. *Numbers 12:13*   15
2. *1 Kings 1:33-35*   15
3. *Leviticus 24:13-23*   16
4. *Jonah 1*   18
5. *2 Chronicles 25:1-28*   20
6. *Genesis 2:4b–3:24*   21
7. *1 and 2 Kings*   23
8. *1 Kings 1:1–2:12a*   25

B. Chiastic symmetry   26
1. *1 Kings 19:14*   26
2. *Genesis 12:16b*   27
3. *Genesis 9:6a*   27
4. *1 Kings 21:1-16*   28
5. *2 Kings 8:7–9:13*   29
6. *1 Chronicles 11:1–12:41*   30
7. *Genesis 25:12–35:26*   31

2. Forward Symmetry   35
      1. Genesis 1:1; Genesis 1:1-31   37
      2. 1 Kings 11:1-8   38
      3. Genesis 2:18-25   39
      4. 1 Kings 11:31-39   41
      5. 2 Kings 9:14–11:20   43

3. Alternating Repetition   47
      1. 1 Kings 2:36-46a   48
      2. Genesis 12:1   49
      3. 1 Samuel 1:12-13   50
      4. 1 Kings 20:16-21   50
      5. 2 Kings 17:6-41   52
      6. 1 Samuel 8:1–12:25   54

4. Partial Symmetry   57
    Inclusion   57
    Epitome   59

    A. Internal inclusion   60
      1. 1 Kings 2:38b, 41   60
      2. 1 Kings 1:24-27   61
      3. Esther 5:9-14   61
      4. Ruth 4:9-11a   63

    B. Framing inclusion   64
      1. 1 Kings 2:12b, 46b   64
      2. Genesis 18:16, 22   65
      3. 1 Samuel 15:10-12, 34-35   65
      4. 1 Kings 12:30-31; 13:33-34   67
      5. 1 Kings 6:1–9:10   68

    C. External inclusion   69
      1. 2 Samuel 14:24, 28   69
      2. Genesis 37:36; 39:1   70
      3. Exodus 6:10-13, 26-30   71

    D. Complex inclusion   73
      1. 1 Kings 4:1-20, 21-25   73
      2. Genesis 1   74
      3. Regnal formulas   74

    E. Introductory epitome   76
      1. Genesis 10:1   76
      2. 1 Kings 18:1   77

F. Concluding epitome   78
    1. Genesis 2:1   78
    2. Exodus 3:14-15   78

5. Multiple Symmetry   81

  A. Composite symmetry   82
    1. 1 Kings 5:1-12   82
    2. 1 Kings 6:9-36   84
    3. 2 Kings 18–20   85

  B. Complex symmetry   88
    1. Ruth 1–4   88
    2. Genesis 11:27–22:24   89
    3. 1 Kings 1–11   92

  C. Compound symmetry   94
    1. Genesis 11:1-9   94
    2. 2 Kings 17:25-34a   96
    3. 2 Kings 21:19-26   97

6. Asymmetry   101

  A. Unmatched subunit   103
    1. 1 Kings 2:39   103
    2. 1 Kings 18:9-14   103
    3. Genesis 1:26-28   105
    4. Genesis 21:1-7   106

  B. Non-correspondence   107
    1. 2 Kings 2:25   107
    2. 1 Kings 1:33-35   108
    3. 1 Kings 11:31-39   108

  C. Transposition   110
    1. Exodus 6:10-13, 26-30   110
    2. Genesis 1–11   111
    3. 1 Kings 3:16–4:34; 9:26–10:29   113

Part II: Structures of Disjunction

7. Narrative Components   119

  Characters   120
  Setting: locale   122
  Setting: time   122
  Narrative voice   124

A. Change in characters   125
    1. *1 Kings 2:1-10*   125
    2. *2 Kings 7:3-11*   126
    3. *1 Kings 1:15-37*   128
    4. *Ruth 2:1–3:18*   129
    5. *1 Kings 18:21-40*   131

B. Change in setting: locale   132
    1. *2 Kings 10:12-17*   132
    2. *2 Kings 18–20*   132
    3. *Genesis 18*   133
    4. *1 Kings 18:6-16*   134
    5. *Numbers 20:22–21:20*   135

C. Change in setting: time   135
    1. *Genesis 24*   135
    2. *1 Kings 2:39*   138
    3. *Genesis 22:4*   139
    4. *2 Kings 18:13*   139
    5. *1 Kings 18:3-4*   139

D. Change in narrative voice   140
    1. *1 Kings 18:12c-13*   140
    2. *1 Kings 21:20-26*   141
    3. *1 Kings 3:16-28*   141

8. Repetition   145

A. Repetition of information   147
    1. *Genesis 5:32; 6:9-10*   147
    2. *2 Kings 8:28–9:2; 9:14-16*   148
    3. *1 Samuel 17:12a*   149

B. Repetition of subject nouns   150
    1. *Genesis 21:25*   150
    2. *1 Kings 12:26*   150
    3. *1 Chronicles 14:3b*   151

C. Interruptions of discourse   152
    1. *Exodus 5:4-5*   152
    2. *Exodus 3:14-15*   152
    3. *1 Kings 22:28b*   153

9. Narrative Sequence   155

Narrative tense and simple past   155
Breaks in narrative sequence   157

The verb "to be" and verbless clauses   159

A. Broken narrative sequence beginning a unit   160

    1. *Genesis 3:1*   160
    2. *Genesis 18:17*   160
    3. *Exodus 3:1*   160
    4. *Genesis 4:1-2*   161
    5. *Jonah 1:4*   162
    6. *Genesis 39:1-6*   162

B. Broken narrative sequence ending a unit   162

    1. *Genesis 1*   162
    2. *Genesis 2:25*   163
    3. *1 Samuel 15:34*   163
    4. *1 Kings 18:6b*   163
    5. *1 Kings 17*   164
    6. *2 Samuel 18:18*   165

C. Broken narrative sequence interrupting a unit   166

    1. *Ruth 1:14b*   166
    2. *Jonah 1:10b*   166
    3. *Genesis 23:10a*   167
    4. *1 Kings 13:1-10*   168
    5. *Genesis 41:47–42:5*   169

Part III: Structures of Conjunction

A. Threads   177

    1. *Genesis 2:4b–3:24; 4:1-16*   177
    2. *1 Kings 1–11*   178
    3. *Judges 17–21*   179
    4. *1 Kings 13*   179
    5. *Genesis 18–19*   180

B. Links   182

    1. *Genesis 2:25; 3:1*   182
    2. *1 Kings 20:43; 21:4*   182
    3. *2 Kings 2:25; 3:1*   182
    4. *Judges 8:33; 9:4*   183
    5. *Ezra 3:13; 4:1*   183
    6. *Genesis 16:16; 17:1*   183

C. Linked threads   184

    1. *1 Kings 12:25*   184
    2. *Ruth 1:22*   184

        3. *Regnal formulas*   184
        4. *Between books*   185
        5. *1 Kings 1–2*   186

   D. Hinges   186
        1. *Genesis 26:33-35; 27:1*   186
        2. *Genesis 2:4*   187
        3. *Genesis 23:1–25:11*   187

   E. Double-duty hinges   188
        1. *2 Kings 17:6*   188
        2. *2 Kings 2:15b*   188
        3. *1 Kings 11:26-43*   189

Conclusion   191

Selected Bibliography   195

Author Index   199

Subject Index   200

Scripture Index   202

LIST OF ABBREVIATIONS

AJSL	*American Journal of Semitic Languages and Literatures*
AnOr	Analecta Orientalia
Bib	*Biblica*
CBQ	*The Catholic Biblical Quarterly*
CBQMS	The Catholic Biblical Quarterly Monograph Series
FF	Foundations and Facets
GBS.OT	Guides to Biblical Scholarship: Old Testament Series
HUCA	*Hebrew Union College Annual*
IJS	Institute for Jewish Studies
Int	*Interpretation*
JBL	*Journal of Biblical Literature*
JJS	*Journal of Jewish Studies*
JSOT	*Journal for the Study of the Old Testament*
JSOTSup	Journal for the Study of the Old Testament Supplement Series
LB	*Linguistica Biblica*
MT	Masoretic Text (= Hebrew Bible)
NRSV	New Revised Standard Version
OTL	Old Testament Library
OtSt	*Oudtestamentische Studiën*
PTMS	Pittsburgh Theological Monograph Series

SBLMS	Society of Biblical Literature Monograph Series
SSN	Studia Semitica Neerlandica
VT	*Vetus Testamentum*
VTSup	Supplements to Vetus Testamentum
ZAW	*Zeitschrift für die alttestamentliche Wissenschaft*

INTRODUCTION

Everyone likes a good story. In every culture and in every age, from childhood bedtime stories to the reminiscences of elders, we capture our world in words and distill it in story. Storytelling—the urge to narrative—is a human universal. Yet individual *stories* are inexorably particular. They are the product of a particular time and a particular culture. Only the very greatest narratives travel on their own merits across the deep cultural and temporal chasms of the world. And even when they do, they arrive in the form of translations that are admixtures of faithful transmission and creative achievement.

Above all else, an individual story is the product of a particular language. A narrative is, in the last analysis, words: storytelling builds worlds, and characters, and actions, out of vocabulary and syntax—nothing more, nothing less. To appreciate any story in its wholeness, we must fathom its words—their sounds, their meanings, their connotations, their collocations, their allusions. And when we read a story in translation, we are utterly dependent upon the translator, whose perceptiveness and penetration of the verbal weave is the limiting precondition of our own access to the original. This book is intended primarily for people who read the Hebrew Bible in translation (though I hope that even those who read it in Hebrew may find something of interest here as well). It is an attempt to explore a few of the ways in which the creators of biblical Hebrew narrative use words, in order to highlight for the English Bible reader significant literary elements of biblical narratives that may otherwise be obscured in translation.

Well-built, compelling narrative worlds arise from well-constructed tales. We shall study a few of the construction techniques, so to speak, of the ancient Hebrew authors. Specifically, we shall look at the ways in which biblical Hebrew handles the building blocks—the literary units and subunits—out of which it constructs its narratives. How does it mark the boundaries between those units? This is an important question, since literary units and subunits (like paragraphs, episodes, scenes, or chapters in modern English literature) are usually thematic units and subunits as well. How does it establish continuity and connection between contiguous units? Without such connections a narrative lacks coherent flow and compelling momentum, and risks disintegration and loss of reader interest. Most importantly, how does biblical Hebrew narrative organize its literary units and subunits internally? Here we will enter unfamiliar territory, for the techniques used by biblical Hebrew narrative are quite different from those we are accustomed to in English literature. We shall see that discerning the inner shape of a literary unit often starts us on the road to insightful interpretation.

We will begin with this last question, since its unfamiliarity will require the lengthiest treatment. Part I of our study will examine a wide variety of symmetrical patterns biblical Hebrew narrative uses to organize its units and subunits, and the interpretive dynamics those patterns can imply. In each case we will begin with a brief description of the pattern and its characteristics, and follow this with analyses of extensive examples of the pattern. Part II will address the question of boundaries between literary units. The treatment here will be shorter, since in many cases biblical Hebrew marks boundaries in ways similar to English narrative. There are, however, one or two peculiarly Hebrew ways of marking boundaries, and we will have to dabble a bit in the Hebrew language to appreciate them. As in Part I, brief treatments of the technique in general terms will precede several examples. I hope that the examples will clarify the discussion of the arcana of Hebrew grammar—or at least earn me the readers' forgiveness for forcing them to slog through it! Finally, and briefest of all, Part III will examine devices that biblical Hebrew narrative uses to connect consecutive literary units and subunits. Somewhat similar devices occur in English literature, although they are not commonly discussed; consequently, once they are described and illustrated, the reader will discern them relatively easily. The approach here will remain the same: brief explanations in general terms followed by a number of examples.

I would be remiss if I did not acknowledge a scholar whose ideas, many years ago, started me on the road that has led eventually to this book: H. Van Dyke Parunak. For a brief time our paths crossed at the University of Michigan. Articles that he wrote at that time stimulated my thinking enormously, and this book has been in gestation ever since. For inspiration, as well as for continued support and friendship over the years, I am grateful to him. What I have done with that inspiration, for better or worse, is my own responsibility. But the originating insights are his.

I am also grateful to the University of Botswana and to Union Theological Seminary in New York. Mr. Drew Kadel of the UTS library graciously extended guest privileges to me during my research stays in New York, and the interlibrary loan staff at UB went beyond the call of duty in procuring otherwise unavailable material for me from all over southern Africa.

Finally, I dedicate this study of story to the memory of one whose study, and whose story, were cut tragically too short.

PART I

STRUCTURES OF ORGANIZATION

Repetition is the most common formal device for organizing a literary unit in biblical Hebrew prose.[1] Repetition, of course, can serve many literary functions in a prose text: repeated words or themes (e.g., keywords or leitmotifs) can unify a passage, create emphasis, or delay action and create suspense.[2] In none of these cases, however, does the repetition necessarily provide the passage with an overall structure. Part I of our study will focus on those cases in which repetition *is* used to organize the parts of a literary unit symmetrically.[3] In this section we must consider issues touching repetition in general; the following sections will examine the various symmetrical patterns that occur as structuring devices in biblical Hebrew narrative.

Symmetry and asymmetry

In two- and three-dimensional visual patterns symmetry refers to correspondence of parts in size and position about an axis. By extension, the term is applied to literary passages whose subunits correspond in length and placement. As in visual symmetry, most often two sets of corresponding subunits are arranged about a center; occasionally

[1] In poetry, other formal devices occur with some frequency as well. Acrostic psalms (e.g., Lamentations 1–4; Psalm 119) are structured by the order of letters in the Hebrew alphabet; numerical poems (e.g., Prov 30:15b-16, 18-19, 21-23, 29-31) by the higher of the x, x+1 numbers with which they begin.

[2] See Robert Alter, *The Art of Biblical Narrative* (New York: Basic Books, 1981), especially 88–113; Shimon Bar-Efrat, *Narrative Art in the Bible* (Sheffield: Almond, 1989); Adele Berlin, *Poetics and Interpretation of Biblical Narrative* (Sheffield: Almond, 1983); Jacob Licht, *Storytelling in the Bible* (Jerusalem: Magnes, 1978); Meir Sternberg, *The Poetics of Biblical Narrative: Ideological Literature and the Drama of Reading* (Bloomington, Ind.: Indiana University Press, 1987). All have extensive and insightful discussions of the uses of repetition.

[3] H. Van Dyke Parunak has shown that this structural use of repetition has its origins in the dominance of oral over written communication in the culture that produced the Hebrew Bible. See his "Some Axioms for Literary Architecture," *Semitics* 8 (1982) 1–16.

more elaborate examples, with three or more sets of correspondences, are found. Correspondence between subunits is effected by repeated elements, and the pattern is schematized by using letters to refer to each subunit: ABCΛ'B'C' or ABCDC'B'A', for instance. The possible variations of symmetrical patterning afford the biblical Hebrew narrator a flexible tool not only for integrating and organizing a literary unit, but for directing the reader's interpretive attention as well.[4] The interpretive impact is twofold. First, structural units are often thematic units (like paragraphs in English prose) or dramatic ones (like scenes). To the degree that symmetrical patterning enables us to discern the extent and limits of a literary unit it can provide clues to the thematic structure of the passage. Second, as we shall see, different forms of symmetry tend toward different interpretive dynamics: reinforcement and intensification, comparison, contrast, reversal, and so forth.

One variation of symmetry deserves particular mention. Hebrew narrative will sometimes violate an otherwise symmetrical pattern with an insertion, deletion, or other disturbance of the patterned regularity. The clearer the fundamental symmetry and the more obtrusive the disturbance, the more the asymmetrical element draws a reader's attention. This gives asymmetry great potential as a literary tool. We will explore this in a separate section.

Repeated elements

In principle, repetition can involve any element, from phonemes (i.e., sounds: alliteration, assonance, and the like) to large, thematically coherent units. In practice, phonemic repetition is more typical of poetry than of prose. At particularly significant junctures, however, Hebrew narrative prose may take on more properly prosodic characteristics such as balance, parallelism, rhythm, and sound patterning. Phonemic repetition, then, does occur in prose, but as an organizing device it is relatively rare; only a few examples will figure in the discussions that follow.

---

[4] In past generations a few scholars studied the use of symmetry in the Bible, but only in recent years has it become a topic of widespread interest. See, in the bibliography, the studies by J. A. Bengel, Thomas Boys, E. W. Bullinger, D. A. Dorsey, John Forbes, John Jebb, N. W. Lund, Roland Meynet, and Victor Wilson. The books of Dorsey and Wilson became available to me only after the completion of this work. Both books show clearly how the analysis of the surface structure of biblical Hebrew texts is reaching new maturity. Wilson analyzes selected texts (predominantly narrative) from both testaments; Dorsey examines each book of the Hebrew Bible. In the main, their identification of symmetries is judicious and is put to effective use in interpretation.

It is more common in prose for repeated roots, words, word pairs,[5] and whole phrases to appear as structuring elements. The efficacy of such repetitions as structuring devices depends upon the likelihood that they will be perceived, at least unconsciously, by an attentive reader or hearer. Several factors influence this likelihood. The more extensive the repetition and the closer together the repeated elements, the more evident it is. Exact repetition is striking, but approximate repetition can be effective as well. Forms of the same word (e.g., *melek,* "king" and *mělākîm,* "kings") are easier to perceive as repetitions than are different words related to the same root (e.g., *melek* and *yimlōk,* "he shall rule as king"). Words or forms that are aurally or orthographically similar, including paronomasias, are more likely to be perceived as repetitions than are words, even forms of the same word, that are quite different (e.g., the echo of *māh-lāk,* "What is the matter with you?" and *mālak,* "he has become king," is more evident to both eye and ear than that of *nātan,* "he gave" and *bětittěkā,* "when you gave"). Repetitions of conceptually significant words (e.g., nouns, verbs) are more noticeable than those of ordinary conjunctions, prepositions, and the like. Repetitions of less common words (e.g., *nāgîd,* "ruler"), including unusual conjunctions and prepositions, are more striking than those of more common words (e.g., *melek,* "king").

Repeated syntactic elements such as grammatical forms, word order, length and complexity of sentences, and the like can sometimes establish correspondence between subunits. For instance, Hebrew narrative regularly uses a particular word order and a particular verb form, called the "consecutive," to indicate that the events being narrated flow sequentially.[6] Use of a different order and form indicates some sort of break in the flow (for example a flashback, simultaneity, insertion of background information, or the like). Such breaks are unusual enough that their repetition can effect a link between two subunits, especially if those subunits are relatively short and close together.

"Thematic" or "conceptual" repetition, i.e., repetition that involves similarity of thought without any similarity of language, is more difficult to identify and assess. That it occurs is beyond question. The use of

---

[5] "Word pairs" are common words that occur frequently in combination with each other, either as a fixed phrase ("ups and downs"; "room and board") or as regularly associated terms like "lightning" and "thunder." Often the words are similar in meaning ("family and friends") or diametrically opposed ("night and day"). The literatures of several ancient Semitic languages, including biblical Hebrew, use such pairs of words as corresponding structural components. The technique has been studied by a number of scholars, and long lists of such word pairs have been identified. See, in the bibliography, the studies of Avishur and Dahood.

[6] See the discussion of "narrative sequence" in Part II, below.

stereotyped word pairs (e.g., "justice" and "righteousness"; "heaven" and "earth"; see note 5) is one example; synonymous and antithetic parallelism in Hebrew poetry is another. But identification of a structure solely or primarily on the basis of conceptual repetition runs the risk of relying too heavily on subjective judgment to be convincing. Where thematic repetition involves stereotyped word pairs attested elsewhere in the Hebrew Bible the risk is lessened. Where it does not, as is frequently the case in large-scale structures, other, more objectively demonstrable repeated elements are essential to support the structural analysis.

Organizing elements and organized units

Repetition can occur on any level of a text, from the smallest sound patterns to large thematic units that encompass several biblical books. There is a congruence between the repeated elements, the subunits they mark, and the scope of the whole unit they organize. In general, the smaller the repeated element, the more limited the unit it can organize. Phonemic repetition, for example, can mark a syllable and can unify and structure a phrase or a clause, but it is unlikely to be the principal organizing device in a lengthy scene. A single word may mark a sentence or two, and even be a leitmotif through a scene, but the repetition of single words is unlikely to be the main organizing device in a literary unit comprising several chapters. This is hardly surprising since, as was noted above, the efficacy of repetition depends upon the likelihood that it will be perceived. As literary units increase in scope, the memorability of smaller repeated elements fades as they are submerged in the wealth of textual data and the narrative complexity with which the reader must cope.

It is on larger levels of organization, therefore, that thematic or conceptual repetition becomes more decisive. When we look for the structure of a literary unit of several chapters or longer we have no choice but to resort to major themes as the principal organizing device. It is essential in doing so not to misconstrue or misrepresent the thematic content of a subunit in order to manufacture an echo. Themes should be central to their subunit, and they should be expressed to the extent possible in vocabulary used in the text itself. This is the point at which subjective judgment is most influential and at the same time most inescapable. The analyst can do little more than present his or her conscientious readings to others in the hope that others' judgment will provide the critical control the text itself does not afford.

Balance of subunits

Corresponding subunits in the overall structure of the literary unit will be of comparable size, but that "comparability" can take different forms. There is often a very approximate equivalence in length, such that a subunit of one or two verses is unlikely to correspond to a subunit of twenty verses. More fundamental than approximate equivalence, however, is relative equivalence in terms of the overall structure. In other words, in a structure ABB'A', most often A and A' will be approximately equal in length, as will B and B'; but sometimes the equivalence is only proportional: if AB is notably longer than B'A', then A and B will each be proportionately longer than A' and B'. Occasionally the equivalence is looser still, such that the most one can say is that if A is longer than B, then A' will be longer than B'. Since equivalence of length is another form of repetition, the connection of corresponding subunits is strengthened by their equivalent length. Conversely, the looser the equivalence in length, the stronger must be other connective elements to support the correspondence. Where two subunits are considerably disparate in length they are unlikely to be perceived as corresponding unless there are strong patterns of verbal repetition.

Interpretation

Prose narrative naturally expects linear reading, i.e., progressive reading from one subunit to the next (e.g., from A to B, etc.) as the story unfolds through the text. Symmetrically organized narrative offers additional avenues for interpretive access as well. For instance, in a symmetrical structure certain positions (ends, centers) are often points of greater emphasis. Further, symmetry invites two levels of intratextual comparison. We can juxtapose corresponding units (e.g., A and A'), and we can consider corresponding sequences before and after the center (e.g., in a passage organized ABCA'B'C' we can compare the entire sequence ABC to the entire sequence A'B'C').[7] As we will see below, different symmetrical patterns make different use of these comparisons.

---

[7] Earlier scholars used the term "panel" to refer to one of the sets of corresponding subunits. The term derives from visual art, where it refers to the two matching halves of a diptych. Since, as we shall see, some forms of literary symmetry can involve three or more sets of subunits, a broader term like "sequence" seems preferable.

1. REVERSE SYMMETRY

Reverse symmetry (sometimes called "envelope symmetry") is the commonest symmetrical pattern in biblical Hebrew narrative.[1] It obtains when corresponding elements occur in reverse order on either side of the center of the structure; in other words, the first element corresponds to the last, the second to the second last, and so on. There are two varieties of reverse symmetry, one whose center comprises a single element, the other a balanced pair. A single-centered structure, e.g., ABCB'A', is called "concentric"; a double-centered structure, e.g, ABCC'B'A', is called "chiastic."[2] In practice it is occasionally difficult to determine whether a reverse symmetry is chiastic or concentric. When the central subunit(s) can be analyzed either as a single literary unit with a complex

---

[1] In recent decades numerous books and articles have contributed to the unearthing of envelope structures in the biblical text, following the lead of such earlier scholars as Nils Lund, *Chiasmus in the New Testament* (Chapel Hill: University of North Carolina Press, 1942). Unfortunately, not all of these efforts have been well thought through. There are signs that this phase of relatively untrammeled experimentation is being tamed by the identification of sober guidelines that can help the interpreter determine when a structure is solidly rooted in the text and when it is more likely the product of his or her own imagination. See, in the bibliography, the works of Bar-Efrat ("Some Observations"), Boda, Butterworth, Clark, Dorsey (especially pp. 33–35), and Watson.

[2] The word derives from the Greek letter "chi," which is shaped like an X. When one connects the corresponding elements of a simple, two-line passage like

He made <u>three thousand</u> <u>proverbs</u>

and of <u>songs</u> <u>a thousand and five</u> (1 Kings 4:32 [Heb 5:12]), structure or as two corresponding units, a certain degree of subjective judgment is inevitable. See, for example, the discussion of 1 Kings 1:1–2:12a below.

Interpretation of a passage that exhibits reverse symmetry must consider corresponding subunits as well as the entire sequence before and after the center. In many cases comparison reveals contrast. When one considers corresponding subunits the contrast is generally between states or single actions: the situation in subunit B will be reversed in subunit B' (high to low, rich to poor, alive to dead, etc.). In whole sequences, however, the plot itself often runs in opposite directions: a process of growth, success, victory becomes a process of disintegration, failure, defeat, or vice versa.

The turning point regularly, though not always, is found in the central subunit(s). These are generally, therefore, the most important part of the whole structure (though often not the longest). The importance of the center is more marked in concentric narrative than in chiastic, although here too the central pair of subunits may receive greater emphasis than others and will frequently encompass the actions on which the plot turns.

There are other points of emphasis as well, though this is less consistent than the emphasis on central subunits. The first and last subunits of a reverse symmetry often receive stronger emphasis than other subunits. Sometimes, in a concentric pattern, there is an explicit or implicit link between these outermost subunits and the central one. Moreover, in a concentric structure whose sequences preceding and following the central subunit contain an odd number of members (not counting the center), the central subunit of each sequence is sometimes more significant than the others (see, for example, Jonah 1, below).

The examples that follow begin with those in which the repeated elements and the corresponding subunits they mark are small (e.g., phonemes marking words, words marking phrases and clauses), and conclude with those in which they are longer.

---

the resulting figure is an "X." Some scholars would therefore restrict the term "chiastic" to double-centered symmetries that comprise only four elements (ABB'A'). Others would apply it much more broadly, to all reverse symmetries, including single-centered structures. However, the distinction between single- and double-centered envelope structures holds greater promise for interpretation than the distinction between those of four elements and all others. Consequently I will use "chiastic" to mean double-centered structures and "concentric" to mean single-centered ones.

A. CONCENTRIC SYMMETRY

1. Numbers 12:13[3]

In Numbers 12 Aaron and Miriam complain against Moses, and YHWH rebukes them both. Miriam, however, is punished further; she contracts a case of "leprosy."[4] At Aaron's behest, Moses prays for her healing. The sounds and words of his prayer are concentric: *ʾēl nāʾ rĕpāʾ nāʾ lāh*. A literal translation would be: "God please heal please her." The *l* that is repeated in the outermost syllables is their only audible consonant;[5] the second and second-last syllables are repetitions of the word *nāʾ*, "please." The entire sentence centers on the word *rĕpāʾ*, the imperative verb "heal."

The line opposes God *(ʾēl)* and Miriam *(lāh*, "her"), punisher and punished, and centers on the reversal of the relationship between them, from punishment to healing *(rĕpāʾ)*. The reversal is mediated by Moses' repeated entreaty *(nāʾ*, "please").

2. 1 Kings 1:33-35

David, old and infirm (see 1 Kings 1:1-4), is nonetheless capable of impressive rhetorical style. His speech contains three parts: an introductory command to Nathan, Zadok, and Benaiah; a series of seven commands outlining the ceremony of inauguration for his son Solomon; and a reprise of the two-part statement that acts as a leitmotif throughout the chapter (see vv. 13, 17, 20, 24, 27, etc.). The second part is concentrically arranged:

A. [33]You shall mount Solomon upon my own mule.
B.   You shall lead him down to the Gihon spring.
C.   [34]There Zadok the priest and Nathan the prophet shall anoint him king over Israel.
D.   You shall sound the trumpet.
C'.   You shall say, "Long live King Solomon!"
B'.   [35]You shall come up after him.
A'. He shall sit upon my throne, and he shall reign in my stead.

---

[3] See also Jacob Milgrom's similar analysis in *Numbers* (Philadelphia: Jewish Publication Society, 1990) 98.

[4] As scholars have long pointed out, biblical "leprosy" refers to a variety of skin disorders such as psoriasis, eczema, and others, but almost certainly does *not* refer to Hansen's disease.

[5] The Hebrew consonant aleph *(ʾ)* is, for all practical purposes, silent. The final *h* on *lāh* is likewise silent, just as it would be in English.

The concentric structure is not simply a secondary function of the natural order of events. This is shown by the verbal and conceptual links between corresponding clauses ("being seated" in A and A'; "lead down / come up after" in B and B'; "king" in C and C'). It is shown even more forcefully by a comparison of the two later accounts of the same ceremony, the narrator's description in 1:38-40 and Jonathan's in 1:44-46, neither of which has any trace of concentric organization.

Differently from many other concentric structures, the emphasis on the central element seems misplaced here. Surely the anointing of Solomon is more important than the trumpet blast. In the larger context, however, the sound of the trumpet is the thread of continuity that carries the reader from Solomon's ceremony at Gihon (1:39) to the festivities of the doomed Adonijah at nearby En Rogel (1:41). Similarly there is little sense of contrast in the situations preceding and following the trumpet, but rather a sense of continuity. In the larger context, however, David's speech marks the turning point of the whole chapter. From the moment the moribund David takes this decisive action, Adonijah's fortunes tumble and Solomon's are in the ascendant.

3. Leviticus 24:13-23[6]

While the legal corpora of the Hebrew Bible are not, strictly speaking, narrative, they are nevertheless embedded in narrative prose contexts. This formal declaration of the law of talion, for instance, occurs in a scene where YHWH commands Moses and the community to action (24:13) and the action is duly carried out (24:23). (The translation is literal, and most of the verbal repetition in corresponding subunits of the Hebrew text is retained and underlined in the translation.)

A. [13]YHWH spoke to <u>Moses,</u> saying:
B.   [14]"Take the <u>mocker outside the camp</u>.
       All who heard will lay their hands on his head,
       and the whole congregation will <u>stone him</u>.

---

[6] John Forbes, *The Symmetrical Structure of Scripture, or, The Principles of Scripture Parallelism Exemplified in an Analysis of the Decalogue, the Sermon on the Mount, and Other Passages of the Sacred Writings* (Edinburgh: T & T Clark, 1854) treats vv. 16-22 as chiastic, and cites Thomas Boys, *A Key to the Psalms* (London: L. B. Seely & Sons, 1825) 41. (Unfortunately I have not been able to locate a copy of Boys's work.) The passage has also been studied by Lund, *Chiasmus in the New Testament* 57, who recognizes the concentric structure; by J. P. Fokkelman in *Narrative Art in Genesis: Specimens of Stylistic and Structural Analysis* (2d ed.; Sheffield: JSOT Press, 1991) 33; and by Yehuda T. Radday, "Chiasmus in Hebrew Biblical Narrative," in John W. Welch, ed., *Chiasmus in Antiquity: Structures, Analyses, Exegesis* (Hildesheim: Gerstenberg, 1981) 87.

C.   ¹⁵You shall <u>speak to the Israelites,</u> saying:

D.   'Each and every one, when they mock their <u>god,</u>
            shall bear responsibility for their own sin.
            ¹⁶But whoever blasphemes the name of Y<small>HWH</small> shall be put to
            death.

E.   The whole congregation shall stone such a one: <u>alien and
                citizen alike,</u>
                one who blasphemes the Name shall be put to death.

F.   ¹⁷Anyone, when he <u>kills a human</u> life, <u>shall be put to
                    death.</u>

G.   ¹⁸Whoever <u>kills a beast</u>'s life <u>shall make restitution,</u>
                        live beast for live beast.

H.   ¹⁹Anyone, when he <u>injures</u> another,
                            <u>as</u> he gave, <u>so</u> he is to be given—

I.   ²⁰fracture for fracture,
                                eye for eye
                                tooth for tooth—

H'.   <u>As</u> he <u>injured</u> a person, <u>so</u> he is to be <u>injured.</u>

G'.   ²¹Whoever <u>kills a beast shall make restitution.</u>

F'.   Whoever <u>kills a human shall be put to death.</u>

E'.   ²²You shall have one law,
                it shall be for <u>alien and citizen alike,</u>

D'.   For I am Y<small>HWH</small>, your <u>God.</u>'"

C'.   ²³And Moses <u>spoke to the Israelites.</u>

B'.   And they <u>took</u> the <u>mocker outside the camp,</u>
        and they <u>stoned him</u> with rocks.

A'. The Israelites did as Y<small>HWH</small> had commanded <u>Moses.</u>

The entire unit is concentric, but it is complex. Its central part is the articulation of the law of talion (subunits D through D'), cast as a speech Moses is to deliver, whose formulation is given him by Y<small>HWH</small>. The speech is surrounded by a frame that involves both direct discourse and narrative. The frame presents a case study of the application of the law enunciated in the center. The two parts are best considered separately.

Although no single subunit of the central section stands in contrast to its corresponding subunit, the entire structure pivots around subunit I, the most memorable and most laconic formulation of the law of talion, whose essence is a classic reversal: "the punishment fits the crime." The first and last subunits focus on the name of Y<small>HWH</small>: in D its sanctity is protected by capital law; in D' it is proclaimed by Y<small>HWH</small> himself. The sequences before and after the center have an odd number of members, and the center of each sequence (F, F') has special significance: the capital penalty for human murder.

The frame situates the legal formula in a narrative setting, the divinely decreed punishment of one who has "blasphemed" the Name (presumably of YHWH) and "mocked" (24:10-12). The "mocker" was a man born of an Egyptian father and an Israelite mother, but he had left Egypt with the Israelites. This raises some ambiguity: should he be treated as an alien or a citizen? The formulation of the law rules this ambiguity out as irrelevant and imposes capital punishment (subunits D, E and E').[7]

4. *Jonah 1*[8]

Between a narrative prologue (1:1-3) and a narrative epilogue (1:16), the action of Jonah 1 is concentrically arranged. Corresponding subunits are sometimes linked by common vocabulary (indicated by underlining in the summary below), more often by common theme, and usually by common style (that is, both subunits are either narrative [N] or dialogue [D]).

A.   YHWH <u>throws</u> a wind <u>into the sea</u> (1:4 [N])
B.   The sailors cry out to their gods (1:5a [N])
C.   They attempt to save the ship (1:5b [N])
D.   The captain <u>speaks</u> to Jonah (1:6 [D])
E.   The sailors seek to learn how to save themselves (1:7a [D])
F.   They learn Jonah's responsibility (1:7b [N])
G.   They <u>ask</u> Jonah questions (1:8 [D])
H.   Jonah's profession of faith (1:9 [D])
G'.   The men <u>ask</u> Jonah a question (1:10a [D])
F'.   The men had learned Jonah's responsibility (1:10b [N])
E'.   They seek to learn how to save themselves (1:11 [D])[9]
D'.   Jonah <u>speaks</u> to the sailors (1:12 [D])
C'.   The men attempt to save the ship (1:13 [N])
B'.   They pray to YHWH (1:14 [D])
A'.   The sailors <u>throw</u> Jonah <u>into the sea</u> (1:15 [N])

---

[7] The man is oddly anonymous, although his Israelite mother, his maternal grandfather, and his tribal forefather are all named. This is a more subtle invocation of the law of talion: the man who blasphemes the divine name shall lose his own.

[8] This analysis is based on that of Rudolf Pesch, "Zur konzentrischen Struktur von Jona 1," *Bib* 47 (1966) 577–81. In her valuable study *Rhetorical Criticism: Context, Method, and the Book of Jonah* (Minneapolis: Fortress, 1994) Phyllis Trible identifies many other small-scale symmetries in the chapter, although she does not accept Pesch's overall pattern.

[9] In some modern translations the last words of the verse ("For the sea [is] growing increasingly stormy") are treated as narrative. Grammatically it is equally possible and, in view of the concentric structure, more likely that they are part of the sailors' speech.

Additional links between corresponding subunits include striking anthropomorphisms in A ("the ship thought about breaking up") and A' ("the sea stood still in its wrath"), and the word pair "sea" and "dry land" that appears in the central subunit (1:9) and also links C (the sailors throw the cargo "to the sea") and C' (the men try to row back "to the dry land"). Note too that the requirements of the concentric structure explain the otherwise puzzling flashback in 1:10b, where reference is made only after the fact to Jonah's admission that he was fleeing from YHWH. By recounting Jonah's admission at this point the narrator creates a narrative subunit F' to correspond to subunit F and focuses Jonah's speech in v. 9 on a profession of faith in YHWH rather than complicating it with a confession of the prophet's own misbehavior.

The first and last subunits contrast ironically: in A, YHWH "throws" a storm "into the sea"; in A', the men "throw" Jonah "into the sea." On the surface of things Jonah's destiny has undergone a reversal from life to death. Yet the deeper irony, reflected in a verbal leitmotif in the text, is that this apparent reversal is in fact a continuity. Jonah's goal is to escape YHWH. In pursuit of this goal he "goes down" (*yrd*, 1:3b) to Joppa, he "goes down" (*yrd*, 1:3b) into the ship, he "goes down" into the hold (*yrd*, 1:5), and he even falls deeply asleep (*yrdm*, from the root *rdm*, 1:5b). Far from being a guilt-induced self-sacrifice, his plea to be thrown into the sea is another attempt to elude the divine grasp, and his descent to the depths merely continues the "going down" that has been his direction since the first.[10]

On the other hand, subunits B and B' reveal the true reversal in the chapter: the sailors, who had cried out to their own gods in B, pray to YHWH in B'. What accomplishes this change is, again ironically, the disobedient prophet himself, who in ch. 4 will reveal his unwillingness to cooperate in the conversion of pagans (4:2). Jonah's profession of faith in the central subunit (1:9) convinces the sailors that YHWH is creator of "sea and dry land," and so they turn to YHWH to save them from their doom and eventually vow sacrifices to him (1:16). Like Jonah's continuity, the sailors' reversal is reflected in a verbal leitmotif, the connotations of the word "fear" (*yr*) throughout the chapter. The sailors are first afraid (*yr*, 1:5) of the storm. Then, after Jonah has told them that he "fears" (*yr*, 1:9, but here in its religious sense of "reveres") YHWH, they "fear with great fear" (*yr yrh gdwlh*, 1:10) what the presence of Jonah in their ship might mean. Finally, when they have escaped danger, they "fear [that is, revere] YHWH with great fear" (*yr t-yhwh yrh gdwlh*, 1:16).

---

[10] Jonathan Magonet, *Form and Meaning: Studies in Literary Techniques in the Book of Jonah* (2d ed.; Sheffield: Almond, 1983) 17.

As in the passage from Leviticus, the middle member of each sequence stands out. Here the captain's speech balances Jonah's second speech (D and D'). The former subtly recalls YHWH's speech from 1:1: in both, Jonah is addressed with a double command: "Get up!" *(qûm)* and "Cry out!" *(qĕrāʾ)*; thus, unknown to the captain, the echo of YHWH's words in his mouth reminds Jonah of his divine mission. In Jonah's second speech, "throw me into the sea" recalls YHWH's action in 1:4 of "throwing a great wind into the sea," and represents Jonah's last, desperate attempt to avoid his divine mission.

5. 2 Chronicles 25:1-28[11]

As several commentators have shown, the late narrative literature of the Hebrew Bible continues to use symmetry as a structuring device. The Chronicler has modified the account of the reign of Amaziah by expanding the description of his war with Edom (compare 2 Chr 25:5-13 with 2 Kings 14:7) and by inserting the surprising claim, completely absent from 2 Kings, that after his victory over Edom Amaziah undertook to worship Edomite gods. These modifications have transformed the linear, non-symmetrical account of 2 Kings 14:1-22 into a concentric passage.

A. Introduction to Amaziah's reign (25:1-4)
B.   War with Edom: Amaziah's victory (25:5-13)
C.   Amaziah's idolatry (25:14-16)
B'.   War with Israel: Amaziah's defeat (25:17-24)
A'. Conclusion to Amaziah's reign (25:25-28)

Two interpretive strategies are useful in this case. In addition to the dynamic of contrast and reversal implied in the concentric structure, we can compare the Chronicler's account with its source in 2 Kings to determine how the Chronicler has modified the source and thereby revealed his own particular concerns.

The introduction and conclusion to the reign are taken more or less intact from 2 Kings. The principal modification is the omission of 2 Kings 14:4, which identified Amaziah's major cultic offense as failure to "remove the high places" (that is, the local hilltop sanctuaries outside Jerusalem). Since the Chronicler intends to introduce an accusation of full-fledged idolatry he cannot retain this reference to a lesser infidelity as explanation of the charge that Amaziah's heart was not true to YHWH (25:2).

---

[11] M. Patrick Graham, "Aspects of the Structure and Rhetoric of 2 Chronicles 25," in idem, et al., eds., *History and Interpretation: Essays in Honour of John H. Hayes* (Sheffield: JSOT Press, 1993) 78–89.

Subunits B and B' contrast two wars, one of victory over foreigners and one of defeat at the hands of fellow Israelites. The Chronicler's modifications to the source are many and significant in these subunits. First, his expansion of the account of war with Edom from a single verse to nine verses enables it to balance the account of the war with Israel structurally. It also tightens the logic of the whole account. Amaziah hires, then dismisses, Israelite mercenaries (25:6, 10). Angry at being dismissed before battle (perhaps because it deprives them of a share in the spoils victory over Edom will win), the Israelite mercenaries sack Judahite cities on their way home (25:13). This explains Amaziah's challenge to Joash of Israel in 25:17: he seeks satisfaction for Israelite depredations in his territory. Second, the insertion of a theological aside in 25:20b explains Amaziah's perdurance in pride as YHWH's doing in order to punish the king for his idolatry. This links Amaziah's defeat causally to 25:14-16, which is the Chronicler's own insertion. Finally, the Chronicler inserts the phrase "and Obed-Edom with them" into 25:24. This reference too inevitably recalls Amaziah's worship of the gods of Edom (25:14-16), since the name Obed-Edom, literally translated, means "servant of Edom," and can refer specifically to cultic service.

Subunit C, the center of the concentric structure, is entirely from the Chronicler's hand. It identifies the turning point in Amaziah's reign as the moment when he fell into two grievous religious evils: first, he began worshiping Edomite gods, presumably in addition to YHWH rather than in place of him; then, when taken to task for this behavior by a prophet of YHWH, he refused to heed the warning.

6. Genesis 2:4b–3:24[12]

In Gen 2:4b–3:24 there are seven scenes, arranged concentrically (ABCDC'B'A'). Corresponding scenes share similar themes, main characters,[13] and locale.

A. 2:4b-17
    Theme: creation of *hāʾādām*[14]

---

[12] For more details of this analysis see Jerome T. Walsh, "Genesis 2:4b–3:24: A Synchronic Approach," *JBL* 96 (1977) 161–77, and Pierre Auffret, *La Sagesse a bâti sa maison* (Fribourg: Editions Universitaires, 1982) 25–47.

[13] In Scenes C and C' the characters are complementary: in C the snake initiates a dialogue with the woman; in C' YHWH God initiates a dialogue with *hāʾādām* (and briefly with the woman as well).

[14] The Hebrew text regularly speaks of the male character in these chapters as *hāʾādām*. This is not a proper name ("Adam"), since it includes the definite article

Characters: YHWH God (active); *hāʾādām* (passive)
Locale: the earth outside the garden, moving into the garden

B. 2:18-25

    Theme: creation of woman and animals; relationships among creatures
    Characters: YHWH God (active); *hāʾādām* (gives names); animals, woman (passive)
    Locale: unspecified location in the garden

C. 3:1-5

    Theme: dialogue about eating the fruit
    Characters: snake ("cleverest of the animals"), woman
    Locale: in the garden, not at the center[15]

D. 3:6-7

    Theme: narrative about eating the fruit
    Characters: the woman and her husband[16]
    Locale: center of the garden

C'. 3:8-13

    Theme: dialogue about eating the fruit
    Characters: YHWH God, *hāʾādām*, the woman
    Locale: in the garden, not at the center[17]

B'. 3:14-21

    Theme: punishment of all creatures; hostile relationships among them
    Characters: YHWH God (active); *hāʾādām* (gives name); woman, snake (passive)
    Locale: unspecified location in the garden

A'. 3:22-24

    Theme: expulsion of *hāʾādām*
    Characters: YHWH God (active); *hāʾādām* (passive)
    Locale: inside the garden, moving to the earth outside the garden.

In this passage each scene contrasts with its corresponding scene:

"the." Nor does it mean "man" in a gendered sense, which is the Hebrew word *ʾîš* (used in 2:23-24, 3:6, and 3:16, and sometimes translated "husband"). *Hāʾādām* is primarily the term for "humankind," here personified as the first ancestor of all human beings. Thus the Hebrew story is not, strictly speaking, about "the first man and woman," as representatives of all subsequent men and women; it is about "the first human being," as representative of all subsequent human beings.

[15] The woman says that they may not eat of "the tree which is in the center of the garden." Contrary to much traditional iconography, this implies that she and the snake are not standing at the tree, since in that case she would have said "this tree."

[16] The woman's partner is not called *hāʾādām* ("the human being") here, but *ʾîšāh*, "her husband."

[17] In 3:8 *hāʾādām* and the woman ran away from the tree and hid themselves among the trees of the garden.

A. *hā'ādām* is placed in the garden
B.   character relationships are established in harmony
C.   the snake makes statements[18] to the woman
D.   the woman and her husband eat of the tree
C'.   YHWH God asks questions of *hā'ādām*
B'.   character relationships are reestablished, but with disharmony
A'. *hā'ādām* is driven from the garden.

Furthermore, the sequences before and after the center contrast in their sense of movement. Scenes A–D move gradually from outside the garden to its center. (Scene B is in the garden somewhere, with no particular attention paid to its precise location; scene C is not at the garden's center, but focuses our attention in that direction by its topic of conversation.) Scenes D–A' reverse the journey.

The turning point of the action is clearly the humans' eating of the fruit in Scene D. This pivotal character is enhanced by the concentric structure of the scene itself, whose lines are closer to poetry than to prose. In a nearly literal translation:

> [6]Then the woman saw that the tree [was] good for food,
> and pleasant for the eyes, and desirable for wisdom.
>   So she took of its fruit and ate and gave also to her man with her, and he ate.
> [7]Then the eyes of both opened up, and they saw that they were naked,
> and they sewed fig leaves together, and they made for themselves loincloths.

The first couplet, almost verbless, depicts the woman standing before the tree, mulling over the advantages of acting. The last couplet, with four verbs equally distributed in each half-line, tolls the inexorable knell of the wages of sin. Between them stands a single line, charged with verbs, in which first the woman, then her husband, succumb to the snake's charm.

The first and last scenes have a special connection to the center. In Scene A *hā'ādām* receives the command not to eat of the tree of knowledge under pain of death. He violates the command in Scene D. As a result he is deprived of access to the tree of life in Scene A' (3:22).

7. 1 and 2 Kings[19]

Concentric symmetry is also found over very large expanses of text, although in such cases the repeated elements that link corresponding

---

[18] Though most translations render the snake's first words as a question, "Did God say . . . ?" they are in fact a misstatement, "To think that God said . . . ," that the woman attempts to correct.

[19] See George Savran, "1 and 2 Kings," in Robert Alter and Frank Kermode, eds., *The Literary Guide to the Bible* (Cambridge, Mass.: Harvard University Press, 1987)

subunits are almost inescapably thematic. The two books of Kings (which the Hebrew text tradition treats as one) form a single concentric structure:

A. Solomon and the United Monarchy (1 Kings 1–11)
B.   The separation of the northern kingdom (1 Kings 12)
C.   Kings of Israel and Judah (1 Kings 13:1–16:20)
D.   Civil war: the Omrid dynasty begins (1 Kings 16:21-34)
E.   Elijah, the prophets, and the Omrids (1 Kings 17–2 Kings 1)
F.   Elisha succeeds Elijah (2 Kings 2)
E'.   Elisha, the prophets, and the Omrids (2 Kings 3:1–9:13)
D'.   Civil war: the Omrid dynasty ends (2 Kings 9:14–11:20)
C'.   Kings of Israel and Judah (2 Kings 12–16)
B'.   The fall of the northern kingdom (2 Kings 17)
A'. The kingdom of Judah alone (2 Kings 18–25)

Some of the corresponding subunits contrast with one another. The glories of the imperial monarchy under Solomon (subunit A) contrast starkly with the tragic destiny of the beleaguered kingdom of Judah under its last kings in A'. The northern kingdom, Israel, begins its independent career in B and is wiped out by the Assyrians in B'. Similarly the Omrid dynasty begins in civil rebellion in D and ends in a bloodbath in D'.

On the other hand, the sequences as a whole do not contrast, nor does the structure as a whole reflect a sense of reversal. Rather the whole story portrays the progressive disintegration and dissolution of Israel, from empire to two petty kingdoms to the eventual destruction of each. If there is a reversal at all, it is to be seen in the attention focused on prophets, particularly in the central subunit. Note how 2 Kings 2 takes place *between* reigns, not *within* a specific regnal account.[20] Just as crossing the Jordan removes the departure of Elijah from ordinary space (represented by the guild prophets who remain on the hither bank), so Elijah's departure takes place in a time outside of ordinary time. Hidden beneath an apparent historical account of kings and

---

148, and Jerome T. Walsh, *1 Kings* (Collegeville: The Liturgical Press, 1996) 371–74. Similarly, but with less detail, Yehuda T. Radday, "Chiasmus in Hebrew Biblical Narrative," 61–62.

[20] There are a few places in 1–2 Kings where material falls between reigns in this fashion, but it is usually a matter of only a few verses and there is usually a literary explanation. In 1 Kings 16:21-22, for instance, the civil war makes it unclear who will be Zimri's successor, and the literary placement of the verses reflects the political interregnum. Only in 2 Kings 2 does such a lengthy passage stand outside the regnal succession formulas. On the structural significance of the regnal formulas see below under "Partial Symmetry."

kingdoms lies the deeper story, the real story, of which political vicissitudes are merely epiphenomena: the story of the word of God and its bearers, around whom the true history turns.

8. 1 Kings 1:1–2:12a

The first dramatic story in the account of King Solomon's reign describes how he came to succeed David on the throne of Israel, thwarting the expectations of the heir apparent, Adonijah. The narrative centers on four scenes in David's chambers:

A. King David is dying (1:1-4)
B.   Adonijah exalts himself (1:5-8)
C.   Adonijah holds a feast (1:9-10)
D.   Nathan conspires to make Solomon king (1:11-14)
E.   Four scenes in David's chambers (1:15-37)
D'.   Nathan and others make Solomon king (1:38-40)
C'.   Adonijah's feast is disrupted (1:41-50)
B'.   Adonijah abases himself (1:51-53)
A'. King David dies (2:1-12a)

Contrast is clear between some of the corresponding subunits (e.g., B and B', C and C'), as well as between the sequences preceding and following the center. In the first half Adonijah, the heir apparent, celebrates his royal expectations which, in view of David's infirmities, are not likely to be long delayed. In the second half an unexpectedly decisive David decrees the succession of Solomon, and Adonijah's future falls quickly from festive to fatal. The moment of reversal takes place in the privacy of David's chambers.

This passage is an example of the difficulty the analyst can have in deciding whether to identify a reverse symmetry as concentric or chiastic. If we take the four scenes as a single subunit E (a subunit that would comprise about one third of the entire text), the structure is concentric. On the other hand, the four scenes themselves are arranged in alternating fashion, beginning with two scenes wherein David is completely passive, followed by two scenes wherein he takes active initiative.[21]

E. Two scenes wherein David is passive
   a.   Bathsheba's audience with David (1:15-21)
   b.   Nathan's audience with David (1:22-27)
E'. Two scenes wherein David is active
   a'. David summons Bathsheba (1:28-31)
   b'. David summons Nathan and others (1:32-37)

---

[21] On the overlap of AA'BB' and ABA'B' structures see the discussion below of "Forward Symmetry."

Read this way the story is double-centered, with the turning point at the moment when David seizes the initiative, namely, exactly between E and E'.

In the final analysis the difference is one of emphasis. Either reverse symmetry highlights the contrast of the two parts of the whole. A concentric reading points up the links between the first, middle, and last subunits and the progression they involve: David is moribund (subunit A) and, in spite of a brief return of the old vigor (E), is soon to die (A'). A chiastic reading stresses rather the contrast between subunits E and E', thereby underlining the return of David's decisiveness in spite of the inescapable consequences of his old age.

B. Chiastic symmetry

1. 1 Kings 19:14

The famous "still, small voice" *(qôl děmāmâ daqqâ)* Elijah hears on Mount Horeb involves a chiastic sequence of syllable-initial consonants: *q-d-m* // *m-d-q*. The formulation is as striking in Hebrew as it is in English. *Qôl* means a "voice" or a "sound"; it can be articulate or inarticulate, the voice of human or animal, or any natural sound. *Děmāmâ* means "silence"; a *qôl děmāmâ* is literally a "sound of silence," or a silent sound. Finally, *daqqâ* is a tactile word, not an aural one, and means "thin," like sheer cloth or underfed cattle.

The "reversal" that is betokened by the chiastic structure is the self-contradictory phrase itself. It is an oxymoron, mysterious and puzzling, a quality lost in translations that render it "a thin, whispering sound" or the like. The NRSV comes closest with "a sound of sheer silence," but even this weakens the jarring juxtaposition of aural and tactile terms. Better yet would be "a slender, silent sound."

The intrinsically contradictory nature of the phrase is emblematic of the puzzling contradictions that color the whole chapter.[22] Elijah, fleeing Jezebel's threat against his life (19:3), asks YHWH to take his life (19:4), then later complains that his life is in danger (19:10). Fortified by divinely supplied food and sent back to his mission (19:7), he makes his way instead in the opposite direction, into the heart of the desert to the mountain where God dwells, and where YHWH is surprised by his arrival (19:9). There he insists upon his faithfulness in YHWH's service, yet by protesting the failure of his work implies that he no longer sees any point to continuing (19:10). Even after a powerful and mysterious en-

---

[22] Several recent commentators read 1 Kings 19 as Elijah's attempt to resign his prophetic ministry. See the discussion in my *1 Kings* 264–65.

counter with Yhwh (19:11-12), Elijah is unmoved. He is no longer willing to "stand before Yhwh" (i.e., serve Yhwh) as he had in the past (17:1; 18:15), and as Yhwh orders him to do again (19:11), but stands instead "at the mouth of the cave" (19:13) and repeats his complaint in exactly the same words as before (19:14). Then, in a final reversal, when Yhwh concedes and commissions Elijah to "anoint" Elisha as his successor (19:16), Elijah does not do what Yhwh tells him, but "invests" Elisha as a privileged servant (19:19, 21) and continues to pursue his own prophetic ministry throughout the reign of the current king (1 Kings 21) and his successor (2 Kings 1).

2. Genesis 12:16b[23]

In Genesis 12 Abram, knowing that his wife Sarai's beauty puts him in danger, passes her off as his sister and allows her to be taken into Pharaoh's harem. In return, Pharaoh rewards Abram with a long list of goods. The odd order in which these goods are enumerated is due to their chiastic arrangement: flocks-and-herds[24] / jackasses / men servants // women servants / jenny asses / camels. The central elements are clearly the most important, human beings as opposed to livestock. There is little sense of reversal, however, except insofar as the four internal subunits correspond as male to female.

On the other hand, the whole story has a loosely chiastic plot involving a reversal. The patriarch goes down into Egypt to escape famine (12:14), the matriarch is taken into Pharaoh's harem (12:15), the patriarch reaps rewards because of his wife (12:16a) // Pharaoh suffers plagues because of the patriarch's wife (12:17-19a), he returns her to the patriarch (12:19b), and he expels the patriarch from the country (12:20). It is precisely at the turning point of this development that the chiastic series of 12:16b is situated.

3. Genesis 9:6a[25]

Talion law (see the example of Lev 24:13-23 above) can call for chiastic formulation as well as concentric. After the Deluge, which, according

---

[23] Forbes, *The Symmetrical Structure of Scripture* 38–39, citing Thomas Boys, *Key to the Psalms* 37–38. The structure is also noted by Lund, *Chiasmus in the New Testament* 43.

[24] In the Hebrew text of Gen 12:16 the phrase is similarly hyphenated, though that is quite rare in the Hebrew Bible. That punctuation links the two Hebrew words into a single complex idea (the technical term is hendiadys), thereby enabling them to act as a unit and to balance the single word "camels" in the chiastic structure.

[25] J. P. Fokkelman, *Narrative Art in Genesis* 34–35.

to Gen 6:11, was the divine response to the "violence" that filled the earth, God decrees a talionic punishment for murder.

šōpēk	The one who sheds
dam	the blood
hā'ādām	of a human being
bā'ādām	for[26] a human being
dāmô	his blood
yiṣṣāpēk	shall be shed.

As in any situation of talion law, the fundamental reversal is that "the punishment fits the crime." This is reflected in an exact balance of words, but with reversed values: "one who sheds" / "shall be shed" (active versus passive); "blood" / "his blood" (the murdered person's blood versus the murderer's blood). At the center the reversal is more subtle. Instead of the expected opposition of victim to murderer we have the victim mentioned twice and the murderer not mentioned at all: the victim, though dead, remains in mind and mouth; the murderer, though living, disappears into the silence of the text.

4. 1 Kings 21:1-16

In 1 Kings 21:1-16 there are six chiastically arranged scenes that correspond in theme and usually in locale.

A. 21:1-3
> *Theme:* Ahab asks to buy Naboth's vineyard, but is refused.
> *Locale:* Naboth's vineyard.

B. 21:4-7
> *Theme:* Jezebel promises Ahab that she will obtain Naboth's vineyard for him.
> *Locale:* Ahab's palace.

C. 21:8-10
> *Theme:* Jezebel details a plot to the elders of Jezreel.
> *Locale:* Ahab's palace.

C'. 21:11-14
> *Theme:* The elders carry out Jezebel's plot in detail.
> *Locale:* Jezreel.

B'. 21:15
> *Theme:* Jezebel announces to Ahab that he can take possession of the vineyard.
> *Locale:* Ahab's palace.

---

[26] The traditional translation, "by a human being," is mistaken. The preposition *b-* here points not to the agent or means of the action, but to the grounds for the action. See Fokkelman, *Narrative Art in Genesis* 35.

A'. 21:16
>*Theme:* Ahab takes possession of Naboth's vineyard.
>*Locale:* Naboth's vineyard.

Contrast is more obvious on the level of the complete sequences than on that of individual pairs of corresponding subunits. In the first half Ahab's failure to obtain Naboth's vineyard (Scene A) leads to a promise (B) and a plot (C). In the second half the plot succeeds (C'), the promise is kept (B'), and Ahab takes possession of the vineyard (A'). The four internal scenes are related as expectation/realization, but the contrast between the opening and closing scenes imbues the whole narrative with a feeling of reversal.

The reversal is accomplished in the central scenes. Jezebel details her plot in a letter and the elders of Jezreel carry it out successfully. The two scenes are strongly emphasized by extensive verbal repetition. Although in themselves they are related as command and compliance rather than as contrasting, together they bring about the change in situation of both Ahab (he can obtain the vineyard) and Naboth (he loses vineyard and life).

In this story, too, the structural reversal points to something greater than a simple turn in the plot. The story is not simply about power wreaking injustice on a helpless commoner. It is about *royal* power wreaking injustice, and shamelessly abusing both religious observance and law in the process, although it was the throne's duty to uphold law and justice, and to sustain the relationship of deity and people. Behind this story of the seizure of an Israelite landowner's vineyard, then, lies a darker drama: the abdication of royal responsibility for the mechanisms of social stability, and thus the betrayal of YHWH's people by the king himself.

5. 2 Kings 8:7–9:13

A series of more or less independent stories can also be arranged symmetrically. There is a collection of stories set during the time of the prophet Elisha in 2 Kings 3–9, the last four of which are organized in chiastic fashion:[27]

---

[27] The organization of the first ten stories is much more complex, but the basic structure is also a chiastic arrangement of the four longest stories:
- A. War with Moab: the problem of drought (3:4-27)
- B. Elisha raises the Shunammite's son (4:8-37)
- B'. Elisha cures Naaman's leprosy (5:1-27)
- A'. War with Aram: the problem of famine (6:24–7:20).

A. Elisha names Hazael to kingship in Aram (8:7-15)
B.   Jehoram's reign over Judah (8:16-24)
B'.   Ahaziah's reign over Judah (8:25-29)
A'. Elisha names Jehu to kingship in Israel (9:1-13)[28]

In this case there is little feeling of reversal. Subunits A and A' contrast in their location—outside of Israel, within Israel—but the dominant impression is of the continuity of the four stories. Each deals with a change of ruler; the A and A' subunits, indeed, inaugurate changes of dynasty. Moreover, they correspond to one another in another way as well: they complete commissions given by YHWH to Elisha's former master, Elijah, at Mount Horeb (1 Kings 19:15-16).

6. 1 Chronicles 11:1–12:41[29]

Between two descriptions of David's coronation as king by the leaders of "all Israel" (that is, the northern confederation of tribes as distinct from "Judah," the southern tribes), the Chronicler depicts how David's support had previously grown from his original group of outlaws (David's "warriors," 11:10) to "a great army, like an army of God" (12:22). The report is organized chiastically, by geographical references:

A. David becomes king of all Israel at Hebron (11:1-9)
B.   David gains support at Hebron (11:10-47)
C.   David gains support at Ziklag (12:1-7)
D.   David gains support at "the stronghold" (12:8-15)
D'.   David gains support at "the stronghold" (12:16-18)
C'.   David gains support at Ziklag (12:19-22)
B'.   David gains support at Hebron (12:23-37)
A'. David becomes king of all Israel at Hebron (12:38-40)

The geographical basis of the pattern is all the more evident in that from a chronological point of view the passage is in chaos. According to the Chronicler's source in the books of Samuel, David's presence at a "stronghold in the wilderness" (1 Samuel 22–23) precedes his establishment of a base at Ziklag (1 Samuel 27), which in turn precedes his settling at Hebron (2 Samuel 2).

---

[28] Though the figure of Jehu and the theme of his coming to the throne connect 9:1-13 to what follows in 9:14–10:36, there are signs in the passage that 9:14 begins a new literary unit. See the remarks below, p. 43.

[29] H.G.M. Williamson, "'We are Yours, O David': The Setting and Purpose of 1 Chronicles xii 1-23," *OtSt* 21 (1981) 164–76. The verse numbers cited in this treatment correspond to those in English Bibles. Since the Hebrew text divides English 12:4 into two verses, the Hebrew numbering is one higher from that point to the end of ch. 12.

In this case reverse symmetry does not support an interpretive approach based on contrast. Corresponding subunits reinforce one another, as do the two sequences. Subunits A and A' describe the coronation of David, the first emphasizing the covenant between "all Israel" and David, the second focusing on the celebration itself. Subunits B and B' describe the individuals (B) and armies (B') that were gathered around David at Hebron. Subunit B begins the chronological disorder of the entire passage: David's "mighty men" had been with him since his outlaw days at "the stronghold" (2 Sam 23:13-14), but the context—particularly 11:10, which speaks of "kingdom" and "all Israel"—makes it clear that the Chronicler has the days of David's reign at Hebron in mind. Subunits C and C' identify tribal groups and individuals that had joined David at Ziklag, Benjaminites (C) and Manassites (C'), while subunits D and D' identify further groups as joining him even earlier, Gadites (D), more Benjaminites and Judahites (D').

The sequences contrast only in the sense that subunits A–D move back in time, while D'–A' retrace the same time span forward. This may, however, be one key to interpreting the passage. The Chronicler does not otherwise describe David's career before he became king at Hebron. In other words, in contrast to the books of Samuel and Kings, Chronicles' presentation of David begins with his coronation at Hebron. This passage is the only glimpse we have of how David's kingship came to pass. The emphasis, for the Chronicler, is on the theological principle, "[Yhwh] turned the kingdom over to David, Jesse's son" (10:14b), and earlier biographical information derived from the Chronicler's sources is subordinated to that principle.

7. Genesis 25:12–35:26

Chiastic patterning can also serve to organize a very long cycle of stories such as those about Jacob in the book of Genesis. The overall reverse symmetry of the Jacob cycle is evident even to the casual reader:

A. Jacob cheats Esau of his birthright and flees from him (25:19–28:9)
B.   Jacob encounters God at Bethel (28:10-22)
C.   Jacob works for Laban at Paddan-Aram (29:1–31:55)
B'.   Jacob encounters God at the Jabbok (32:1-32)
A'. Jacob returns and is reconciled with Esau. (33:1–35:29).

But this reverse pattern can be analyzed in much greater detail.[30]

---

[30] See Michael Fishbane, "Composition and Structure in the Jacob Cycle (Gen. 25:19–35:22)," *JJS* 26 (1975) 15–38, and idem, *Text and Texture: Close Readings of Selected Biblial Texts* (New York: Schocken, 1979) 40–62. The analysis has been taken

A. The descendants of Ishmael (25:12-18)
B.   Rebekah struggles in childbirth; Jacob and Esau born (25:19-26)
C.   Jacob obtains Esau's birthright *(bkrh)* (25:27-34)
D.   Rebekah in a foreign palace; foreign pact (26:1-33)[31]
E.   Blessing *(brkh)* taken from Esau (27:1-46)
F.   Jacob flees Esau, encounters God on his journey (28:1-22)
G.   Jacob arrives at Haran (deception, wages) (29:1-30)
H.   Jacob's wives are fertile (29:31–30:24)
H'.   Jacob's flocks are fertile (30:25-43)
G'.   Jacob leaves Haran (deception, wages) (31:1-55)
F'.   Jacob returns to Esau, encounters God on his journey (32:1-32)
E'.   Blessing-gift *(brkh,* 33:11) returned to Esau (33:1-20)
D'.   Dinah in a foreign palace; foreign pact thwarted (34:1-31)
C'.   Jacob receives God's blessing *(brkh)* (35:1-15)
B'.   Rachel struggles in childbirth; Benjamin born (35:16-22)
A'. The descendants of Jacob (35:23-26)

Almost all of the corresponding subunits show contrast: subunit A names a descendance collateral to the line of the promise, which passes through Abraham's other son, Isaac, to Jacob; A' names a descendance within the line, since Jacob becomes "Israel," and all his sons share in the promises. In B the matriarch recovers from difficult childbirth; in B' she dies. In C Jacob wrests the birthright by guile; in C' he receives the blessing gratuitously. In D Abimelech discovers the truth about Rebekah before any of the Philistines can lie with her (26:10); in D' Dinah is "taken" by a foreign prince, who lies with her (34:2).[32] In E Jacob steals the blessing from Esau, again by guile; in E' Jacob gives Esau rich gifts, which he terms a "blessing." In F Jacob flees; in F' he returns. Even the two encounters with the deity contrast: one is a dream of peaceful communication between heaven and earth, with the promise freely bestowed by God on Jacob; the other is a waking struggle with a mysterious being whose attributes (darkness of night, violence, connection with a ford) are more chthonic than celestial, and from whom Jacob wins a blessing by force. In G Jacob's arrival in Haran is marked

---

up, with some differences of detail, in Gary A. Rendsburg, *The Redaction of Genesis* (Winona Lake: Eisenbrauns, 1986) 53–69, who credits Fishbane with its discovery. The presentation here is based on the work of both authors, again with some differences in detail.

[31] On the function of 26:34-35 see below, pp. 186–87.

[32] Some scholars are unsure whether Dinah was the victim of forcible rape, because of the ambiguity of the Hebrew form *wᵉnh.* Whatever it means, however, it is clear that Shechem is the active party. Dinah, like Rebekah in the corresponding subunit, is always the object of verbs and never the subject.

by hospitality that leads to Laban's deception of Jacob; in G' Jacob's departure is marked by Jacob's deception of Laban (31:20) and leads to a grudging covenant and permanent separation. Only H and H' are not in contrast: the fertility of Leah and, eventually, of Rachel (H) is balanced by the fruitfulness of Jacob's flocks and herds (H').

On the other hand, there is little contrast between the complete sequences before and after the center. In A–H Jacob is crafty in getting what he wants, whether by coercing Esau or deceiving Isaac. Nonetheless, God freely commits himself to Jacob at Bethel, and Jacob makes a conditional promise to God in return (28:20-22). In H'–A' Jacob is still crafty, deceiving Laban (31:20) and forcing God at the Jabbok to bless him. (In fact, we may not be wrong to see in the rich gifts Jacob prepares for Esau less a desire for fraternal reconciliation than a ploy to mollify Esau's anger. Notice that Jacob separates himself from Esau as soon as possible, despite a promise to join him: 33:12-17.) At Bethel, Jacob keeps his conditional promise (35:3-7) and God again freely commits himself to Jacob (35:9-15).

Nevertheless, there has been a notable change. The Jacob who returns is not quite the same as the Jacob who left. His deception of Esau is no longer damaging. The abundance of Jacob's presents to Esau, whether due to remorse or fear, bespeaks Jacob's willingness to share the benefits the blessing has brought him. His self-centeredness has expanded to include wives and children, whom he protects from Esau's anticipated anger by sending several droves of gift animals ahead of them. Perhaps most significantly, Jacob gets a new name, Israel, conferred on him twice by God after his return from Paddan-Aram (32:28; 35:10).[33]

In general terms the reversal takes place in Paddan-Aram. One motif that tracks the dynamics of the story is a play on the words "birthright" *(bĕkôrâ),* "blessing" *(bĕrākâ),* "your firstborn son" *(bĕkôrĕkā),* and "firstborn daughter" *(bĕkîrâ).* Jacob first extorts the birthright from Esau, which gives him some claim to the paternal blessing. But he compounds his crime and steals the blessing itself from his father, the blind Isaac, by posing as the firstborn son though he was the younger. Jacob gets his comeuppance in Paddam-Aram when he unwittingly, in the dark of night, takes as wife Laban's firstborn daughter Leah, who is posing as her younger sister Rachel, Jacob's beloved.

The trickster tricked is not, however, the deepest reversal of the story, nor does it occur in the central subunits, where we expect the pivotal events to be found. In fact, as we have seen, in the course of the whole cycle Jacob's personality is moderated but does not undergo

---

[33] Compare the Abraham cycle of stories, where the turning point coincides with a name change from "Abram" to "Abraham." See below under "Multiple Symmetry."

profound change. At its deepest level this is not Jacob's story but the story of the promise to Abraham, to Isaac, and to Jacob himself ("your offspring will be like the dust of the earth," 28:14). Until the central subunits Jacob has no children, though the text avers that he has worked seven years since taking both Leah and Rachel as wives (29:30). Only in subunit H does Leah begin to bear him children; and only at the very end of subunit H (30:22-24), that is, at the very center of the structure, is Rachel's barrenness overcome with the birth of Joseph.

2. FORWARD SYMMETRY

Forward symmetry, as its name implies, is a pattern in which corresponding subunits occur in the same, rather than in reverse, order. In theory two varieties of forward symmetry are possible. In the first, which we shall call "parallel symmetry," each subunit in the first sequence corresponds to a subunit in subsequent sequences, and the corresponding subunits occur in the same order in each sequence; parallel symmetry is schematized ABCA'B'C'. Parallel symmetry is quite common, with sequences of greatly varying lengths. Here we will consider only patterns that comprise three or more subunits in each sequence.[1]

The second form of forward symmetry might be called "symmetry of immediate repetition." This pattern repeats each set of corresponding subunits together and orders the sets, rather than individual subunits, sequentially; this would be schematized AA'BB'CC'. Symmetry of immediate repetition appears in prose narrative mainly in two situations. First, thematic and verbal elements will often be repeated in the course of plot development, producing a pattern that is merely a secondary effect of the linear nature of prose narrative. Consequently it affords no distinctive angle of approach for interpretation. For example, in discussing 1 Kings 1:15-37 (see p. 25) I analyzed the four scenes in David's chambers as

    A. Bathsheba's audience with David (1:15-21)
    B.   Nathan's audience with David (1:22-27)
    A'. David summons Bathsheba (1:28-31)

---

[1] Parallel symmetry has often been called "alternation" by scholars who have discussed it in the past. That term, however, implies only two members in each sequence (ABA'B'), a form of symmetry that has its own peculiar characteristics. It is therefore better to reserve the term "alternating repetition" for our later study of this device and to use a broader term for forward symmetries of three or more correspondences.

B'.   David summons Nathan and others (1:32-37).

They could also be analyzed:

A. David is passive; Bathsheba confronts him (1:15-21).
A'. David is passive; Nathan confronts him (1:22-27).
B.   David is active; he summons Bathsheba (1:28-31).
B'.   David is active; he summons Nathan and others (1:32-37).

But this analysis simply reflects the change in David's character that is one constitutive element of the narrative, and does not reveal an organizing pattern independent of the plot development.

Second, symmetry of immediate repetition sometimes involves other repeated elements, unconnected with plot development, that reinforce the pattern, such as the length of corresponding subunits, striking non-thematic verbal or syntactic elements, or the like. In these cases there is a basis for closer examination. But it appears that whenever such a pattern is found in prose narrative there is usually another symmetrical pattern in the passage as well. Such cases, where two independent symmetrical patterns organize the same material, will be treated later as "compound symmetry." Symmetry of immediate repetition, therefore, does not seem to occur as a primary organizing device in biblical Hebrew prose narrative, though it does occur in biblical poetry.[2] Consequently in this section we will be concerned only with parallel symmetry.

Parallel symmetry allows a variation that is rarely found in cases of reverse symmetry, namely the possibility of more than two sequences: ABCA'B'C'A''B''C''. Such extended examples of forward symmetry are not uncommon, though there seems to be an inverse relationship between the number of sequences in the pattern and the length of each. In other words, when the sequence is short, say ABC, it may occur more than twice; when the sequence comprises many subunits, say ABCDEFGH, it is likely to occur only twice. This is not surprising, since the effectiveness of a symmetrical pattern resides in its memorability, and long, complex sequences are harder to remember than shorter ones.

As with reverse symmetry, interpretation must consider not only the linear development of the plot but also the comparison of corresponding subunits and of whole sequences as well. Unlike reverse symmetry, however, the principal dynamic conveyed by forward sym-

---

[2] In two acrostic poems where the basic organizing device is the Hebrew alphabet, several lines begin with one letter of the alphabet, followed by several beginning with the next letter, and so on. In Lamentations 3 the first three lines each begin with aleph, the next three with beth, etc., and Psalm 119 has eight successive lines beginning with aleph, eight with beth, etc.

metry is not usually reversal or contrast but progression. It may take the form of simple succession (before and after), or of consequence (cause and effect), or of emphasis or intensification, but the impression is of forward movement rather than of turning around.

1. Genesis 1:1; Genesis 1:1-31

The first two words of the Hebrew Bible present us with an example of parallel symmetry on the phonemic level: *běrē'šît bārā'* ("In the beginning, [God] created . . .") contains a triple alliteration of consonants, *br' / br'*. This prosodic device intensifies the solemnity of the phrase and urges us forward, as titular words should, to what follows.[3]

In this case the symmetry also foreshadows what will follow. Just as God's creation is announced with an ABCA'B'C' series of consonants, so the creation itself will unfold in an ABCA'B'C' series of days and acts.[4]

A. First day: <u>light</u> (1:3-5)
B.   Second day: <u>firmament</u>, called <u>sky</u>, divides the <u>waters</u> (1:6-8)
C1.   Third day: sea and <u>earth</u> (1:9-10)
C2.   Third day: <u>plants</u> (1:11-13)
A'. Fourth day: <u>lights</u> (1:14-19)
B'.   Fifth day: fish in the <u>waters</u> and birds in the <u>firmament</u> of the <u>sky</u> (1:20-23)
C1'.   Sixth day: animals of the <u>earth</u> (1:24-25)
C+.   Sixth day: humankind (1:26-28)
C2'.   Sixth day: <u>plants</u> for food (1:29-31).

Corresponding subunits are linked by the numerous repeated words underlined above.[5] The two sequences, as well as the corresponding subunits within them, are related as environment and inhabitants. In the first three days God prepares the physical world; in the last three God makes creatures to occupy the various regions of the

---

[3] See the remarks of Gabriel Josipovici, *The Book of God: A Response to the Bible* (New Haven: Yale University Press, 1988) 68.

[4] To be precise, the acts are arranged in two parallel series of *four* acts each, thus ABCDA'B'C'D', but the imposition of a six-day structure has compressed these eight acts into an ABCA'B'C' pattern, with C and C' comprising two acts each. In addition, subunit C' has an unbalanced element, the creation of humankind (1:26-28), that has no counterpart in C. On the function of asymmetry see Section 7, where we will examine this example more closely.

[5] There is one slight variation. On the first day God makes "light" (*'ôr*); on the fourth day God makes "lights" or "lamps." The Hebrew word for "lamp" is *mā'ôr*, which comes from the same root as *'ôr*.

world. From the first to the second sequence there is an intensification from immobile to mobile (and probably therefore in the ancient understanding from non-living to living).

Moreover, in each sequence there is progression from the mysterious to the familiar. The first three days move from light, intangible and unknowable, to sky and sea, distant and alien, to dry land, the earth under our feet. The last three days move from the celestial hosts through fish and birds to land animals and human beings, reflecting humankind's varying sense of closeness to the other sorts of creatures that share the cosmos.[6]

2. 1 Kings 11:1-8

The last chapter of the story of King Solomon begins with a narrator's summary of Solomon's apostasy. The summary falls into two parts, his attraction to foreign women (11:1-3) and the apostasy that attraction led him to (11:4-8). Each part has parallel symmetry, and the two parts are also parallel to one another.

> A. "King <u>Solomon loved</u> many *foreign women*" (11:1a)
> B.   description of the women: nations (11:1b)
> C.   ". . . they will <u>turn your mind away</u> toward their gods" (11:2a)
> A'. "<u>Solomon</u> clung to them in <u>love</u>" (11:2b)
> B'.   description of the women: numbers (11:3a)
> C'.   "and his women <u>turned his mind away</u>" (11:3b).

The second part has a very similar structure:

> A. ". . . *his women* turned his mind away toward **other gods**" (11:4a)
> B.   "his mind <u>was not true to</u> Y<small>HWH</small> his God, <u>like</u> the mind of <u>his father</u>
>   <u>David</u>" (11:4b)
> C.   ". . . Astarte of Sidon and <u>Milcom</u> *(mlkm)* <u>of Ammon</u>" (11:5)
> A'. "Solomon *did* evil in Y<small>HWH</small>'s sight" (11:6a)
> B'.   "he <u>was not fully with</u> Y<small>HWH,</small> <u>like his father David</u>" (11:6b)
> C'.   ". . . Chemosh of Moab and <u>Molek</u> *(mlk)* <u>of Ammon</u>" (11:7)
> A". "This was what he *did* for all *his foreign women* . . ." (11:8).

In the first part the two sequences are progressive. Subunit A describes Solomon's foreign amours in general terms, while the verb "clung" in A' is more pointed in depicting the intensity of his attraction. (In the context of the whole of 11:1-8 it also foreshadows that foreign women are going to replace that to which Solomon ought to be clinging, namely his fidelity to Y<small>HWH</small>.) Subunits B and B' explicate the phrase "many foreign women" of A: B' illustrates the "many," and B

---

[6] On the internal parallels among the six days see below under "Partial Symmetry."

details their foreign provenances. Subunits C and C' are related as expectation and fulfillment. YHWH had warned Israel against foreign marital entanglements that would endanger Israel's faithful adherence to YHWH (C); despite the warning, Solomon embroils himself in foreign marriages and is led astray, just as YHWH had forewarned (C').

The second part continues the same sort of progressive development. Subunit A picks up where the first part left off: Solomon was led astray by his foreign wives; subunit A' presents a theological evaluation of his actions: they were evil. (Note the word pair of opposites: "other gods" in A, "YHWH" in A'.) Subunits B and B' are approximately synonymous, though there is a subtle wordplay in B: "The mind of Solomon *(šlmh)* was not true *(šlm)*." The two words are from the same Hebrew root, *šlm*, which means approximately "to be as one is ideally supposed to be." (In various contexts and forms the word can be translated "to be whole, complete," "to be at peace," "to pay a debt," "to fulfill a promise," etc.) The narrator's wordplay implies that Solomon, *šlmh*, by not being true, *šlm*, was negating his own identity. Subunits C and C' are likewise approximately synonymous, but C' spells out a little more concretely what Solomon's "going after" other gods entailed, namely building sanctuaries for them. The final insult to YHWH is that these sanctuaries are built "across from Jerusalem" (literally "in the face of Jerusalem"), where they are in full view of the Temple of YHWH.

The two parts form a progression as well. The first part (11:1-3) is a bald statement of Solomon's sin. The second part (11:4-8) takes its starting point from the last subunit of the first part, and registers the particulars of Solomon's apostasy in detail. The last subunit, A'', contains verbal links with three preceding subunits to form multiple inclusions;[7] these links are italicized in the text above. The term "he did" marks A'' and A' (11:6a) and thus surrounds the final sequence; "his women" marks A'' and A (11:4a) and thus surrounds the second part; "foreign women" marks A'' and subunit A of the first part (11:1a) and thus surrounds the entire passage.

3. Genesis 2:18-25[8]

Parallelism between sequences is sometimes not a simple affair. In this passage YHWH God, in an attempt to answer *hāʾādām*'s need for companionship, creates first animals, which do not prove to be fit companions, then woman, who does. The process of making woman is

---

[7] On the device of "inclusion" see the section on "Partial Symmetry" below.

[8] On the overall structure of Gen 2:4b–3:24 see "Concentric Symmetry" above, pp. 21–23.

made more solemn by a doubling of each of the elements in the process
of making the animals.

A. Problem:
    a. It is not good for *hāʾādām* to be alone (2:18a);
    b. I will make a companion[9] for him (2:18b).
B.   Yhwh God acts:
    he shapes the animals and brings them to *hāʾādām* (2:19).
C.   *hāʾādām* acts:
    he names the animals (2:20a).
A'. Problem:
    b'. no companion is found for him (2:20b).
B'.   Yhwh God acts:
    (i) he puts *hāʾādām* to sleep and takes one of his ribs (2:21);
    (ii) he builds the rib into woman, and brings her to *hāʾādām* (2:22).
C'.   *hāʾādām* acts:
    (i) he greets the woman (2:23a);
    (ii) he names the woman (2:23b).
A''. Problem solved:
    a'. *hāʾādām* is no longer alone (2:24-25).

In this passage the "A" subunits act as a complex chiastic frame
around each sequence and around the whole.[10] The problem with
which the scene opens is *hāʾādām*'s solitude. A first attempt to resolve
the problem fails; when the second attempt succeeds, the scene is over.
The "B" subunits recount Yhwh God's deeds; the actions in subunit B
correspond to the *second* set of actions in B'.[11] The "C" subunits recount
hāʾādām's deeds, and here too the action in subunit C corresponds to
the *second* action in C'. The intensification of action from the first sequence to the second is accomplished in several ways: the doubling of
Yhwh God's and *hāʾādām*'s actions, the shift from prose to poetry in
2:23 (see below), and the successful solution to the opening problem.
The choice of parallel rather than reverse symmetry to describe the
creation of animals suggests that the dynamic of the passage is not so
much a contrast (the animals are a failure, the woman is a success) as a
progression. Animals have a certain connatural relationship with
hāʾādām: both are made from the earth (*hāʾădāmâ:* 2:7, 19), but it is insufficient to make them true companions. The companionship of the

---

  [9] The literal Hebrew, "a helper over against him," means someone who is
hāʾādām's supportive counterpart.

  [10] On the use of frame verses see "Partial Symmetry" below.

  [11] The treatment of the verbs of action in subunit B as forming one set and of
those in subunit B' as forming two sets is based on the recurrence of the subject
"Yhwh God" at the beginning of each set. The presence or absence of the phrase is
not always reflected faithfully in English versions.

woman is entirely suitable, since she is made from the body of *hāʾādām* himself.

Short as it is, this literary unit uses a surprising variety of symmetrical devices: framing verses, chiasm, parallelism. It is noteworthy that the point at which this narrative breaks into poetry, 2:23, uses the same devices: *hāʾādām*'s speech consists of two poetic lines, both using a six-stress meter. The first line, in 2 + 2 + 2 meter, consists of three verbless cries of recognition; its intense emotion is reflected in the brevity of the three members and the simplicity of the parallel (technically, alternating) symmetry of the last four stresses:

(-). This! At last!
A. Bone
B.   of my bone!
A'. Flesh
B'.   of my flesh!

The second line is more intellectual, using unusual passive verb forms, wordplay, chiastic symmetry, and slower meter (3 + 3):

A. This
B.   shall be called
C.   woman *(ʾiššâ)*
C'.   for from man *(ʾîš)*
B'.   has been taken
A'. this.

The repeated "this" frames the whole couplet and occurs between the two lines, much as the repeated elements of the "problem" in 2:18 unify the whole scene.

4. 1 Kings 11:31-39

Parallel symmetry can involve very long sequences of corresponding units. When this occurs the whole structure is generally limited to two sequences, and there may be occasional flaws in the symmetry. The latter can be accommodated only to the degree that the correspondences of other elements make the overall symmetry unmistakable.

In 1 Kings 11 YHWH has decided to punish Solomon's idolatry by wresting much of his territory from his control. For the sake of David's memory, however, YHWH tells Solomon that he will defer the punishment until the reign of Solomon's son, and YHWH will leave one tribe under his rule (11:11-13). Later in the chapter a prophet, Ahijah of Shiloh, encounters one of Solomon's officials, Jeroboam, in a field outside Jerusalem and delivers to Jeroboam YHWH's oracle pronouncing him the new ruler of the territory Solomon's heir is to lose. YHWH's oracle is almost entirely in parallel symmetry.

A.   ³¹I am tearing the <u>kingdom from</u> Solomon's <u>hand</u>
B.   and I will give you the ten tribes.
C.   ³²The <u>one tribe</u> will be his
D.   for the sake of my servant David
E.   and for the sake of <u>Jerusalem, the city I have chosen</u> from all the tribes of Israel.
F.   ³³for they¹² have forsaken me and bowed down . . . [to other gods]
G.   They did not <u>walk in my ways</u>
H.   <u>by doing what is right in my sight,</u>
I.   <u>my statutes and my</u> decrees,
J.   like <u>David</u> his father.
K.   ³⁴But I will <u>not</u> take the whole kingdom from his hand
                                        but will make him ruler <u>all the days</u> of his life,
                                        <u>for the sake</u> of my servant <u>David</u> whom I chose
                                        and who did keep my commandments and my statutes.
A'. ³⁵I will take the <u>kingship from the hand</u> of his son,
B'.   and I will give it to you, the ten tribes.
C'.   ³⁶To his son I will give <u>one tribe.</u>
D'.   <u>for the sake of</u> a lamp¹³ for <u>my servant David</u> all days before me
E'.   in <u>Jerusalem, the city I have chosen</u> for myself to put my name there.
F'.   ³⁷You I will take and you shall be king over all your heart desires; you shall be king over Israel.
G'.   ³⁸If you heed all I command you and <u>walk in my ways</u>
H'.   and <u>do what is right in my sight</u>
I'.   by keeping <u>my statutes and my</u> commandments
J'.   as did <u>David</u> my servant
+.¹⁴   I will be with you and I will build you a sure house

---

¹² The Hebrew text has unexpected plural forms here and in subunit G. Most English versions follow the ancient Greek translation here and read singular pronouns: "*He* has forsaken me . . ." etc.

¹³ The meaning of the word traditionally translated "lamp" *(nîr)* is disputed. It may mean a "fief" or small possession remaining under the control of the Davidic house.

¹⁴ This sentence has no corresponding subunit in the first sequence. For a discussion of the asymmetries in the passage, see below, pp. 108–110.

as I built for David and I will give you Israel.

K'.   [39]I shall punish <u>David's</u> line <u>for</u> this <u>sake</u> [i.e., "for this reason"], but <u>not</u> for <u>all the days</u>.

The verbal connections between corresponding pairs of subunits are impressive. Only subunits F and F' lack them, and these two subunits express most pointedly the difference between the first and second sequences. Both sequences announce YHWH's decision to take ten tribes from the control of Solomon's house and give them to Jeroboam. The first sequence looks to the past, identifying Solomon's disobedience and the people's idolatry (note the plural "they," in subunits F and G) as the reason for the divine decision. The second sequence looks to the future (subunit F') and insists on the requirement of obedience that is laid upon Jeroboam as condition for his dynastic success.

Progression can be seen in some of the corresponding subunits as well as the sequences as a whole. The shift from past to future is reflected in the focus on Solomon in the first sequence and his son in the second (subunits A and A', C and C'). The same shift occurs in subunits K and K'. In K, YHWH defers his punishment of Solomon's house until after Solomon's death; "all his days" refers to the length of Solomon's reign. In K', however, the purview is future; YHWH promises that the punishment of David's house will not last "all days." In other words, YHWH's fidelity to the Davidic covenant means mercy not only to Solomon himself but, in due course, to the dynastic line: its punishment will end and presumably its rule and glory will be restored.

5. 2 Kings 9:14-11:20

Commentaries usually treat the account of the anointing of Jehu (2 Kings 9:1-13) and the story of his uprising against the royal houses of Israel and Judah (2 Kings 9:14–10:36) as a single literary entity followed by a separate account of the seizure of power in Judah by the Queen Mother, Athaliah, and her eventual downfall (2 Kings 11:1-20). There are indications in the text, however, that this is not its inherent structure. First, Elisha is the immediate motivating force behind the action in 9:1-13 but thereafter disappears completely from the narrative until his death is recounted in 13:14-21. Second, 9:14-16 reintroduces Jehu as "son of Jehoshaphat, son of Nimshi," genealogical information already given in 9:2, and these verses repeat almost verbatim many details from 8:28-29. Together, as several commentators have recognized,[15] these observations argue that 9:14 is the beginning of a literary unit.

---

[15] See, for example, John Gray, *I & II Kings* (2d ed.; Philadelphia: Fortress, 1970) 537–38. He comments on both the introductory nature of 9:14 and the absence of

The complete change of characters and locale from chs. 9–10 (Jehu in Israel) to ch. 11 (Athaliah in Judah) is often seen as marking the division between two separate literary units. However, there is thematic continuity, since both accounts deal with the overthrow of a reigning dynasty and the seizure of power by someone from outside that dynasty.[16] Moreover, attention to the parallel structure of the whole passage shows no break between the two narratives.

A. Death of Joram, king of Israel, son of Ahab (9:14-26)
B.   Death of Ahaziah, king of Judah, grandson of Ahab[17] (9:27-29)
C.   Death of Jezebel, Baalist Queen-Mother of Israel, wife of Ahab (9:30-37)
A'. Death of seventy "sons" of Ahab (10:1-11)
B'.   Death of forty-two "brothers" of Ahaziah of Judah (10:12-17)
C'.   Death of worshipers of Baal in Samaria (10:18-28)
A". Death of Jehu, king of Israel (10:29-36)
B".   Death of seed royal of Ahaziah of Judah (11:1-3)
C".   Death of Athaliah, Baalist Queen-Mother of Judah, daughter of Ahab (11:4-20)[18]

Corresponding subunits are linked in different ways. The "A" subunits all relate directly to the throne of the kingdom of Israel. Joram was the reigning king; Ahab's "sons" (probably direct descendants, but more likely grandsons than sons; the Hebrew word *ben* can be used this way) would include all in the line of royal succession; Jehu seized the throne after he had exterminated Ahab's line. The "B" subunits all relate to the throne of the kingdom of Judah. Ahaziah was the reigning king; Ahaziah's "brothers" were probably relatives not in the direct line of succession; Ahaziah's "seed" would be his descendants and potential successors. The "C" subunits all relate to worshipers of Baal. Jezebel, the wife of Ahab and mother of Joram, was the champion of the cult of Baal in Israel; the cult's stronghold in Israel was in the capital city of Samaria;

---

prophetic figures thereafter, and speculates that 9:1-13 derives from a prophetic source and 9:14–10:31 from a secular one.

[16] Lloyd M. Barré, *The Rhetoric of Political Persuasion: The Narrative Artistry and Political Intentions of 2 Kings 9–11* (Washington, D.C.: Catholic Biblical Association of America, 1988).

[17] Or perhaps Ahab's nephew. Ahaziah's mother, Athaliah, was either Ahab's daughter (8:18) or his sister (8:26). For our purposes a decision on the historical question is unnecessary.

[18] Francisco O. García-Treto identified the first two-thirds of this pattern in "The Fall of the House: A Carnivalesque Reading of 2 Kings 9 and 10," *JSOT* 46 (1990) 53–54. He treats 9:1-14 and 10:29-31 as a "crowning/decrowning" inclusion around the material I have marked ABCA'B'C'.

Athaliah, daughter of Ahab of Israel[19] and mother of Ahaziah of Judah, introduced the cult of Baal into the kingdom of Judah.

The three sequences progress (though not entirely smoothly), from individuals immediately and closely related to Ahab of Israel (his son, grandson, and wife), through groups more distantly associated with Ahab (his remoter descendants, his grandson's collateral relatives, followers of Ahab's state-supported idolatry), to others still more distantly connected to Ahab (Jehu, his assassin and erstwhile servant [9:25]; Ahaziah's descendants, related to Ahab by blood but no longer part of Israel's dynastic line; Ahaziah's mother, closely related to Ahab by blood but, like the grandchildren she murdered, no longer part of Israel's dynastic family).

Behind this bloodbath stands a prophecy. In 1 Kings 21:22-24 we hear Yhwh's condemnation of Ahab:

> "I will make your house like the house of Jeroboam, son of Nebat, and like the house of Baasha, son of Ahijah, because of how you have incited wrath and led Israel to sin." To Jezebel too Yhwh spoke: "Dogs shall eat Jezebel within the confines of Jezreel." Whoever of Ahab's who dies in the city, dogs shall eat; and whoever dies in open country, birds of the sky shall eat.

The whole passage, then, is a chronicle of death, and more precisely death as it inexorably obliterates the line of Ahab of Israel, spreading from those closest to him to those who belong to him only tangentially. The regularity of the parallel symmetry adds to the sense of inevitability. Yhwh's word cannot be escaped; it reaches from generation to generation and from kingdom to kingdom to effect what God has pronounced.

---

[19] See note 17 above.

3. ALTERNATING REPETITION

Alternating repetition involves only two sets of corresponding elements, but the relationships between them can be of several types. In its simplest form, ABA', alternating repetition is a subtype of concentric symmetry, with the central element often pivotal to the narrative (see the first example below). In a slightly more expanded form, ABA'B', it becomes a subtype of forward symmetry. Still more developed forms may have either an odd (e.g., ABA'B'A'') or even (e.g., ABA'B'A''B'') number of components, but they generally have the same forward thrust as parallel symmetry.

Two other patterns are similar, at least schematically, to alternating repetition, but should be distinguished carefully from it. The first is "inclusion," where a single repeated element marks the beginning and ending of a literary unit; this too could be schematized ABA'. The second is "framing verses," where a series of corresponding subunits is surrounded and separated by a series of relatively brief repeated elements, rather like a chain of inclusions (ABA'B'A''). In each of these patterns there are notable differences between the major subunits ("B") and the repeated elements that frame them ("A"). First, the repeated "A" elements are generally quite a bit shorter; second, unlike the major subunits the repeated "A" elements do not show significant progression or contrast. "Inclusion" and "framing verses" will be treated later, as types of "Partial Symmetry."

As in the other patterns we have examined, alternating repetition invites comparison of the corresponding elements as well as comparison of the successive sequences, although the brevity of two-member sequences lessens the utility of this level of comparison for interpretive purposes. The linear progression of the whole narrative is frequently more productive for interpretation. On the other hand, the potential of the pattern for a concentric reading (ABA'B'A'' could be seen as overlapping ABA' and

BAB' structures) makes the pattern apt for expressing a series of contrasts or changes within that linear progression.

1. 1 Kings 2:36-46a

When David is about to die he urges Solomon to dispose of two people David considers enemies, Joab and Shimei. Solomon's treatment of Shimei is recounted in a three-part narrative, organized ABA'.

A.	Solomon's first interview with Shimei (2:36-38a)
a.	"The king sent and summoned Shimei and said to him . . ." (2:36)
b.	"And Shimei said to the king . . ." (2:37)
B.	Narrative of Shimei's disobedience (2:38b-41)
A'.	Solomon's second interview with Shimei (2:42-46a)
a'.	"The king sent and summoned Shimei and said unto him . . ." (2:42)
b'.	"And the king said to Shimei . . ." (2:44).

Comparison of the two "A" subunits reveals strong contrast. In the first there is the potential for peace between the two: Solomon imposes certain restrictions on Shimei, and the latter accepts them. But by the second interview Shimei has violated Solomon's commands, and Solomon condemns him to death. There is, however, a more subtle contrast as well; it is pointed up by the alternating symmetry of the subunits aba'b'. In the first interview Solomon speaks and Shimei answers. In the second Solomon speaks, asking Shimei for an explanation of his behavior, but at the point where we expect Shimei to respond ("And Shimei said to the king," as in the first interview) the narrator tells us that *the king* continues to speak ("And the king said to Shimei"). The words are unnecessary, since the king is already speaking, and the contrast with the corresponding words in the first interview is thereby highlighted. The contrast is puzzling until we examine subunit B.

The central subunit continues the concentric structure of the whole narrative with a detailed and lengthy composition. The following translation is literal, with repeated words underlined.

A.	[38]. . . And stayed (Hebrew <u>wayyēšeb</u>)
B.	<u>Shimei in Jerusalem</u> many days.
+.	[39]At the end of three years, two slaves of Shimei fled to Achish, son of Maakah, king of Gath.[1]
C.	They <u>told</u> Shimei,
D.	"Your <u>slaves</u> are in <u>Gath</u>."
E.	[40]<u>Shimei</u> got up,

---

[1] This lengthy component has no corresponding subunit in the otherwise symmetrical structure. See the section below on asymmetry for further discussion.

F.	saddled <u>his</u> donkey
G.	and went to Gath, to Achish
F'.	to look for <u>his</u> slaves.
E'.	<u>Shimei</u> went,
D'.	and brought his <u>slaves</u> from <u>Gath</u>.
C'.	⁴¹Solomon was <u>told</u>
B'.	that <u>Shimei</u> had gone from <u>Jerusalem</u> to Gath
A'.	and returned (Hebrew <u>wayyāšob</u>).

The structure strongly emphasizes Shimei's destination, Gath: it is mentioned five times, including in the central phrase. The location is crucial. In the first interview Solomon forbade Shimei to leave Jerusalem, but imposed capital punishment only on his crossing the Kidron (which would have been Shimei's route to his own home, Bahurim, on the Mount of Olives). Gath was in the opposite direction (southwest of Jerusalem rather than east), and a journey to Gath would not require crossing the Kidron. Solomon's claim in the second interview, therefore, that he had imposed capital punishment on any journey outside Jerusalem (compare 2:36-37 with 2:42) is false, and Solomon is shown to be convicting Shimei by falsehood. This is tacitly confirmed by Solomon himself in 2:44 when he points out to Shimei that evil is befalling him not because he disobeyed Solomon's order but because of the evil Shimei had done to David. Solomon's duplicity explains why he continues speaking in 2:44: since he knows his accusation is false he does not allow Shimei an opportunity to respond.

The identification of "Gath" as Shimei's destination, which he reaches in the exact center of the entire concentrically organized passage, is the key to the whole. It marks a turning point for Shimei: his actions will cost him his life; it marks also a turning point for Solomon: his words reveal a side of his character that we have not suspected, a ruthless lack of scruples in pursuing what he wants.

2. Genesis 12:1

When God is about to send Abram on the journey that will eventually bring him to the promised land, God uses an odd phrase: *lek-lĕkā*. The phrase cannot be translated literally; it means something like "Get yourself going." It is extremely rare in the Hebrew Bible, occurring elsewhere only once, Gen 22:2, where again God is speaking to Abraham;[2] grammatically similar forms are found in Josh 22:4 (in the plural)

---

[2] It is noteworthy that the stories of Abram/Abraham, like those of Jacob/Israel, are chiastically organized (for the Abraham stories see below, pp. 89–92; for the Jacob stories see above, pp. 31–34). In that pattern God's first speech to Abram and

and in Song of Songs 2:10 and 13 (in the feminine). In all cases the sense is an urging to undertake a journey of some sort. The phrase has an alternating repetition of consonants, *l - k - l - k*, whose forward symmetry strengthens the force of the imperative verb (*lek* = "Go!") and of the whole phrase.

3. 1 Samuel 1:12-13[3]

One of the possibilities alternating repetition affords the narrator is that of depicting two points of view. Witness the brief scene found between two pieces of discourse in 1 Samuel 1. Hannah is praying. We hear the words of her prayer in 1:11, we watch a scene unfold in 1:12-13, and we hear Eli's chastisement of Hannah in 1:14. The scene:

> A.   [12]And as she continued to pray before YHWH,
> B.   Eli was watching her mouth.
> A'. [13]But Hannah was speaking in her heart.
> B'.   Only her lips were moving;
> A". her voice was not heard.
> B".   And Eli thought her drunk.

The "A" subunits emphasize vocal and/or auditory phenomena and primarily reflect Hannah's point of view. The "B" subunits focus on visual phenomena and reflect Eli's point of view. Because Hannah is silent, only she knows of her "prayer" and of her "speaking in her heart." Eli can see her lips move but misapprehends the meaning of what he sees. The progression of the "A" subunits is from a generalization (Hannah is praying) to greater precision (speaking in her heart, voice not heard). The "B" subunits progress in the opposite direction: from specifics (mouth, lips) to generalization (that she is drunk). The contrary movement of the two progressions reflects the way in which Eli's careful observations lead him to draw exactly the wrong conclusion.

4. 1 Kings 20:16-21

A similar though more ambitious use of alternating repetition to portray different points of view shows us the prelude to battle between

---

Abram's resultant journey to Canaan (Gen 12:1-9) correspond to God's last speech to Abraham and Abraham's resultant journey to sacrifice Isaac (Gen 22:1-19). Among the repeated elements that link these two subunits is the unusual phrase *lek-lĕkā*.

[3] J. P. Fokkelman, *Narrative Art and Poetry in the Books of Samuel: A Full Interpretation Based on Stylistic and Structural Analyses*. 4 vols. (Assen: Van Gorcum, 1981–1993) 4:42–43.

Israelite forces under King Ahab and the Aramean aggressor, Ben-Hadad. In the preceding verses (20:13-15) Ahab has been advised by a prophet that YHWH intends to give Ahab victory over Ben-Hadad, and the prophet has even set out divine directives for Ahab's military strategy. When Ahab asks how he is to achieve the victory the prophet responds, "Thus says YHWH, by the men of the district commanders" (possibly a technical term for some sort of shock troops?). When Ahab continues, "And who shall finish the battle?"[4] the prophet replies, "You." So Ahab musters his whole army, first the "men of the district commanders," and after them all the forces of Israel. We then witness the following scene:

> A. [16]They <u>set out</u> at noon.
> B.   <u>Ben-Hadad</u>, drinking, was drunk in the tents,
> >   he and the thirty-two kings helping him.
> A'. [17]The men of the district commanders <u>set out</u> first.
> B'.   <u>Ben-Hadad</u> sent, and they told him, "People have set out from
> >   Samaria."
> >   [18]He said, "If they have set out for peace, take them alive.
> >   And if they have set out for war, take them alive."
> A". [19]These <u>set out</u> from the city: the men of the district commanders and
> >   the army in their train.
> +.   [20]And they killed one another.
> B"   Aram fled and Israel chased them,
> >   and <u>Ben-Hadad</u> escaped by horse and steeds.
> A'''.[21]The king of Israel <u>set out</u> . . . .

The "A" subunits all focus on the Israelite army, the "B" subunits on Ben-Hadad and the Aramean forces. The progression in the "A" subunits is marked by the verb "to set out," which, in Hebrew, is the first word in each subunit: we watch the Israelite forces emerge gradually from the besieged city of Samaria. The sortie begins in the bright light of noon (A). First to set out are the "men of the district commanders" (A'), as YHWH had commanded. They are followed by the whole army (A") and, also as YHWH had commanded, the king emerges last to bring the battle to an end (A'''). The progression in the "B" subunits shows Ben-Hadad sinking deeper and deeper into drunkenness and disaster. He has in fact been drinking since 20:12. By the time our scene begins at noon he is already drunk (B). He "sends," though his order is not quite

---

[4] The meaning of Ahab's words is uncertain. He asks literally "Who shall bind the battle?"—an idiom that occurs nowhere else in the Hebrew Bible. Many translations take it in the sense of "joining" battle, and therefore translate "Who shall begin the battle?" In view of what follows, however, it seems more likely that the reference is to ending the battle, as in the English idiom of "wrapping things up."

coherent. The Hebrew text has no direct object for the verb: he simply "sends . . ." somebody, anybody.[5] When he learns of the sortie from Samaria he issues oddly phrased orders, as if his thought processes are muddled (B').[6] His part of the scene climaxes with his ignominious flight from the victorious King Ahab (B'').

The genius of this use of alternating repetition is that it allows the narrator to achieve what is almost impossible in a linear medium like literature: the depiction of simultaneity. In the previous example we saw one scene, Hannah praying, from two points of view, Hannah's and Eli's. In this example we see simultaneously two series of actions that take place at the same time but in different places.

There is one asymmetrical element in the passage, the sentence "And they killed one another" (marked "+" above). The sentence in Hebrew is simply three words: literally "each-man killed his-man." The various functions of asymmetry will be explored in greater detail below, but it is worthwhile to signal here the function of emphasis. When a symmetrical pattern is strongly enough established to sustain some deviation, that deviation calls attention to itself. Here the sentence intrudes into the alternating repetition. It marks the moment where the points of view of Israel and Aram coincide—the moment of actual battle. It is noteworthy in another respect as well. Before and after the battle not only are Israel's and Aram's points of view separate, but their identities are also clear. Here, at the moment of actual encounter, there is no longer Israelite or Aramean, but simply one human being killing another.

5. 2 Kings 17:6-41

This chapter has long been recognized as a theological explanation of the fall of the kingdom of Israel, according to the Deuteronomic school (the creative force behind the books of Joshua, Judges, 1–2 Samuel, and 1–2 Kings). Its structure, however, affords a more nuanced reading of that explanation.[7] Alternating repetition structures the passage on several levels.

---

[5] Some translations supply a direct object because of the oddness of the Hebrew text (e.g., the NRSV supplies "scouts"). But the oddness of the text is precisely its point: Ben-Hadad is drunk, and he is not thinking tactically.

[6] We would expect either "If they have set out for peace, take them alive; if they have set out for war, kill them!" or perhaps "Whether they have come out for war or for peace, take them alive." The phrasing of what we actually hear him say betrays his condition.

[7] There are several indicators of this structure, e.g., the verbal links between 17:6 and 17:24 and the use of the phrase "until this very day" to end three of the four

A. Israelites (17:6-23)
>   a. Israelites deported by the king of Assyria to many cities (17:6)
>   b. Israelites had abandoned the worship of YHWH (17:7-23)
>   > A_1. Israel's sin (17:7-12)
>   > B_1. YHWH's response (17:13-14a)
>   > A_2. Israel's sin (17:14b-17)
>   > B_2. YHWH's response (17:18a)
>   > A_3. Judah's sin (17:18b-19)
>   > B_3. YHWH's response (17:20)
>   > A_4. Israel's sin (17:21-22)
>   > B_4. YHWH's response (17:23)

B. Foreigners (17:24-34a)
>   a'. Foreigners imported by the king of Assyria from many cities (17:24)
>   b'. Foreigners undertake the worship of YHWH (17:25-34a)[8]

A'. Israelites (17:34b-40)

B'. Foreigners (17:41)

The innermost series of alternating subunits, in 17:7-23, is linked both thematically and verbally. The A_n subunits and the B_n subunits are related as crime and punishment. The A_n subunits describe the sins of Israel and Judah with increasing intensity. The people of Israel followed the errant ways of the kings of Israel in practicing the irregular cults (high places, sacred objects of stone and wood) of the nations who had lived there before them (A_1). What was worse, they rejected YHWH's laws and commandments and turned to idols and to the Canaanite god Baal (A_2). Still worse, even Judah, where YHWH's own temple sat in the capital at Jerusalem, followed the practices Israel had fallen into (A_3). Worst of all (from a Deuteronomic perspective), the Israelites worshiped the golden calves Jeroboam had set up at Bethel and Dan (A_4). The B_n subunits interlock with a series of phrases: "by the hand of my servants the prophets" (B_1); "he turned them away from his face" (B_2); "he threw them from his face" (B_3); "he turned Israel away from his face, as he had predicted by the hand of all his servants the prophets" (B_4). Here too there is a progression. In (B_1) YHWH merely warns the people of Israel and Judah. In (B_2) he punishes Israel but leaves Judah. In (B_3) he punishes "all the descendants of Israel" (i.e., of the patriarch Jacob); no exception is made for Judah. Finally, (B_4) summarizes the whole series.

The intermediary level reveals the main dynamic of the whole passage. It is not simply a condemnation of Israel for its idolatry and

---

major sections. (The first words of v. 34 should be read with what precedes them rather than with what follows.)

[8] We will examine the structure of this subunit later, under "Compound Symmetry."

abandonment of YHWH, but a comparison of the Israelites with the foreign peoples brought by the Assyrians to replace the depleted population (subunits a and a'). (The tactic was apparently typical of the Assyrians: disperse conquered peoples through foreign territories and replace them with exiles from elsewhere; mutual distrust and lack of solidarity among the resultant mixed populations would hamper any effective resistance to Assyrian domination.) According to Deuteronomic theology Israel's sin, the wrong for which YHWH allowed the Assyrians to conquer and exile them, was their abandonment of YHWH and their worship of other gods in place of YHWH (subunit b). By contrast the foreigners imported into Israel, from whom YHWH had never asked any sort of worship, were quick to incorporate worship of the local deity, YHWH, into their cultic practices (b').

The first level of alternating repetition shows a great disparity of length. Subunits A and B are much longer than the corresponding subunits (A contains 18 verses while A' is only 7; B contains 9 while B' is only 1). For this reason subunits A' and B' act as a recapitulation of the whole; they do not advance the argument to a new stage.[9] Subunit A' repeats the condemnation of Israel for its abandonment of YHWH and worship of other gods. Subunit B' repeats the startling notice that the foreigners had taken up the worship of YHWH alongside their own.

6. 1 Samuel 8:1–12:25[10]

Alternating repetition can structure a large block of text as well as shorter passages. 1 Sam 8:1 marks the beginning of a new stage in the narrative of Samuel. At the end of ch. 7 we have a narrator's remark summarizing Samuel's whole career (7:15-17). In 8:1 Samuel is old, and the question of his successor looms. His sons prove unworthy, and the people want Samuel to name someone to the unprecedented office of king. The story of Saul's accession to kingship in Israel covers chs. 8–11 and climaxes with Samuel's lengthy speech in ch. 12 about the implications of the new institution of monarchy among YHWH's people.

---

[9] More properly subunits A' and B' constitute a concluding epitome, a device we will examine below, under "Partial Symmetry."

[10] See J. P. Fokkelman, *Narrative Art and Poetry in the Books of Samuel* 4:532–38. Fokkelman cites the work of three other scholars on this text: V. Philips Long, *The Reign and Rejection of King Saul: A Case for Literary and Theological Coherence* (Atlanta: Scholars, 1989) 175; Dennis J. McCarthy, "The Inauguration of Monarchy in Israel," *Int* 27 (1973) 401–12; and Matitiahu Tsevat, "The Biblical Account of the Foundation of the Monarchy in Israel," in idem, *The Meaning of the Book of Job and Other Biblical Studies: Essays on the Literature and Religion of the Hebrew Bible* (New York: Ktav; Dallas: IJS, 1980) 77–99.

A. 1 Sam 8:1-22
    Main characters: Samuel, the people
    Location: Assembly of the people at Ramah
    Issue: The people request a king; Samuel warns them, then agrees.

B. 1 Sam 9:1–10:16
    Main characters: Saul, Samuel
    Location: Journey from home and return
    Issue: Saul's secret anointing

A'. 1 Sam 10:17-27
    Main characters: Samuel, the people
    Location: Assembly of the people at Mizpah
    Issue: Samuel chooses Saul by lot and establishes the kingship.

B'. 1 Sam 11:1-13
    Main character: Saul
    Location: From Jabesh to Gibeah to Jabesh
    Issue: Saul's first victory

A". 1 Sam 11:14–12:25
    Main characters: Samuel, the people
    Location: Assembly of the people at Gilgal
    Issue: Samuel renews the kingship and addresses the people about kingship.

The three "A" subunits all describe assemblies of the people under the leadership of Samuel, and all project an attitude of great reserve about the institution of kingship. All three assemblies take place at sites closely associated with him: 7:16-17 says, "Each year he went around to Bethel and Gilgal and Mizpah and judged Israel in all these places. Then he would go back to Ramah, since his home was there; he judged Israel there too." Since the people initiate the first assembly, it takes place at Samuel's home in Ramah, where they gather to meet him. Samuel calls the next two assemblies at other places where he regularly exercises authority over Israel.

There is a progression in the three assemblies. In the first Samuel resists the people's desire for a king until Yʜᴡʜ tells him to agree to it, but he takes no action toward choosing a candidate. In the second Samuel begins by reproaching the people for their insistence on a king. He then casts lots to reveal the divinely chosen king, who turns out to be Saul. (Since Yʜᴡʜ has already identified Saul to Samuel in the previous subunit, and Samuel has secretly anointed him, there is no doubt for Samuel—or for the reader—about who will be chosen.) In the third Samuel again reproaches the Israelites for having demanded a king, but assures them that Yʜᴡʜ will not abandon them for that sin as long as they remain faithful to Yʜᴡʜ in the future.

The three assemblies have another thread of progression as well. In the first Samuel warns the people in detail about the ways in which

kingship will impinge upon their lives and encroach upon their free-
dom. A king will take their sons and daughters, their best properties
and servants, and tax their crops and herds (8:11-17). In the second assembly Samuel writes in a book the "customary practice" of the king—
presumably a listing of royal rights and duties—and deposits the book
in the sanctuary of YHWH (10:25). This is no doubt an attempt to cir-
cumscribe the king's powers and protect both God and the people from
royal abuses. In the third assembly, which contains Samuel's last long
address to the people, he implicitly contrasts his own behavior with
what he has warned Israel to expect (8:11-17), and what Israel has indeed already experienced (11:7-8), at the hands of a king. He claims "in
the presence of YHWH and of his anointed" (that is, the king: 12:3) that
he has never taken so much as an ox or donkey from them, accepted
bribes, or otherwise acted improperly, and the people freely acknowledge his integrity.

The "B" subunits contain much more dramatic narratives, both fea-
turing Saul, and betray little of the doubt about kingship in general or
Saul in particular that characterizes the "A" subunits. The first describes how Samuel comes to encounter Saul and anoint him as king at
YHWH's behest. The second describes Saul's first accomplishment as
publicly acknowledged king. It is a two-edged victory wherein Saul
liberates the embattled population of Jabesh-Gilead, but only by exer-
cising absolute authority over the military muster of all of Israel and
Judah. The two subunits are linked by an explicit motif, relatively
minor in both, that will nevertheless become a major motif as the story
of King Saul develops. The spirit of YHWH "rushes upon" Saul in both
stories (10:6, 10; 11:6). As Saul's tragic tale continues in later chapters,
and his relationship with David becomes more and more paranoid, the
"spirit of YHWH" that possesses him will be described as an "evil" spirit
(1 Sam 16:14, 23).

4. PARTIAL SYMMETRY

Some symmetrical patterns, while they affect our reading of an entire literary unit, only involve some of its subunits. Such patterns can be called "partial symmetry." The commonest type of partial symmetry is inclusion; in inclusion the repeated elements that establish the pattern mark the beginning and end of the literary unit. A less common partial pattern, epitome, is found at the beginning or the end, but not at both.

Inclusion

In inclusion the repeated element is usually a word or phrase[1] at or near the beginning and end of the unit; these act as a kind of frame or border around the unit and indicate its limits. Because they mark the beginning and end of a passage they are important for revealing the internal structure of any larger units of which the passage may be a subunit; this in turn can highlight thematic organization as well. Furthermore, as in concentric structure, a position at the extremes of a unit can be emphatic; thus the repeated element itself is often of special significance within the unit it surrounds.

The whole literary unit may be made up of several subunits, but they are generally much longer than any subunit marked by the inclusive repetition. In other words, a repeated word or phrase may form an inclusion around a lengthy speech but not around a passage of only one or two short sentences. Or a repeated sentence may form an inclusion around a series of scenes but not around a short single scene. The reason for this is straightforward. When the inclusion involves subunits of a length comparable to the subunit(s) they surround, the whole

---

[1] Thematic inclusion is certainly possible, and almost certainly present in biblical narrative. But it is so difficult to demonstrate convincingly in the absence of clearer verbal repetitions that, in our examples, we will not rely on it.

structure manifests reverse symmetry (ABA') and the inclusive subunits A and A' are simply the outermost subunits of the structure. To
signal the relative brevity of inclusive elements schematically I will use
lower-case letters (a, a') to indicate them and upper case X to represent
other blocks of material, whatever their structure.[2] As usual, corresponding upper case letters (A, A') will indicate symmetrically corresponding subunits.

For analytic purposes several subtypes of inclusion can be distinguished, although these are no more than categories of convenience and
there is some overlap among them. The subtypes differ primarily in the
connection of the repeated elements to the material they surround and
secondarily in the complexity of the repeated elements themselves. The
simplest forms of inclusion involve repeated elements that are integral
parts of the material they surround and do not form separable subunits
within the whole. We shall term this "internal inclusion." When there is
only one element repeated at the beginning and end of the unit we have
a single internal inclusion (aXa'). If there are several repeated elements
the inclusion is multiple. Multiple repeated elements may be ordered in
parallel (abXa'b') or chiastically (abXb'a'); the latter is more common.
Repeated elements must fall quite close to the beginning and end of the
literary unit; the farther repeated elements are from those points the less
effectively they function as an inclusion.

When the repeated elements mark small literary units separable
from the subunit(s) they surround, the inclusion functions more clearly
as a frame. We will therefore call this structure a "framing inclusion"
and schematize it by separating the inclusion from the remaining material: a X a'. Here too the repeated elements can be single or multiple,
parallel or chiastic. Framing inclusion has the potential for several repetitions and can thus be used to connect a whole series of literary units:
a X a' X a'' X a'''.

Sometimes the repeated elements do not belong to the literary unit
they surround but to the units that precede and follow it: X_1a X_2a'X_3.
This can be called "external inclusion";[3] biblical scholars have long

---

[2] The distinction is sometimes easier in theory than in practice. Our earlier
analysis of the Jacob cycle (see pp. 31–34 above) treated the first and last subunits as
part of the chiastic structure. In view of the fact that they are genealogies while the
remaining subunits are narratives, one could analyze B through B' as the chiasm
and the surrounding genealogies as an inclusion. This analysis is the more persua-
sive when we see that genealogies surround the chiastic arrangement of Abraham
stories as well (see pp. 89–92).

[3] H. Van Dyke Parunak may have been the first to distinguish between "internal" and "external" inclusion. Parunak points out that external inclusion is often
used "to set off material that is peripheral to the course of the argument" ("Oral

identified it by the technical term "resumptive repetition." In the history of the development of the text the device often indicates the point where an editor inserted new material (X_2 above) into a preexisting document, then resumed use of the original document by repeating something from just before the insertion (a, a'). In the literary structure of the resultant text the repeated element is attached to the material to which it originally belonged, but it points to the separate and presumptively unitary character of the inserted material as well. It also calls attention to the location of the surrounded material. Particularly if it is a later insertion, it was inserted precisely at this point, not elsewhere. This invites us to examine its connection to what precedes and follows it.

In all these forms of inclusion the interpretive strategies used for forward and reverse symmetry are appropriate: comparison of the corresponding units (a, a') and, in the case of multiple inclusions, of the corresponding sequences (ab, b'a'). There may be dynamics of progression or contrast, but the relative subordination of the inclusive elements to the larger whole will often weaken or eliminate those effects.

Finally, what we may call "complex inclusion" links two or more successive literary units and involves two distinct repeated elements, one that marks the beginning of each unit and another that marks the end: aXb a'X'b'. The structure easily permits several repetitions: aXb a'X'b' a''X''b'', etc. The similarity of this pattern to parallel symmetry suggests its likely interpretive dynamic: comparison of corresponding elements and progression from one unit to the next, although the progression will be effected more by the main subunits (X, X') than by the inclusive ones.

Subunits surrounded by an inclusion may have their own symmetrical pattern (for example, aBCB'C'a', alternating repetition within an inclusion). In such cases we may speak of "composite symmetry"; this will be discussed in a later section. Similarly the individual literary units in a series linked by framing or complex inclusions (i.e., the "X" subunits) may correspond structurally, though they need not.

Epitome

Epitome is a device through which the organization of a short subunit at the beginning or end of a literary unit reflects the organization

---

Typesetting," *Bib* 62 [1981]160). This is true; however, he does not distinguish "external" inclusion from "framing" inclusion, which does not subordinate the material it frames.

of the whole. If the epitome comes at the end of the unit (schematized ABab), it acts as a concluding summary; if it comes at the beginning (abAB), it acts as a sort of introductory outline or table of contents. The device occurs in both poetry and prose, but it has not been widely identified or studied.[4] In most of the examples the repeated elements are generally thematic, not verbal. For the analyst as well as the casual reader this makes epitome more difficult to recognize than forms of symmetry based on verbal repetition.

Interpretation of epitome depends on whether it comes at the beginning or end of the literary unit. If it comes at the beginning it reduces the level of tension by announcing the course of narrative development in advance. Generally that lessening of suspense permits the reader to attend to other aspects of the story—characterization, allusions to other texts, motif development, or the like. Alternatively the presaged narrative development may be incomplete, and an unannounced component may enter the story (e.g., abABC or, as in the case of 1 Kings 18:1 below, abACB). The disruption of symmetry focuses attention on the unexpected material and thus highlights it.[5] If the epitome comes at the end of the literary unit it recapitulates and thus emphasizes by repetition the principal themes of the unit.

A. INTERNAL INCLUSION

1. 1 Kings 2:38b, 41

We have already examined the concentric structure of the narrative scene in 1 Kings 2:38b-41 (see pp. 48–49). The first and last words of the scene, although they are from different roots (*yšb*, "to dwell," and *šwb*, "to return"), are identical in the consonantal text *wyšb*).[6] Although we treated this above as the first subunit of the concentric structure, it functions also as an internal verbal inclusion, with its own pointed effect. It implies that Shimei's "staying" in Jerusalem for three years was a sincere attempt to conform to Solomon's strictures, and that his "return" to Jerusalem from Gath had, in the long run, changed nothing. He had violated the letter of Solomon's prohibition but not its spirit.

---

[4] Parunak gives some examples of epitome at the beginning of the unit, which he calls "introductory summary" ("Oral Typesetting," 163).

[5] See the section on "asymmetry" below.

[6] In ancient Hebrew the vowel sounds, though pronounced, were not written. This allows a type of repetition for which no adequate English equivalent is available. The closest we might come would be the visual echoing of words spelled alike but pronounced differently, like "polish" (to scour) and "Polish" (from Poland).

2. 1 Kings 1:24-27

A literal translation of Nathan's speech to David, preserving the Hebrew word order as far as possible, runs:

> [24]Nathan said, "<u>My lord the king</u>, you have said that Adonijah shall be king after me, and he shall sit upon my throne. [25]For he has gone down today and sacrificed bull and fatling and flock in quantity, and he has invited all the king's sons, the army commanders, and Abiathar the priest. Right now they are eating and drinking before him, and they have said, 'Long live King Adonijah!' [26]But me, your servant, and Zadok the priest, and Benaiah son of Johoiada, and Solomon, your servant, he did not invite. [27]If this situation has come from my lord the king, you did not inform your servants who will sit upon the throne of <u>my lord the king</u> after him."

Except for the last word ("after him"), Nathan's speech begins and ends with the phrase "my lord the king," which is found once more toward the end of the speech. This highlights the importance of the phrase, which is part of a complex and ironic wordplay in the speech. Nathan feigns to believe that David has decreed the succession of Adonijah. Nathan knows that is false, but he intends to provoke David against Adonijah and thereby win David to supporting Nathan's choice for king, Solomon. By painting Adonijah's feast as an enthronement ceremony Nathan forces on David the question of who is really in charge: is David still the king, or has Adonijah usurped his authority? That dilemma comes to expression in two very similar-sounding phrases: "my lord the king" *(ʾădōnî hammelek)*, which occurs at the beginning and end of the speech, and "King Adonijah" *(hammelek ʾădōnîyāhû)*, which occurs in the exact middle of the speech.[7]

3. Esther 5:9-14

As the book of Esther approaches its climax it brings Haman to his highest peak of expectation before extinguishing his hopes and eventually his life in favor of Mordecai. The moment of reversal is preceded by two scenes, the first banquet given by Queen Esther (5:1–8), and Haman's gloating return to his own home (5:9–14). The second scene is marked by a subtle but significant inclusion with three repeated elements in parallel

---

[7] There is another example of inclusion within Nathan's speech. His list of people Adonijah did not invite to the feast, 1:26, begins and ends with an identification of Nathan himself and then of Solomon as "your servant." Nathan's implication is that he and Solomon (and everyone in between) are loyal to David, whereas Adonijah and his invited guests are not.

order. Unfortunately, some of the inclusive terms can be reflected only by
a strained translation:

> [9]Haman <u>went out</u> that day <u>rejoicing *(śāmēaḥ)* and-good *(wĕṭôb)*</u> of heart . . .
> [10] . . . [13]
> [14]Zeresh his wife and all his friends told him, "Let them make a pole fifty
> cubits high, and in the morning speak to the king to have them hang
> Mordecai on it. Then <u>go in</u> to the banquet with the king <u>rejoicing
> *(śāmēaḥ)*</u>." <u>And-good-was *(wayyîṭab)*</u> the advice in Haman's opinion, and
> he made the pole.

The first set of repeated elements is the contrasting word pair "to go
out" *(yṣ²)* and "to come in" *(bw²)*. Both verbs are very common in Hebrew and would be insufficient in themselves to establish a symmetrical pattern. In this case, however, the verbs have another link: both
refer to Queen Esther's banquets. In 5:9 Haman is leaving the first banquet and in 5:14 his wife and friends are assuring him that he can attend the second banquet in confident good spirits. That link, together
with the other two repeated elements, helps establish the inclusion and
the two verbs' place in it.

The other two repeated elements are consecutive in both verses,
though in 5:14 they are separated by a syntactic break: the first element
ends the speech of Haman's wife and friends; the second begins a statement by the narrator. There is a change as well in the grammatical construction of the second element. In 5:9 the word is an adjective *(ṭôb,*
"good"; in this context "happy, content") from the root *ṭwb*; in 5:14 the
word is a verb *(yîṭab*, "to be good, to go well"; in this context "to be sat-
isfactory, pleasing"), from the related root *yṭb*.[8]

The parallel order of the three repeated elements (abcXa'b'c') suggests a dynamic of forward development and intensification. The development is primarily expressed in the shift from the adjective *ṭôb* to
the verb *yîṭab*. When Haman "went out" from Queen Esther's first banquet his self-satisfaction was a state of being ("good of heart"), quickly
marred by the sight of Mordecai (5:9b). Having been "well advised"
and having acted accordingly, he can "go in" to the Queen's second
banquet actively anticipating the elimination of the man whose presence so offends him. The shift from first (past) banquet to second (future) banquet, from emotional state to action, from rejoicing in his
present status to rejoicing over future victory heightens Haman's
hubris. This in turn increases dramatic tension and prepares for the
irony of his imminent downfall.

---

[8] The two three-letter roots *ṭwb* and *yṭb* probably derive from an older, two-letter
root, *ṭb*.

4. Ruth 4:9-11a

After Naomi's closest kinsman renounces his right to purchase the property of Naomi's dead husband and sons, Boaz agrees to purchase it and to marry Naomi's widowed daughter-in-law, the Moabite woman Ruth. Boaz's negotiations with the unnamed kinsman take place "at the gate" (4:1), that is, in the venue for public, legal decisions. His speech, then, is a legally binding agreement, which he requires the assembled people to witness. The speech itself involves a single internal inclusion, but the following narrative line, which introduces the assembly's response, extends the inclusion to three elements, chiastically arranged (ab cXc' b'a').

> [9]Boaz said to the elders and all the people,
> "You are witnesses today that I have purchased everything that was Elimelech's and everything that was Chilion's and Mahlon's from Naomi's hand. [10]Ruth too, the Moabite, Mahlon's wife, I have purchased as my wife, to establish the dead man's name over his inheritance, that the dead man's name might not disappear from among his brothers and from the gate of his homeland. You are witnesses today."
> [11]All the people who were in the gate and the elders said, "Witnesses [yes, we are] . . . ."

The structural effect of the repeated elements here is complicated. The single inclusion (the phrase "You are witnesses today") unifies Boaz's speech by marking its beginning and its end. The chiastic triple inclusion reinforces that effect. However, it also links the unit of Boaz's speech, with its narrative introduction, to the following unit of the assembly's response, with its narrative introduction, to produce an alternating repetition:[9]

A. Narrative introduction to Boaz's speech (4:9a)
B.   Boaz's speech (4:9b–10; "You are witnesses . . .")
A'. Narrative introduction to the assembly's response (4:11a)
B'.   The assembly's response (4:11b–12; "Witnesses . . .")

This structure is in turn reinforced by the repetition of the word "witnesses" as the first word of the assembly's response.

Although chiastic patterns often indicate a reversal in the plot development, several factors work against that as an interpretive strategy in this case. First, the surrounded material, Boaz's speech, does not carry through the reverse structure, as we might expect if it contained a

---

[9] On the double-duty use of structural links see Part III, "Structures of Conjunction."

plot reversal. Second, the repeated elements are identical before and after the surrounded speech; there is no suggestion of change that might be attributed to an intervening turn in the plot. Third, the repeated elements in 4:11a that establish the chiastic pattern are not properly part of the literary unit of Boaz's speech, and therefore their chiastic effect is much weaker. The larger pattern of alternating repetition gives the whole passage a sense of forward motion rather than of reversal.

B. Framing Inclusion

1. 1 Kings 2:12b, 46b

The lengthy tale of Solomon's consolidation of his kingship recounts how he eliminated people he perceived as threats to his throne: Adonijah, his older brother; Abiathar the priest and Joab the army commander, both of whom had favored Adonijah to succeed David; and Shimei, a long-time foe of David. The tale is framed by two very similar lines:

[12b]His <u>kingship was established</u> firmly (2:12b).

[13] . . . [46a]

[46b]And the <u>kingdom was established</u> in the hand of Solomon (2:46b).

These are a framing rather than an internal inclusion because they are relatively separate from the subunits they enclose. The story of Adonijah's downfall begins with 2:13 and the story of Shimei's execution ends with 2:46a. "Kingship" (*malkût*, 2:12b) may carry a slightly stronger nuance of royal power than the word "kingdom" (*mamlĕkâ*, 2:46b), which is closer to "realm," but both derive from the root *mlk*, "to reign as king," and the difference in meaning is slight enough that it does not obscure the inclusion.

Interpretation in this case is guided by the tension between the inclusion and what it surrounds. According to 2:12b Solomon's royal dominion was already "firmly established" *before* he undertook to eliminate his opponents. When 2:46b simply repeats that "the kingdom was established" it says, in effect, that nothing has changed. Solomon's purge was not needed as a means of consolidating power, since power was already his. If there is any indication of change, it is in the elements of the inclusion that differ from each other. The change of "firmly" to "in his hand" suggests a shift in point of view from an objective assessment of the political scene to Solomon's subjective view. In other words, though his power was never in real danger Solomon himself did not feel secure until he had eliminated anyone he believed to be a potential threat.

2. *Genesis 18:16, 22*

Between the scene where Abraham's mysterious guests promise him that he will have a son by his aged wife Sarah (18:1-15) and the one in which Abraham bargains with YHWH for the safety of Sodom (18:23-33) comes a brief scene in which YHWH first deliberates whether to tell Abraham his plans and then decides to do so (18:17-21). This short scene is framed by an inclusion involving several elements in parallel order (abcde X a'b'c'd'e'):

> [16]The men arose <u>from there</u> and headed <u>toward Sodom. Abraham</u> **went** with them to see them off.
>
> [17] . . [21]
>
> [22]The men turned <u>from there</u> and went <u>to Sodom. Abraham</u> **kept standing** before YHWH.

The first four repeated elements are identical; the fifth is a common word pair of opposites, "to walk, go" *(hlk)* and "to stand still" *('md)*. The forward thrust that is typical of parallel symmetry provides the interpretive strategy. The plot continues in the direction the text has already alluded to ("and afterwards you shall continue on," 18:5), with no reversals. The intervening verses simply reveal to Abraham (and to the reader) YHWH's intention in undertaking this journey.

The change in the fifth element, on the other hand, opens narrative space for a new development in the ongoing plot, namely Abraham's initiative in accosting YHWH and reminding him of the need for justice within a context of punishment (18:23-33). Abraham's campaign failed, however, since not even "ten just people" (18:32) were to be found in the city ("the people of Sodom surrounded the house, young and old, every last person," 19:4). The entire bargaining scene, then, goes nowhere; it is a delaying tactic to build a suspenseful hope ("will there be enough just people in Sodom to save it?") that will ultimately be frustrated. The plot, like Abraham himself, "stands still."

3. *1 Samuel 15:10-12, 34-35*[10]

In this long scene Samuel condemns Saul for his disobedience to YHWH in retaining some of the spoil from the Amalekite campaign and,

---

[10] J. P. Fokkelman, *Narrative Art and Poetry in the Books of Samuel: A Full Interpretation Based on Stylistic and Structural Analyses.* 4 vols. (Assen: Van Gorcum, 1981–1993) 2:110–11.

most seriously, for permitting Agag the Amalekite to live, and tells him that YHWH has decided to take the kingdom away from him. The scene is framed by a lengthy chiastic inclusion with several repeated elements (abcdef X f'e'd'c'b'a'):

> [10]YHWH's word came to Samuel: [11]"I <u>regret that I made Saul king</u>, for he has turned back from following me and not held firm to my word." But <u>Samuel was angry</u>, and he cried out to YHWH all <u>night</u>. [12]Samuel got up early and went to meet Saul in the morning. Samuel was told, "Saul came to <u>Carmel</u>—see, he set up a monument for himself—then he circled and crossed and <u>descended</u> to <u>Gilgal</u>."
> [13] . . . [33]
>
> [34]Samuel went to <u>Ramah</u>, while Saul <u>ascended</u> to his house at <u>Gibeah</u> of Saul. [35]Samuel did not see Saul again until the <u>day</u> of his death. Indeed, <u>Samuel mourned</u> for him, but YHWH <u>regretted having made Saul king</u> over Israel.

The "a" elements are identical (YHWH "regretted having made Saul king"). The other repeated elements are not identical, but their similarities are sufficient to sustain the analysis. The "b" elements ascribe different moods to Samuel (anger/grief); the "c" elements are a contrasting word pair (night/day), as are the "e" elements (descended/ascended); the "d" and "f" elements are place names in both subunits, though the names are all different. The chiastic series of elements could be expanded, for instance, to include the name "Saul," which occurs between the "c" and "d" elements in each subunit, and by the loose word pair ("house"/"monument") that occurs between the "d" and "e" elements in each subunit.

Like chiastic symmetry generally, chiastic symmetry in an inclusion can point to a plot reversal. Here the entire dialogue between Samuel and Saul establishes the reversal of Saul's fortunes because of his (unwitting?) disobedience and YHWH's condemnation. Certainly Saul, at the beginning of the unit, appears unaware of any divine displeasure (15:13, 20), but by the end of the scene he has accepted the situation (15:30). The reversal is signaled in the inclusion itself in several ways. Saul's movement contrasts: he descends (15:12), then ascends (15:34). He is associated at first with a "monument," presumably in commemoration of his military victory over the Amalekites (15:12), but at the end he returns to his "house," as if he might be retiring from public life (15:34).

By contrast, YHWH's attitude is immutable: he regrets making Saul king (15:11), and even Saul's protestations of innocence (15:15, 21) and eventual confessions of guilt (15:24, 30) do not change the divine decision (15:35). Samuel too is constant, though his attitude is at considerable odds with that of YHWH. His first reaction is anger at YHWH for rejecting Saul (15:11), and even though he carries out YHWH's commission he remains dissatisfied with it and grieves for Saul (15:35), a grief that will merit him a mild rebuke from YHWH (16:1).

4. 1 Kings 12:30-31; 13:33-34

When an inclusion surrounds apparently independent stories it invites the reader to consider their connection anew. In 1 Kings 12:32–13:32 there are three stories: a brief introductory account of Jeroboam's establishment of a dedicatory feast for the sanctuary at Bethel (12:32-33), a story of how the ceremony was disrupted by an unnamed man of God from Judah who condemned the altar Jeroboam had set up to honor the deity of the golden calf (13:1-10), and a story of that man of God's subsequent encounter with a local Bethel prophet, which resulted in the man of God's disobedience to YHWH's command and his eventual death (13:11-32). The stories are framed by a chiastic inclusion:

> 12:30This thing came to be sin, and the people went after the one [golden calf] as far as Dan. 31He made the sanctuaries of the high places, and he made priests from among the whole people, who were not of the sons of Levi.
> 12:32 . . . 13:32
> 33After this thing, Jeroboam did not turn from his evil way. He turned and made from among the whole people priests of the high places, whoever wanted it he consecrated to be priests of the high places. 34And in this thing came to be the sin of the house of Jeroboam, to eliminate and obliterate it from upon the face of the earth.

In this case the chiastic inclusion does not point to a reversal in the plot. (The turning point in the story of Jeroboam is his decision to build the golden calf sanctuaries in Dan and Bethel: 12:26-31.) Or perhaps it is better said that it points to a reversal that does *not* take place. Between the two inclusive subunits several things have happened. Jeroboam has been confronted by a man of God, speaking "in the word of YHWH" (13:1), who condemned his cultic improprieties and demonstrated the power of his condemnation with a miraculous withering and healing of Jeroboam's hand. Later that same man of God, after being led astray by a local prophet of Bethel, was killed by a lion. The miraculous character of this violence was evidenced by the wonder of lion and donkey standing guard over the body until the Bethel prophet retrieved it (13:28). The Bethel prophet himself subsequently took up the same condemnation against Jeroboam's sanctuaries that the man of God from Judah had proclaimed and, indeed, extended the condemnation to "all the sanctuaries of the high places that are in the cities of Samaria" (13:32). Surely Jeroboam heard of these events as well: they were publicly known and discussed (13:25). Yet, despite all the evidence he has of divine disfavor, he does not repent and turn from sin but persists in his evil ways (13:33). This intransigence is aptly reflected in the almost verbatim repetition of inclusive elements before and after the prophetic events.

There is a small but subtle intensification in one of the repeated elements that does not always come through clearly in translations. In 12:30 the narrator tells us "this thing *(haddābār hazzeh)* came to be sin"; in 13:33 we read *"in* this thing *(baddābār hazzeh)* came to be the sin of the house of Jeroboam." What had been Jeroboam's own sin carries within it the evil that will eventually infect a dynasty, Jeroboam's whole "house."

5. 1 Kings 6:1–9:10

The relative independence of framing inclusions from the material they surround allows them to connect a long series of literary units. The center of the story of Solomon is his construction and dedication of the Temple (1 Kings 6:1–9:10). The entire account is punctuated with framing verses, all of which are general references to "building" *(bnh)* or "finishing" *(klh)* the "house (of YHWH)." Two particularly significant framing verses in the series use the verb "to complete" *(šlm,* a wordplay on *šlmh,* "Solomon") instead of "to finish."

Except for two subunits, the entire first part (1 Kings 6–7) recounts the construction of the Temple in detail; the two subunits are 6:11-13, a word of YHWH to Solomon, and 7:1-12, the construction of the palace complex, which was adjacent to but separate from the Temple itself. When those two passages are set aside, the organizing function of the framing verses is clear.

a₁. Frame verse (6:1): ". . . he <u>built *(bnh)*</u> <u>the house of YHWH</u>."
X.   **WORK IN STONE (6:2-8)**
a₂. Frame verse (6:9a): "He <u>built *(bnh)* the house</u> and he <u>finished *(klh)*</u> it."
X.   **WORK IN WOOD: structural (6:9b-10)**
a₃. Frame verse (6:14): "Solomon <u>built *(bnh)* the house</u> and he <u>finished *(klh)*</u> it."
X.   **WORK IN WOOD: decorative (6:15-36)**
a₄. Frame verses (6:37-38): ". . . <u>the house was finished *(klh)*</u> in all its details and in all its specifications. He <u>built *(bnh)*</u> it in seven years."
X.   **WORK IN BRONZE BY HIRAM OF TYRE (7:13-40a)**
a₅. Frame verse (7:40b) in summary passage (7:40b-45): ". . . and Hiram <u>finished *(klh)*</u> doing all the work that he did for King Solomon on <u>the house of YHWH</u>."
X.   **WORK IN BRONZE AND GOLD BY SOLOMON (7:46-50)**
a₆. Frame verse (7:51a): "He <u>completed *(šlm)*</u> all the work which King Solomon did on <u>the house of YHWH</u>."

After the several scenes and prayers of the dedication ceremony (1 Kings 8), the framing inclusion returns:

a$_7$. Frame verse (9:1): "When Solomon had <u>finished *(klh)* building *(bnh)* the house of Y</u>HWH . . ."

X. SOLOMON'S VISION OF YHWH (9:2-9)

a$_8$. Frame verse (9:10): "At the end of twenty years, during which Solomon <u>built *(bnh)*</u> the two houses, <u>the house of Y</u>HWH and the king's house . . ."

And, finally, at the very end of the account of Solomon's constructions,

a$_9$. Frame verse (9:25b): "He <u>completed *(šlm)* the house</u>."

The principal function of the framing inclusions in 1 Kings 6–7 is organizational; they subdivide the construction process, primarily according to matériel. The reappearance of the framing verses in 9:1 and 10 links Solomon's vision of YHWH to the Temple account despite the fact that the vision did not take place until Solomon had finished building "the king's house and every desire that Solomon wished to make" (9:1)—in other words, until at least thirteen years after the Temple was completed and its dedication ceremony was over (7:1; 9:10a). Finally, the frame verse in 9:25 incorporates the passages about King Hiram and conscripted labor (9:10-14, 15-24) into the larger framework of the Temple account, and forms a loose inclusion with Solomon's first mentions of "building a house" for YHWH (5:3-5), that encompass other passages about King Hiram and conscripted labor (5:1-12, 13-18).

C. EXTERNAL INCLUSION

1. 2 Samuel 14:24, 28

One of the causes of Absalom's disaffection toward his father David was the treatment he received from David after he pardoned Absalom for the murder of his brother Amnon. At Joab's urging David allowed Absalom to return from self-imposed exile in Geshur, but refused to meet his son in person. The scene of Absalom's return from Geshur to Jerusalem ends with:

> [24]The king said, "He may go around to his house, but he is not to see my face." So Absalom went around to his house, <u>and he did not see the king's face</u>.

After two years of ostracism Absalom pressures Joab to get him reinstated in David's good graces. The scene of Absalom's interview with Joab and his eventual reconciliation with David begins with:

> [28] Absalom stayed in Jerusalem for two full years, <u>and he did not see the king's face.</u>

The connection of these two verses with their adjoining subunits is much closer than their connection with the intervening material, which is a brief description of Absalom's physical beauty and his family. The inclusion is therefore external to the material it surrounds.

One effect of an external inclusion is to isolate and unify the intervening material. In this case that effect is analogous to parentheses: the description of Absalom is felt as an interruption in the progress of the narrative.[11] This detour into description permits the reader to feel, as Absalom did for two long years, that the story's action has stalled, and to feel this despite the clear indication that a lot of things are happening (Absalom has four children in those two years! 14:27). It also supplies background information that will prove important eventually, though not immediately. Absalom's good looks (14:25) no doubt explain part of his popular appeal (15:1-6), but his crowning beauty, his rich growth of hair (14:26), will prove his bane (18:9). Absalom's three sons are not named, but his daughter's name honors his sister Tamar, whose rape and rejection by her half-brother Amnon was the start of the still-unresolved tension between David and Absalom.

2. Genesis 37:36; 39:1

The story of Joseph in Egypt is interrupted by the story of Judah and Tamar in Genesis 38. The Joseph story breaks off with 37:36:

> [37:36] The Midianites sold him <u>into Egypt,</u> to <u>Potiphar, an officer of Pharaoh, captain of the guard.</u>

It picks up again in 39:1:

> [39:1] Joseph was brought down <u>to Egypt,</u> and <u>Potiphar, an officer of Pharaoh, captain of the guard,</u> an Egyptian man, bought him from the hand of the Ishmaelites who had brought him down there.

The characters, setting, etc. in Genesis 38 set it apart completely from the surrounding Joseph narrative, an independence that identifies this as an external inclusion. But, as in the previous example, the inclusion points up the fact that the hiatus in the story happens precisely *here,* be-

---

[11] This is no doubt why external inclusions are often treated as "resumptive repetitions," and the material they enclose as later editorial insertions.

tween the inclusive elements, and invites the reader to reflect on the effects of breaking the Joseph narrative at precisely this point. One effect is background. Judah is an important figure in the Joseph story. It is he who first proposes selling Joseph for profit instead of killing him (37:26-27) but who later offers himself as Joseph's slave to assure the safe return of Benjamin (44:18-34). It is surely not irrelevant that Judah himself was in the meantime bereft of two sons (38:7-10). He learns through experience the grief Jacob felt at the loss of Joseph and can anticipate what Jacob would endure if he lost a second son. A second effect is to signal the passage of time, as we saw also in the previous example. By the time we encounter Joseph again he has risen from slavery to mastery over Potiphar's entire household (39:2). The years that pass in the course of Judah's story allow time for Joseph's advancement.

The parallel symmetry of the inclusion (ab X a'b') restores the forward impetus of the Joseph story after the interlude about Judah.

3. Exodus 6:10-13, 26-30

When Yhwh sends Moses to Pharaoh to demand the release of the Israelites from Egypt, Moses objects that he is too inept a speaker to carry out the divine commission. Yhwh responds by assigning Moses' brother Aaron to be his spokesman. The dialogue is interrupted abruptly, between Moses' objection and Yhwh's response, by a long genealogy (6:14-25) that is preceded and followed by a chiastic inclusion (ab X b'a'):

    a.   Dialogue of Yhwh with Moses (6:10-12)
    b.   Narrator's report: Yhwh spoke to Moses and Aaron (6:13)
    X.   Genealogies related to Moses and Aaron (6:14-25)
    b'.   Narrator's report: Yhwh spoke to Moses and Aaron (6:26-27)
    a'.   Dialogue of Yhwh with Moses (6:28-30)

The inclusive subunits are much more closely connected to the surrounding story than to the genealogical lists they surround, and therefore constitute an external inclusion. Each subunit of the chiastic inclusion contains several repeated elements, themselves organized in very complex patterns:

    a. [10]<u>Yhwh spoke to Moses</u>: [11]"Go, <u>speak to Pharaoh, king of Egypt</u>, that he should send the Israelites from his land." [12]<u>Moses spoke before Yhwh:</u> "<u>But</u> the Israelites did not listen to me. <u>How will Pharaoh listen to me? I am unrefined of lips.</u>"
    b. [13]Yhwh spoke to <u>Moses and</u> to <u>Aaron</u> and commissioned them to the Israelites and to <u>Pharaoh, king of Egypt, to bring the Israelites out from the land of Egypt</u>.

[14] . . . [25]

b'.   [26]This was the <u>Aaron and Moses</u> to whom Y<small>HWH</small> said, "<u>Bring the Israelites out from the land of Egypt</u> in their hosts." [27]They spoke
to <u>Pharaoh, king of Egypt, to bring the Israelites out from Egypt.</u>
This was <u>Moses and Aaron.</u>

a'.   [28]On the day when Y<small>HWH</small> spoke to Moses in the land of Egypt, [29]<u>Y<small>HWH</small></u>
<u>spoke to Moses:</u> "I am Y<small>HWH</small>. <u>Speak to Pharaoh, king of Egypt,</u> every-
thing I tell you." [30]<u>Moses said before Y<small>HWH</small>:</u> "But I am <u>unrefined of</u>
<u>lips. How will Pharaoh listen to me?</u>"

The complexity of the patterning is noteworthy. The "a" subunits
have six repeated elements that are virtually identical.[12] Except for the
last two, they are in strict parallel order (ABCDEF/A'B'C'D'F'E'). The
"b" subunits share three repeated elements, which are further repeated
in b' to produce a concentric pattern (ABC/A'C'B'C"A"). While this is
unusually complex, we will see below in considering "multiple symmetry" that such multi-leveled symmetry is not uncommon.

As with the other external inclusions we have seen, the intervening
material supplies the reader with background. Moses' objection to
Y<small>HWH</small>'s commission has been left hanging (6:12). After the genealogy
Y<small>HWH</small> will answer the objection by including Aaron in the commission
(7:1). Aaron has already appeared in the larger narrative context
(4:27–5:21) and been identified as Moses' brother (4:14), and their
Levite ancestry has been announced (2:1; 4:14), but this is scant information indeed about foundational figures in Israel's history. The genealogy will situate Moses and especially Aaron in the family of the
promise, from their forebears among the sons of Jacob to Aaron's descendants to the second generation—that is, from those who left the
promised land to those who returned there.

The presence of symmetry on several levels and in several forms offers a variety of interpretive approaches. First is the overall chiastic pattern of the inclusion. As usual this focuses our attention on the central
element, the genealogy, with its strong emphasis on the line of Aaron
(note the narrative rather than strict genealogical formulation of 6:20,
23, 25). The inclusion, however, balances this by putting Moses alone in
the emphatic first and last positions (the "a" subunits).[13] The final effect, then, is to present Moses and Aaron as a unit, a team, born of the
same parents and sent on the same mission by Y<small>HWH</small>.

---

[12] The only variations are: in 6:12 Moses "spoke" *(dbr)* before Y<small>HWH</small> while in 6:30
Moses "said" *(ʾmr)* before Y<small>HWH</small>, and the grammatical construction "listen to me" is
slightly different in 6:12 *(yišmāʿēni)* and in 6:30 *(yišmaʿ ʾēlay)*.

[13] The center of the genealogy, 6:20, balances Aaron and Moses as well.

The concentric structure of the "b'" subunit of the inclusion strengthens this impression of balance (6:26-27). The mission, "to bring the Israelites out of the land of Egypt," is encompassed by "Aaron and Moses" and "Moses and Aaron" (the chiastic ordering of the names adds its own bit of weight to balancing the two characters) in the emphatic first and last positions. At the center an emphatic pronoun, "they," sets the two as an indissoluble team before "Pharaoh, king of Egypt."

Finally, the parallel ordering of the repeated elements in the "a" subunits keeps the story moving. YHWH's dialogue with Moses, which ends with Moses' unanswered objection in 6:12, is reprised after the genealogy, before the narrator proceeds to YHWH's response.[14]

D. Complex inclusion

1. 1 Kings 4:1-20, 21-25[15]

The narrator of 1 Kings describes Solomon's royal administration in glowing terms. He considers both the internal administration of the kingdom itself and the way in which Solomon's imperial hegemony over other kingdoms brought peace and abundant wealth to the people of Israel. These two purviews, internal and external administration, are separated and connected by a complex inclusion (aXb a'X'b').

a.   [1]King <u>Solomon was king over all Israel</u>.

X.   [2]. . .[19]

b.   [20]<u>Judah and Israel</u> were numerous as sand at the sea, eating, drinking, rejoicing.

a'.   [21]And <u>Solomon was ruler in all kingdoms</u> from the Euphrates through Philistia to Egypt's border.

X'.   [22]. . .[24]

b'.   [25]<u>Judah and Israel</u> dwelt secure, each under his vine and fig tree, from Dan to Beer-Sheba. . . .

Each paragraph is unified by its political horizon. Solomon's internal administration produces a society where prosperity, orderliness, and joy are the norm. Solomon's imperium over all the lands surrounding Judah and Israel produces peace and security throughout his own kingdoms.

---

[14] The repetition is so exact and the parallel order so protracted that the two variations in Moses' second speech stand out: he omits "the Israelites did not listen to me" and reverses the order of his other two clauses. We will examine these asymmetries in more detail in a later section.

[15] The chapter and verse numbers follow those in standard English versions. The Hebrew text numbers 4:21-25 as 5:1-5.

The parallel arrangement of the complex inclusion corresponds to the enlargement of horizon from local to international and from effect (prosperity in Judah and Israel) to cause (tribute from vassal states).

2. *Genesis 1*

We examined above the parallel symmetry that organizes the six days and eight acts of creation (see pp. 37–38). There is another level of parallel symmetry internal to the days and acts. In the case of the acts of creation the symmetry is loose since not every element is repeated for every act, and the parallelism is loose since one or another element is occasionally out of order. But the general pattern for the eight[16] acts runs:

A. "God said"
B.   Creative command
C.   "And so it was" (lacking in 1:3-5)
D.   Statement of fulfillment (lacking in 1:9-10, 29-31)
E.   "God saw that it was good" (lacking in 1:6-8).

The six days, on the other hand, do not fit this parallel pattern because there are multiple acts on the third and sixth days. The six days are better seen as linked by a lengthy complex inclusion (aXb a'X'b' a''X''b'', etc.). Each day begins with "God said" *(wayyōʾmer ʾĕlōhîm)*, and ends with "It was evening and it was morning, the nth day."

The forward movement of the complex inclusion urges the story forward; at the same time the exactness of the repetitions reinforces the effect of the parallelism in the eight acts and gives the whole account a stately, formalized cadence appropriate to its exalted subject matter. Finally, the enumeration builds suspense as it nears the symbolically important number seven, a suspense that increases as the account of the sixth day grows to almost twice the length of any other day.

2. *Regnal formulas*

By far the most extensive series of complex inclusions is the set of formulas used by the editor of 1–2 Kings to organize the history of Israel and Judah after the death of Solomon. With few exceptions each regnal account begins with the following information:

a₁.   the year of the king's accession, synchronized with the reign in the other kingdom;

---

[16] The asymmetrical subunit on the creation of humankind, 1:26-28, does not follow the pattern.

a_2. the age of the king at his accession (only for kings of Judah);
a_3. the length of the king's reign and the name of his capital city;
a_4. the name of the king's mother (only for kings of Judah).

In general, each regnal account ends with:

b_1. a referral to other sources of information;
b_2. information about the king's death and burial;
b_3. the name of the king's successor.[17]

With few disruptions[18] this pattern is followed from 1 Kings 11:41 to the end of 2 Kings, whether the regnal account is very short (e.g., Joash of Israel, 2 Kings 13:10-13) or very long (e.g., the regnal formulas framing Ahab's reign are in 1 Kings 16:29 and 22:39-40).

The regularity of the regnal formulas affords two approaches to interpretation. First, the aXb a'X'b' pattern of a complex inclusion is akin to forward symmetry and has the same forward movement. In the case of the regnal formulas the manifold parallel symmetry of the repeated elements within the regnal formulas strengthens this forward impetus considerably and sustains the regnal formulas as the primary organizing device for the history of the divided monarchy.

Second, the ordering of the regnal accounts is significant. There are two subtypes of introductory regnal formulas, one corresponding to kings of Israel and one corresponding to kings of Judah, distinguished by two pieces of information missing from the former—the king's age at his accession and the name of his mother. The author(s) and editor(s) of Kings could have separated the histories of the two realms on this basis and produced a "History of Israel" and a "History of Judah," but they did not.[19] Instead they interwove the two by reporting each king's reign as an unbroken account, while treating the kings in strict order of their accession to the throne irrespective of which realm they ruled. The result is a history of *kings* (as the books are named), not of *kingdoms,* and an implied theological assertion that the *people* whose history is recounted are one people, YHWH's people, though living in two territories and under two lines of kings.

---

[17] Part or all of the information about the king's death, burial, and successor may be missing if it was already given in the regnal account, for instance in telling of an assassination or *coup d'état.*

[18] Out of a total of nearly forty kings, two regnal accounts lack the beginning formula, a few lack the ending one. There is one instance where two reigns are interwoven (aXa'XbXb'). In all cases there are narrative reasons for the deviations.

[19] This is the more noteworthy in view of the fact that the books of Kings cite regularly as their sources of information one book called "The Chronicles of the Kings of Israel" and one called "The Chronicles of the Kings of Judah." See, for example, 1 Kings 14:19, 29.

E. Introductory Epitome

1. Genesis 10:120

The genealogy of the descendants of Noah (Gen 10:2-31) is separated into three sections corresponding to Noah's three sons.[21] A parallel framing inclusion with two repeated elements ("Noah's sons," "after the flood") surrounds the whole (10:1, 32). The opening framing inclusion contains the names of the three sons; corresponding to this the closing framing inclusion has only a general reference to "generations" and "nations." The order of the intervening genealogies, however, corresponds chiastically to the names in 10:1.

frame:		¹*These are the generations of Noah's sons,*
a.		*Shem,*
b.		*Ham,*
c.		*and Japheth.*
		Children were born to them after the flood.
C.		²"The children of Japheth . . ." (10:2-5)
B.		⁶"The children of Ham . . ." (10:6-20)
A.	²²"The children of Shem . . ." (10:22-31)	
frame:		³²*These are the families of Noah's sons,*
a–c.		*by their generations, in their nations;*
		from these the nations were dispersed in the earth after the flood.

Since there is little narrative material in the passage the epitome does not announce narrative development in advance. Rather it sets the parameters for subsequent elaboration, namely all the nations of the world, since all are descended from Noah. By naming Shem first the text assures Israelite readers (who are descended from Shem) that what follows is not irrelevant antiquarian data but is germane to themselves; it then expands the readers' focus from their own people outward to a distant universal horizon. Finally the text narrows the focus to nearer nations and, eventually, to the line of Eber (*'ēber*), the eponymous ancestor of the Hebrews (*'ibrîm*), and therefore of the readers themselves.[22] By withholding the most immediately pertinent information until the end the narrator maintains the readers' interest throughout.

---

[20] Parunak, "Oral Typesetting," 163.

[21] Note that the three sections themselves are marked by a complex inclusion as well. Each begins with a title, "The children of X," and ends with a variation of the phrase "by their families, their languages, in their lands, in their nations" (10:5b, 20b, 31b).

[22] Genesis 10:21 is a striking asymmetry within this pattern since it falls after the conclusion of Ham's lineage but before the formulaic opening of the Shem section.

2. 1 Kings 18:1

Yhwh sends Elijah from Zarephath, where he has been hiding from Ahab's vengeance, back to Israel to bring to an end the drought Elijah proclaimed in 1 Kings 17:1. The divine command has two parts, a command to Elijah to present himself to the king and a promise to restore rain:

> [1]After many days, Yhwh's word came to Elijah in the third year [of the drought]: "Go *(hlk)*, appear before Ahab, so that I may give rain over the surface of the ground."

The remainder of 1 Kings 18 has three sections, two of which correspond to the two parts of Yhwh's command. In 18:2-19 Elijah "went" *(hlk*, 18:2), and he eventually met Ahab (18:17-19; the verb "appear" is not repeated). In 18:41-45 the rain is announced (18:41), and a downpour begins (18:45).[23] The epitome therefore forecasts much of the subsequent story. But between the two passages that correspond to Yhwh's command in 18:1 falls the lengthy scene of Elijah's contest with the prophets of Baal atop Mount Carmel (18:20-40), which has no counterpart in 18:1. Schematically, therefore, the chapter is abACB, where "C" is the scene of the contest. Commentators have long suspected that this scene was originally an independent story and that a later editor is responsible for combining the Carmel theophany with the end of the drought. The absence from 18:1 of any allusion to the Carmel scene is consistent with that understanding. The clear division of the chapter between an Ahab section (18:2-19, 41-45) and a prophets-of-Baal section (18:20-40), with vv. 19-20 accomplishing the transition between them, strongly supports it.

In the present text, however, the Carmel scene surprises the reader because it was unforeseen in 18:1, and the reader is thrown back to 18:1 to reexamine it. The Hebrew has a nuance of purpose ("so that" in the translation given above) that is overlooked in many English versions. Yhwh implies that the provision of rain is somehow contingent upon Elijah's appearance before Ahab, but does not spell out the causal connection more clearly. It is that small logical lacuna that the unexpected and dramatic 18:20-40 fills: Elijah's appearance before Ahab leads to a confrontation between Yhwh, represented by Elijah, and the storm god

---

Its effect is to point up the unique importance of the line of Shem, which leads through Eber to the Israelite reader.

[23] The words used for rain in 18:1 *(māṭār)* and 18:41-45 *(gešem)* are different, but close in meaning.

Baal, represented by his prophets. YHWH's definitive victory over Baal proves YHWH's supremacy over the rain to withhold it (the three years' drought) or return it (18:41-45).

F. CONCLUDING EPITOME

1. Genesis 2:1

We have seen above (pp. 37–38) the parallel symmetry that organizes the six days of creation into two sequences. When the six days are completed the narrator tells us:

> ¹And-were-finished the heavens and the earth and all their hosts.

The phrase "the heavens and the earth" establishes an inclusion with 1:1 (". . . God created the heavens and the earth"), but the phrase "all their hosts" is new. The verse, short as it is, recapitulates the two-part structure of the six days: in the first three days God established the various regions of heavens and earth out of the "formless void"; in the next three days God populated them with the "hosts" that fill the skies, the firmament, the seas, and the land.

2. Exodus 3:14-15

When YHWH appears to Moses on Mount Sinai he commands him to demand from Pharaoh of Egypt the release of the Israelites. Moses offers many objections in a frantic though ultimately futile attempt to escape the divine commission, and in the course of one of those objections Moses has the temerity to ask God for the divine name. Moses' question sets the context:

> Moses said to God, "When I come to the Israelites, and I say to them, 'The god of your fathers has sent me to you,' and they say to me, 'What is his name?'—what shall I say to them?"

In other words, Moses is not just asking for a private revelation of God's name, but for a name by which to name God to the Israelites. God replies:

> ¹⁴And God said to Moses, "I AM THAT I AM." And he said, "Thus you shall say to the Israelites: 'I AM has sent me to you.'" ¹⁵And God said further to Moses, "Thus you shall say to the Israelites: 'YHWH, your fathers' god,

Abraham's god, Isaac's god, and Jacob's god, has sent me to you.' This is my name forever, and this is my remembering for the ages."

The structure of this passage is complicated. The repeated line "And God said [further] to Moses" divides the response into two balanced parts corresponding to the two verses. The first verse is further divided into two speeches by the narrative line "and he said." The second speech in 3:14 begins with the same words as the first speech in 3:15 ("Thus you shall say to the Israelites") and ends with words that recur in the middle of 3:15 ("has sent me to you"). These repetitions act as a complex inclusion linking 3:14b and 3:15a, separating them from 3:14a and 3:15b, and giving a chiastic organization to the whole:

A.   ¹⁴ᵃAnd God said to Moses, "I AM THAT I AM."
B.   ¹⁴ᵇAnd he said, "<u>Thus you shall say to the Israelites</u>:
          'I AM <u>has sent me to you</u>.'"
B'.   ¹⁵ᵃAnd God said further to Moses, "<u>Thus you shall say to the Israelites</u>:
          'YHWH, your fathers' god, . . . <u>has sent me to you</u>.'
A'. ¹⁵ᵇThis is my name forever, and this is my remembering for the ages."

The "B" subunits set up the equation YHWH = I AM, and explicitly direct Moses to inform the Israelites of this name (or perhaps these names). But this is not the whole name that God reveals to Moses; it is only a shortened form of God's full name, which is I AM THAT I AM. There is no directive (and therefore one might surmise that Moses is not permitted) to inform the Israelites of God's full name; this is for him alone to know. Exodus 3:15b is an epitome that reflects this distinction between God's name (the first half of 3:15b corresponds to 3:14a) and how God is to be known (the second half of 3:15b corresponds to 3:14b-15a):

A. "I AM THAT I AM"
B.   "I AM," = "YHWH"
a'. "my name forever"
b'.   "my remembering for the ages."

5. MULTIPLE SYMMETRY

As the name suggests, "multiple symmetry" describes passages in which more than one symmetrical pattern is operative. The symmetries that occur can be any of those we have considered above. This opens the possibility of numerous variations and combinations. For clarity's sake we will consider multiple symmetry in three forms: composite, complex, and compound. In composite symmetry no single symmetrical pattern organizes the entire literary unit; two or more separate patterns organize different parts of the whole. An especially common form of composite symmetry involves an inclusion surrounding material that has its own symmetry (e.g., aBCB'C'a, or aBCC'B'a, or the like). In complex symmetry, on the other hand, there is an overall pattern that organizes the entire piece. Within that pattern one of the repeated elements that links corresponding subunits is the internal symmetrical organization of the subunits themselves. In other words, two corresponding subunits may together form a chiasm (e.g., subunit B will contain abc and subunit B' will contain c'b'a') or a parallelism (e.g., B will contain abc and B' will contain a'b'c'). This sort of multileveled symmetry is particularly effective at unifying a long narrative with many subunits because complex symmetry is one of the ways in which concrete textual elements may reinforce the thematic links that predominate in long narratives. Finally, compound symmetry occurs where an entire literary unit can be analyzed according to two different and distinct symmetrical patterns overlaid on the same material. This last form of organization can perhaps best be understood by analogy with musical counterpoint and, like counterpoint, is a compositional *tour de force.*

Interpretation can approach instances of multiple symmetry on any of the avenues offered by the various symmetrical patterns employed in the passage. However, the situation is frequently an embarrassment of riches, so to speak, particularly in cases of complex and compound symmetry. When multiple symmetries coexist in a passage almost any interpretive strategy can find a stylistic pattern to support it. Paradoxically, therefore, the multiplication of interpretive possibilities weakens the usefulness of symmetry for guiding interpretation, since the various possibilities point in all directions at once. In such cases, as in poetry, stylistic display comes to the fore and becomes something of an end in itself.

A. COMPOSITE SYMMETRY

1. 1 Kings 5:1-12

Once Solomon has established himself on the throne of David, King Hiram of Tyre, his neighbor to the north, begins tentative negotiations to confirm the peace treaty he had with Solomon's father. (This is the meaning of the diplomatic euphemism in 5:1, sometimes translated "Hiram loved David" or "Hiram had been a friend to David.") This suits Solomon perfectly since he has in mind to import materials, especially exotic woods, from Hiram's country for the Temple he plans to build. So his response to Hiram's initiative takes the form of offering a business contract, and Hiram replies in kind. The underlying issue, however, is the unspoken political one of a treaty. This is conveyed in two ways: both parts of the inclusion that frames the passage use diplomatic language, and "cutting" timber evokes the idea of "cutting" a treaty (the standard Hebrew idiom for concluding a treaty), which Hiram and Solomon are said to do in 5:12b. The material surrounded by the inclusion involves an alternation of missive and narrative, marked by opening words.

> *frame:* "<u>Hiram loved David</u>" (diplomatic language, 5:1)
> A.   Solomon's message to Hiram (5:2-6; first word: "and he sent")
> B.   Narrative (5:7; first word: "and it was")
> A'. Hiram's message to Solomon (5:8-9; first word: "and he sent")
> B'.   Narrative (5:10-12a; first word: "and it was")
> *frame:* "<u>the two of them cut a treaty</u>" (diplomatic language, 5:12b).

The alternating opening words mark the inclusive frame as well: 5:1 begins with "and he sent"; 5:12b begins with "and it was." The alternating repetition gives the whole exchange a forward momentum that begins with Hiram's concern about the future of the political alliance and ends with the alliance being confirmed and renewed.

Within the exchange, however, the messages themselves exhibit symmetry. Solomon's message to Hiram has four subunits marked by initial words in chiastic order:

a. "You know . . ." (*ʾattāh yādaʿtā*, 5:3)
b.   "And now . . ." (*wĕʿattāh*, 5:4)
b'.   "And now . . ." (*wĕʿattāh*, 5:6a)
a'. "You know . . ." (*ʾattāh yādaʿtā*, 5:6b).

The structure is underscored by two factors: the pronoun "you" (*ʾattāh*) and the adverb "now" (*ʿattāh*) are very similar in sound, distinguishable only by their initial consonants, and the pronoun "you" is unnecessary (and therefore emphatic) both times that it occurs. The organization balances past (background information, subunits a and b) against future (Solomon's request of Hiram, subunit b', followed by some polite flattery in subunit a'). Concealed in this superficially commercial message is a political one, communicated by an unusual amount of verbal repetition between subunit a, about David, and subunit b, about Solomon: "David my father," "to build a house for the name of YHWH," and "all around" (this last repetition is often obscured in translation). The point of all the repetition is to signal that Solomon's reign will not mark a departure from David's policies, but a continuation and fulfillment of them. Hiram will have his treaty.

Hiram's reply is equally subtle in its overt and covert messages. Its tone of agreement and cooperation signals to Solomon that Hiram is willing to continue the political amity. But in the process Hiram sets forth his own terms for the commercial arrangements, and they are quite different from Solomon's proposals. After a neutral acknowledgment of receipt of Solomon's message (5:8a), Hiram's reply is organized concentrically:

A. "I will do all you desire concerning cedar logs and cypress logs.
B.   My servants will **bring [them] down** from Lebanon to the sea,
C.   and *I* will **build them into** rafts on the sea,
D.   to whatever place you shall inform me,
C'.   and I will **dismantle them** there,
B'.   and *you* shall **take them up.**
A'. And *you* shall do what I desire by supplying food for my household."

The balanced structure, and in particular the verbal repetition in the "A" subunits, reflects the parity in political relationships. Hiram wishes the two kings to treat each other as equals—"friends," as David and Hiram were (5:1)—not as lord and vassal. On the other hand, the reverse symmetry points up contrasts between the corresponding subunits. What Solomon desires (subunit A) and what Hiram desires (A') may not entirely coincide. The oppositions of bringing logs down (B) and taking them up (B') and of building rafts (C) and dismantling them (C') strengthen the feeling of contrast between the two kings' purposes.

The covert message addresses those conflicting purposes. Hiram's reply to Solomon contains three unnecessary, and therefore emphatic, pronouns (in subunits C, B', and A'), whose distribution does not conform to the concentric symmetry. They clearly demarcate where Hiram's responsibilities lie and where Solomon's, and the division of labor between them is not as Solomon had proposed. Solomon had offered to send Israelite workers to Lebanon to help in the lumbering process. Hiram, however, insists that his own people will do all that is to be done up to the point where the logs arrive in Israelite waters. Thus Tyrian labor (and income, of course) is maximized, and no foreigners are allowed to step on Hiram's soil.

2. 1 Kings 6:9-36[1]

We have already considered how framing inclusions organize the account of the construction of Solomon's Temple (see pp. 68–69). Some of the subunits of that account have their own internal organization. The two sections on work in wood, for instance, are presently interrupted by the account of YHWH's first appearance to Solomon and the framing inclusion that follows it (which is probably, in this case, a true "resumptive repetition"). When that interruption is set aside the material proves to be a single subunit with both composite and complex symmetry:

A. **FROM COURTYARD TO SANCTUARY (6:9b-10, 15-20b)**
   a.   cedar roof of the house (6:9b)
   b.   dimensions of external structure (6:10)
   c.   wood paneling inside the house (6:15)
   a'. cedar walls inside the house, and their purpose (6:16)
   b'.   dimensions of the nave (6:17)
   c'.   cedar decorations of the nave (6:18)
   a". fixing of the sanctuary inside the house, and its purpose (6:19)
   b".   dimensions of the sanctuary (6:20a)
   c".   gold decorations in the sanctuary (6:20b)
B. **THE SANCTUARY (6:20-22, 23-28)**
   d.   altar of cedar (6:20c)
   e.   house covered with gold (6:21a)
   f.   gold chains before the sanctuary (6:21b)
   e'.   whole house covered with gold (6:22a)

---

[1] See Bezalel Porten, "The Structure and Theme of the Solomon Narrative (1 Kings 3–11)," *HUCA* 38 (1967) 93–128, and Jerome T. Walsh, "Symmetry and the Sin of Solomon," *Shofar* 12 (1993) 11–27, and idem, *1 Kings* (Collegeville: The Liturgical Press, 1996) 107–108.

d'. whole altar covered with gold (6:22b)
g. cherubim made (6:23a)
h. height of cherubim (6:23b)
i. length of cherubim's wings (6:24-25a)
h'. height of cherubim (6:25b-26)
g'. cherubim placed in sanctuary (6:27a)
i'. spread of cherubim's wings (6:27b)
g". cherubim plated with gold (6:28)
A'. FROM SANCTUARY TO COURTYARD (6:29-36)
j. walls decorated with cherubim, palms, flowers (6:29)
k. floors plated with gold (6:30)
l. doorway from sanctuary to nave (6:31)
j'. doors decorated with cherubim, palms, flowers (6:32a)
k'. doors plated with gold (6:32b)
l'. doorway from nave to courtyard (6:33-34)
j". doors decorated with cherubim, palms, flowers (6:35a)
k". doors plated with gold (6:35b)
l". the courtyard (6:36).

Composite symmetry is clearest in the central section, which involves three concentric patterns (defe'd', ghih'g', and g'i'g"), the second and third of which share a common element. Complex symmetry is seen in the overall concentric arrangement (ABA') and the similar organization of the corresponding sections A and A', each of which comprises a triple, three-part parallel symmetry.

The combination of forward and reverse symmetries points to an interpretive dynamic that combines forward momentum with reversal. In this case the combination is ingenious, because the passage offers a comprehensive though not exhaustive description of Solomon's Temple as one might be led through it by a guide. The view begins as if from a distance, with structural elements—roof and exterior dimensions. The reader enters gradually into the building, noting the layout and the larger features, walls, paneling, and interior rooms. Reaching the innermost part of the Temple, the Holy of Holies, the reader sees the details of the furniture, the altar and the cherubim, and marvels at the ubiquitous gold. The tour turns, and the reader exits from sanctuary to nave, and from nave to courtyard, this time noting impressive decorative features at each step of the way.

3. 2 Kings 18–20

The account of Hezekiah's reign is segmented by a chiastic series of inclusions that describe the movements of various characters in the narrative. The whole is framed by the complex inclusion of regnal formulas that structures most of 1–2 Kings.

inclusion: FORMULAIC INTRODUCTION (18:1-2)

A. THE EARLY REIGN (18:3-12)
   a. Hezekiah's piety results in military success (18:3-8).
   b. Shalmaneser attacks Samaria but spares Judah (18:9-12).

B. SENNACHERIB AND HEZEKIAH (18:13-37)
   c. Sennacherib invades Judah (18:13-16; see 19:35-37).
   d. The king of Assyria sends envoys (18:17; see 19:8).
   e. Hezekiah's representatives meet the envoys (18:18; see 18:36-37).
      f. The Rab-Shaqeh's first speech (18:19-25)
      g. The Judahite representative's answer (18:26)
      g'. The Rab-Shaqeh's retort (18:27)
      f'. The Rab-Shaqeh's second speech (18:28-35)
   e'. Hezekiah's representatives return to him (18:36-37).

B'. HEZEKIAH AND ISAIAH (19:1-8)
      h. Hezekiah's message to Isaiah (19:1-4)
      h'. Isaiah's response to Hezekiah (19:5-7)
   d'. The king of Assyria's envoys return to him (19:8).

B". SENNACHERIB, HEZEKIAH, AND ISAIAH (19:9-7)
      i. The king of Assyria's insult to Yʜwʜ (19:9-13)
      j. Hezekiah's prayer to Yʜwʜ (19:14-19)
      i'. Yʜwʜ's response to the king of Assyria (19:20-28)
      j'. Yʜwʜ's response to Hezekiah (19:29-34)
   c'. Sennacherib returns home (19:35-37).

A'. THE END OF THE REIGN (20:1-21)
   a'. Hezekiah's piety results in restoration of health (20:1-11)
   b'. "Berodach-Baladan" offers Judah a treaty (20:12-19)

inclusion: FORMULAIC CONCLUSION (20:20-21)

Within the inclusive regnal formulas are five major subunits. The three central ones recount a single event, the invasion of Judah by Sennacherib of Assyria during the reign of King Hezekiah.[2] Those three subunits are simultaneously linked and separated by an unusual use of inclusions. Three inclusive frames begin in 18:13-18, each recounting the movement of one party (subunits cde); the three frames end at different points, however, with the returns of each party recounted in chiastic sequence (subunits e'd'c'). The three scenes are further linked by a type of "additive" process: the characters in the first scene (subunit B: Sennacherib and Hezekiah, both represented by subordinates), plus the characters in the second scene (subunit B': Hezekiah and Isaiah, who represents Yʜwʜ), equal the characters in the third scene (subunit B").

---

[2] Historians differ on their reconstruction of the period, some speculating that accounts of two separate Assyrian incursions may have been conflated in this passage. It is clear, however, that as far as the narrative of 1 Kings is concerned only one invasion is in view, whatever the historical events were.

Each scene consists of an exchange of messages, and in each scene the exchange has a different symmetrical pattern. In these cases, however, the patterns are not indicators of the most effective interpretive strategies. In subunit B the pattern is chiastic. Comparison of the corresponding parts, however, reveals a dynamic of intensification rather than reversal. In subunit f the Rab-Shaqeh addresses Hezekiah's representatives, warning Hezekiah not to rely on Egypt or on YHWH; in f' he addresses all the populace within earshot, warning them not to rely on Hezekiah or on YHWH. The intensification is already signalled in subunits g and g', where Hezekiah's representatives ask the Rab-Shaqeh to speak to them alone rather than to the people at large, and he refuses.

In the much shorter subunit B' the exchange of messages is a simple parallel of address and response: Hezekiah addresses the prophet Isaiah, requesting intercession for divine help, and Isaiah responds with reassurance. The exchange of messages in subunit B" uses alternating repetition; in essence it interlaces two instances of the message-and-response structure of the preceding subunit. The messages also interweave dynamics of reversal (Sennacherib insults YHWH; YHWH condemns Sennacherib) and of forward movement (Hezekiah implores YHWH for salvation; YHWH promises Hezekiah divine protection).

The first and last main subunits (A and A') correspond in their internal structure to form an alternating repetition (an example of complex symmetry). This would generally point to development and intensification as the interpretive strategy, but the situation is complicated by the essentially concentric pattern of the whole account (ABA'), which suggests a degree of contrast between A and A'. Comparison of their corresponding subunits reveals both dynamics. Subunits a and a' show intensification. In both Hezekiah's piety is singled out for praise. In subunit a that piety is rewarded by protection: when Hezekiah rebels against the king of Assyria he incurs no punishment; in subunit a' the king's piety is rewarded by a personal rescue from imminent death plus deliverance of the city from the present threat of Assyrian invasion. Subunits b and b', on the other hand, show contrast. In subunit b Shalmaneser of Assyria attacks the neighboring kingdom of Israel and destroys it, but this military action poses no threat to Hezekiah's Judah; in subunit b' "Berodach-Baladan"[3] makes friendly overtures to Hezekiah, which Isaiah subsequently and unexpectedly prophesies will lead to the despoliation of Judah.

---

[3] This king's name is represented more accurately in Isa 39:1 as "Merodach-Baladan." The Babylonian form is "Marduk-apal-idinna." The form "Berodach-Baladan" in the Hebrew text of 2 Kings 20:12 may be a misspelling or it may represent a dialectal variation.

B. Complex Symmetry

1. Ruth 1–4[4]

The entire book of Ruth has a single, grand chiastic organization, in which some corresponding subunits show parallel symmetry.

A. FAMILY HISTORY (1:1-5)

B.   **OBLIGATIONS OF KINSHIP (1:6-22)**

[frame: the women's journey (1:6-7)]

     a.   relationships among the women (1:8-18)

[frame: the women's journey (1:19a)]

     b.   Naomi and the women of Bethlehem (1:19b)

     c.   Naomi names herself "Mara" (1:20-21)

[frame: the women's journey (1:22)]

C.   **RUTH AND BOAZ (2:1-23)**

[inclusion: background (2:1)]

     d.   dialogue: Ruth and Naomi discuss Ruth's going to glean (2:2)

     e.   narrative: Ruth goes (2:3)

     f.   dialogue: Boaz inquires about Ruth's identity; overseer responds (2:4-7)

     f'.   dialogue: Boaz addresses Ruth (2:8-16)

         (i) tells her to stay

         (ii) blesses her

         (iii) gives her food

         (iv) protects her from the young men

         (v) Ruth complies (2:17)

     e'.   narrative: Ruth returns home (2:18a)

     d'.   dialogue: Ruth reports to Naomi and gets advice (2:18b-22)

[inclusion: afterward (2:23)]

C'.   **RUTH AND BOAZ (3:1-18)**

     d.   dialogue: Ruth and Naomi discuss Ruth's going to the threshing floor (3:1-5)

     e.   narrative: Ruth goes (3:6-7)

     f.   dialogue: Boaz inquires about Ruth's identity; Ruth responds (3:8-9)

     f'.   dialogue: Boaz addresses Ruth (3:10-13, 15a)

         (i) blesses her

         (ii) asks her to stay

         (iii) promises to deal with kinsman

         (iv) gives her food

         (v) Ruth complies (3:14, 15b)

---

[4] Stephen Bertman, "Symmetrical Design in the Book of Ruth," *JBL* 84 (1965) 165–68. I have made a few minor adjustments to Bertman's presentation.

e'.	narrative: Ruth returns home (3:16a)
d'.	dialogue: Ruth reports to Naomi and gets advice (3:16b-18)

B'. OBLIGATIONS OF KINSHIP (4:1-17)

a'.	relationships between men (4:1-13)
b'.	Naomi and the women of Bethlehem (4:14-16)
c'.	the women name the child Obed (4:17)

A'. FAMILY HISTORY (4:18-22)

The family histories with which the story begins and ends contrast sharply. Subunit A recounts the past, a family line that failed because of the childless death of all the males. Subunit A' looks to the future and the glorious Davidic lineage that will issue from the union of Boaz and Ruth. The B subunits involve both contrast and similarity, the latter signalled by the parallel symmetry of their own subunits. Most obvious is the contrast of gender: relationships among women are counterposed to relationships between men. There is also a contrast of moods: Naomi's bitterness and desolation are balanced by the joy of the wedding and Naomi's unexpected blessing from YHWH. But the deeper comparison of these subunits is a similarity: in each case one person renounces the ties that the relationship entails (and in both cases the renunciation is blameless), and in each case one person accepts those ties. The C subunits, with their very similar internal organizations, are similar too in their development. In each Ruth takes the initiative and takes a risk; when Boaz recognizes her he responds to her positively, and her plans succeed. Together the two subunits accomplish the reversal of the whole story: from a situation of desolation and destitution Naomi and Ruth obtain first the means of individual survival (subunit C), then of familial continuation (subunit C').

2. Genesis 11:27–22:24[5]

The collection of stories about Abraham is chiastically arranged, with most corresponding subunits showing parallel internal arrangements.

inclusion: Genealogy of Terah (11:27-32)

A. YHWH COMMANDS ABRAM TO LEAVE HIS FATHER'S HOME-LAND (12:1-9)

B. THREATS TO THE PROMISE OF AN HEIR; THE PROMISE OF LAND (12:10–13:18)

---

[5] Gary A. Rendsburg, *The Redaction of Genesis* (Winona Lake: Eisenbrauns, 1986) 27–52. He credits Umberto Cassuto with first identifying the underlying structure, though Rendsburg's analysis is much more detailed than Cassuto's. I have made some changes in Rendsburg's presentation. In an earlier work Dixon Sutherland analyzed the structure of the passage in a similar but not identical fashion; see his "The Organization of the Promise Narratives," *ZAW* 95 (1983) 337–43.

a.   Sarai in a foreign harem (12:10-20)
b.   Abram separates from Lot (13:1-13)
c.   YHWH promises Abram the land
     and Abram builds an altar in honor of YHWH (13:14-18)
C.   **ABRAM SAVES SODOM, RESCUES LOT (14:1-24)**
d.   Nations at war in the Valley of the Salt Sea (14:1-12)
e.   Abram rescues Lot (14:13-16)
f.   Melchizedek blesses Abram; Abram refuses a tenth of Sodom's goods (14:17-24)
D.   **THE PROMISE OF PROGENY (15:1–16:16)**
g.   YHWH makes a covenant with Abram (15:1-20)
h.   Ishmael's birth is announced (16:1-16)
D'.   **THE PROMISE OF PROGENY (17:1–18:15)**
g'.   YHWH makes a covenant with Abraham (17:1-27)
h'.   Isaac's birth is announced (18:1-15)
C'.   **ABRAHAM TRIES TO SAVE SODOM; LOT IS RESCUED (18:16–19:38)**
f'.   Abraham challenges YHWH; YHWH agrees to spare ten righteous in Sodom (18:16-33)
e'.   Sodom is destroyed; Lot is rescued (19:1-28)
d'.   Nations are born in the Valley of the Salt Sea (19:29-39)
B'.   **THREATS TO THE PROMISE OF AN HEIR; THE PROMISE OF LAND (20:1–21:34)**
a'.   Sarah in a foreign harem (20:1-18)
+.   Birth of Isaac (21:1-7)[6]
b'.   Abraham separates from Ishmael (21:8-21)
c'.   Abraham gains rights to the well at Beer-Sheba
      and plants a tamarisk tree in honor of YHWH (21:22-34)
A'. YHWH COMMANDS ABRAHAM TO SACRIFICE HIS SON (22:1-19)
inclusion: Genealogy of Nahor (22:20-24)

The overall reverse pattern is reinforced by the name changes of Sarai/Sarah and Abram/Abraham, which take place at the center of the structure (17:5, 15). The entire cycle is unified by the theme of the promise of an heir and the series of perils that threaten its fulfillment, and the turning point in the plot is reached with the annunciation of Isaac's birth in subunit h'.

The inclusive genealogies fill out the collateral lines of Abraham's family, the descendants of his two brothers: Lot, son of Abraham's brother Haran, who died before the family left Ur of the Chaldeans (11:27-32), and the descendants of his remaining brother, Nahor (22:20-24). Comparison of corresponding subunits reveals a mixture of contrast and intensification. Subunits A and A' involve both dynamics. The

---

[6] Nothing in subunit B (12:10–13:18) corresponds to the birth of Isaac. See the further discussion of this passage in the section on asymmetry.

contrast of generations (father, son) combines with an intensification of action: in A Abram simply separates from his father geographically; in A' his intention is to kill his son—and along with him his hope of the promised heir.

Subunits B and B' each comprise three sections. Intensification is the stronger dynamic, reflected in the parallel order of the corresponding subunits (a, b, c / a', b', c'). The "a" subunits depict Sarai/Sarah passed off as the sister of Abram/Abraham and taken into the harem of a foreign king. Within the similarity there is intensification; this has long been noted by scholars. The moral tone of subunit a' is notably higher: the claim that Sarah is Abraham's sister has a basis in fact; God protects Sarah from adultery; Abraham's reward is compensation for the offense offered to Sarah rather than payment for her; Abraham intercedes for the deceived king and thereby ends his punishment. In addition, Abraham is allowed to remain in the land rather than being forced to depart from it. The "b" subunits both involve separation from a potential heir so as to leave the way clear for a son of Sarah to inherit. There is an intensification, however, in that Lot is only a nephew, whereas Ishmael is Abraham's first-born son. The "c" subunits both involve erecting a holy place in honor of Yʜᴡʜ. They are additionally related as promise and fulfillment. In subunit c Yʜᴡʜ promises Abraham that he will possess the entire land; in c', through a treaty with Abimelech, Abraham receives title to the well he dug at Beer-Sheba, thus beginning the acquisition of land promised in c.

Sodom and Lot figure in both subunits C and C'. Comparison reveals both contrast and intensification, though in this case the contrast is stronger. This is reflected in the reverse order of the corresponding subunits (d, e, f / f', e', d'). Subunits d and d' both take place in the valley of the Dead Sea; in d nations are at war; in d' new nations are conceived and born. In subunits e and e' the fate of Sodom and of Lot is in jeopardy. In e Abram rescues Lot and the property of Sodom; in e' Lot is likewise rescued, but not by Abraham, and Sodom is destroyed. In subunit f Abram encounters "the priest of God Most High," who blesses him for his rescue of Sodom, and Abram declines the offer of a reward from the King of Sodom. In subunit f' Abraham encounters Yʜᴡʜ in person, questions the justice of the divine plan, and wins from God an agreement to spare Sodom for the sake of a few righteous people. A wordplay also links subunits f and f'. In the Hebrew consonantal script the roots "ten" (*ʿśr*) and "rich" (*ʿšr*) are identical. In subunit f Abram gives Melchizedek a tenth (*mʿśr*) of everything he has captured (14:20), and he refuses the King of Sodom's reward lest the latter claim to have made Abram rich (*hʿšr*, 14:23). But in subunit f' Abraham obtains Yʜᴡʜ's concession to spare Sodom if ten (*ʿśrh*) righteous people be found in it (18:32).

Finally, subunits D and D' likewise involve both intensification and contrast. The second covenant with Abraham is more specific than the first: in D he is promised an heir who will be his own offspring; in D' he is promised an heir *by Sarah,* one from whom will descend "nations and kings of peoples" (17:16). Contrast is found between the two birth annunciations. In the context of the promise Ishmael's birth seems to fulfill the promises made in ch. 15, but the ensuing angelic visitation to Hagar makes it clear that Ishmael, though his destiny will be great (16:10), is not the expected heir (16:12). The second annunciation, though it names Isaac only by allusion,[7] assures Abraham that this will be the long-awaited child of the promise.

3. 1 Kings 1–11

The whole account of Solomon's reign forms a single chiasm, with each pair of corresponding elements manifesting parallel internal structure.

A. A PROPHET INTERVENES IN THE ROYAL SUCCESSION (1:1–2:12a)
- a. Nathan gains the throne for Solomon (1:1–2:9)
- b. Formulaic notice of David's death (2:10-12a)

B.   SOLOMON ELIMINATES THREATS TO HIS SECURITY (2:12b-46)
- c.   Adonijah (2:12b-25)
- d.   (Abiathar and) Joab (2:26-35)
- e.   Shimei (2:36-46)

C.   THE EARLY PROMISE OF SOLOMON'S REIGN (3:1-15)
- f.   Narrator's evaluative summary (3:1-3)
          (foreign marriage; building projects; high places)
- g.   Solomon's first encounter with YHWH (3:4-15)

D.   SOLOMON USES HIS GIFTS FOR THE PEOPLE (3:16–4:34)
- h.   "a discerning mind" (3:16-28)
- i.   "riches" (4:1-28)
- j.   "honor above kings" (4:29-34)

E.   PREPARATIONS FOR BUILDING THE TEMPLE (5:1-18)
- k.   Negotiations with Hiram (5:1-12)
- l.   Conscripted labor (5:13-18)

F.   SOLOMON BUILDS THE TEMPLE (6:1–7:51)
          (including Solomon's second encounter with YHWH)

F'.   SOLOMON DEDICATES THE TEMPLE (8:1–9:10)
          (including Solomon's third encounter with YHWH)

E'.   AFTER BUILDING THE TEMPLE (9:11-25)
- k'.   Negotiations with Hiram (9:11-14)
- l'.   Conscripted labor (9:15-25)

---

[7] Sarah's laughter (*ṣḥq,* four times in 18:12-15) is part of a series of punning allusions to Isaac's name *yiṣḥāq.* See also 21:6; 26:8 (Abimelech sees Isaac *mṣḥq* with Rebekah).

D'.	**SOLOMON USES HIS GIFTS FOR HIMSELF (9:26–10:29)**
h'.	"a discerning mind" (10:1-13)
i'.	"riches" (9:26-28; 10:14-22, 26-29)
j'.	"honor above kings" (10:23-25)

C'.   THE TRAGIC FAILURE OF SOLOMON'S REIGN (11:1-13)

f'.   Narrator's evaluative summary (11:1-8)
        (foreign marriages; building idolatrous high places)
g'.   Solomon's fourth encounter with YHWH (11:9-13)

**B'.   YHWH RAISES UP THREATS TO SOLOMON's
        SECURITY (11:14-25)**

c'.   Hadad of Edom (11:14-22)
d'.   Rezon of Damascus (11:23-25)
e'.   Jeroboam of Israel (next section[8])

A'. A PROPHET DETERMINES THE ROYAL SUCCESSION (11:26-43)

a'.   Ahijah prophesies the throne for Jeroboam (11:26-40)
b'.   Formulaic notice of Solomon's death (11:41-43).

Detailed analysis of this structure is available elsewhere.[9] It is enough here to point out that the general dynamic is contrast, as the overall reverse symmetry would suggest. Subunit A wins Solomon the throne; A' deprives his son of it. Subunit B removes what Solomon perceives as three threats to his security; B' tells of threats he does not remove. Subunit C portends blessed glory; C' is the culmination in idolatry and condemnation. In subunit D Solomon uses the gifts YHWH gave him for the benefit of his people; in D' they redound only to his own benefit. E recounts a treaty with Hiram and prepares for the building of the Temple; E' shows cracks in the amity between Tyre and Israel and extends the oppression of conscripted labor to endless building projects. Only F and F' are essentially in harmony: the building of the Temple climaxes in an extravagant ceremony of dedication. Even here, however, an element of contrast is not absent. In both F and F' Solomon receives a divine word in response to his actions of constructing and dedicating the Temple, but in each case YHWH's word focuses less on the glory of the Temple and more on the conditional character of Solomon's reign: he must exhibit faithful obedience to YHWH if his kingdom is to endure.

---

[8] The material on Jeroboam does double duty. He is the third adversary YHWH raises up against Solomon, thus balancing the three perceived threats Solomon executed in subunit B. (See below, pp. 108–110). He is also the person who will succeed to the throne at the instigation of a prophet, as Solomon himself did in subunit A.

[9] The outline is taken from Walsh, *1 Kings* 151. See the discussion there for details; see also Walsh, "Symmetry and the Sin of Solomon."

C. Compound symmetry

1. Genesis 11:1-9[10]

The brief story of the building of the tower of Babel explains the linguistic and geographic dispersion of humankind. Several different structural forces are at work in the story, giving it an unusual density.

The first and simplest structure is a division of the story into two parts. The first verse supplies background information (11:1); then follow accounts of the deeds of humans (11:2-4) and the deeds of YHWH (11:5-9), each ending with the phrase "dispersed across the face of all the earth." A chiastic series of words and phrases runs through the whole story:

a.   "all the earth one language" (11:1a)
b.   they settled "there" (11:2b)
c.   "each one [said] to his neighbor" (11:3a)[11]
d.   "Come on, let's make bricks *(hābāh nilbĕnāh)*" (11:3b)
e.   "let's build for ourselves . . ." (11:4a)
f.   ". . . a city and tower" (11:4a)
f'.   "the city and the tower" (11:5a)
e'.   "which the humans had built" (11:5b)
d'.   "Come on, . . . let's confuse *(hābāh . . . wĕnābĕlāh)*" (11:7a)
c'.   "each one [will not hear] his neighbor's speech" (11:7b)
b'.   YHWH dispersed them "from there" (11:8)
a'.   "language of all the earth" (11:9a).

The reverse symmetry points to one of the basic dynamics in the story: God humbles the proud projects of humans. Many of the repeated phrases convey contrast: the "one" language of all the earth (phrase a) is no longer "one" in phrase a'; settling (b) gives way to scattering (b'); reciprocal speech (c) becomes mutual deafness (c'); cooperative labor (d) dissolves in unintelligible confusion (d').[12] Only in the center of the structure, phrases e through e', is there a sense of continu-

---

[10] J. P. Fokkelman discusses the Tower of Babel story in *Narrative Art in Genesis: Specimens of Stylistic and Structural Analysis* (Assen: Van Gorcum, 1975; 2d ed.; Sheffield: JSOT Press, 1991) 11–32. My treatment of the concentric structure is based on his. See also Isaac M. Kikawada's slightly different analysis in "The Shape of Genesis 11:1-9," in Jared J. Jackson and Martin Kessler, eds., *Rhetorical Criticism: Essays in Honour of James Muilenberg* (Pittsburgh: Pickwick, 1974) 18–32.

[11] This standard Hebrew idiom for "one another" is often obscured in translation.

[12] Fokkelman points out the rich wordplay in the story. "Let's make bricks" *(nlbnh lbnym,* 11:3a), "bricks for stone" *(lbnym l'bn,* 11:3b), "let's build for ourselves" *(nbnh lnw,* 11:4), "let's confuse" *(nblh,* 11:7), "to confuse" *(bll,* 11:9) all play on the consonants *b, l, n.* The foundational pun is in phrases d and d', where the consonants of "brick" *(lbn)* are reversed in the cohortative form "let's confuse" *(nblh).* Al-

ity; here the contrast is rather that of points of view. Phrases e and f represent the plans of humans, phrases f' and e' God's evaluation of them. The turning point occurs when the story shifts from the human point of view to the divine, namely at 11:5, when YHWH comes down to see the city and tower the humans have built.

The contrast of the two halves of the story is prominent on the level of imagery as well. The people gather in one place (11:1-2; centripetal horizontal movement); they decide to build a tower whose top reaches heaven (11:4; vertical ascent). YHWH comes down to examine their doings (11:5) and decides to come down to confuse their language (11:7; vertical descent); YHWH scatters them across the earth (11:8-9; centrifugal horizontal movement).

A more involved structure emerges when we consider the alternating repetition of narrative and discourse. The first narrative subunit (11:1-2) sets the scene. The subsequent discourses (11:3a, 4, 6-7) are separate monologues, not conversations, and each of them is linked to the narrative subunit that follows it by repeated words and phrases. The final narrative subunit (11:8-9) is bounded by an internal inclusion that has verbal links to the opening verses as well. Thus the whole structure can be schematized:

A. Narrative introduction (11:1-2: "<u>all the earth</u>," "<u>there</u>")
B.   Discourse (11:3a: "let's make <u>bricks</u>")
C.   Narrative (11:3b: "the <u>bricks</u>")
B'.   Discourse (11:4: "let's <u>build a city and a tower</u>")
C'.   Narrative (11:5: "<u>the city and the tower which they built</u>")
B".   Discourse (11:6–7: "let's <u>confuse there</u> their <u>language</u>")
a'. "YHWH dispersed them from <u>there</u> across the face of <u>all the earth</u>" (11:8a)
C".   Narrative (11:8b-9a: "he <u>confused there</u> the <u>language</u> of all the earth")
a". "From <u>there</u> YHWH dispersed them across the face of <u>all the earth</u>" (11:9b)

This is not all. Verbal and syntactic parallels link the three discourses. Each includes the word "Come on!" *(hbh)* and continues with two plural cohortative sentences ("let's . . ."), one of which supplies the verbal link with the following narrative. The forward impetus of this careful parallel construction slows gradually, as each cycle of discourse and narrative becomes significantly longer than the preceding one. Their increasing length adds emphasis to each successive stage of the episode, and the focus intensifies from bricks and mortar, materials appropriate to ordinary constructions, through transcendent projects and purposes that evidence the builders' extreme hubris, to the divine response such hubris elicits.

---

though Fokkelman does not mention it, there is a further wordplay implied. The root *nbl*, although it is not used in this passage, means "fool."

2. 2 Kings 17:25-34a

We examined the overall structure of 2 Kings 17:6-41 above (see pp. 52–54). In the whole passage the dominant symmetry is alternating repetition. In the subunit that describes how the foreigners unexpectedly began to worship Yʜwʜ alongside their own deities the patterns are different and manifold. The subunit is structured in two parts, each with compound symmetry.

The first part (17:25-28) entails both chiasm and immediate repetition. The chiastic structure is based on formal characteristics, including verbal repetition:

A. Narrative: "fear Yʜwʜ" (17:25)
B.   Speech: "the custom of the god of the land" (17:26)
B'.   Speech: "the custom of the god of the land" (17:27)
A'. Narrative: "fear Yʜwʜ" (17:28)

The symmetry of immediate repetition is primarily thematic (problem *versus* solution), but it also involves significant verbal repetition:

A. Problem: "Yʜwʜ sent among them lions, and they killed them."
A'. Problem: "he has sent among them lions, and they are making them die."
B.   Solution: "one of the priests . . . exiled from there . . . dwell there . . . and teach."
B'.   Solution: "one of the priests . . . exiled from Samaria . . . dwelt in Bethel . . . and taught."

The combination of reverse and forward symmetries points to interpretive dynamics of both contrast and continuity. The continuity, of course, lies in the development from problem to solution or, more precisely, from ignorance to knowledge. Contrast is clearest in the reversal from not worshiping Yʜwʜ to worshiping Yʜwʜ, but it is also present in the irony of the king of Assyria being obliged to restore to Israel one of the priests he had previously removed.

The second part of the subunit combines immediate repetition with a concluding epitome in chiastic order. Both structures are built on the four participial sentences that begin each subunit. As the following very literal translation shows, the immediate repetition involves the word order of verb and direct object:

A. "and the nations were each making their gods. . . ." (*wayyihyû ʿōśîm gôy gôy ʾĕlōhāyw*, 17:29–31)
A'. "and they were fearing Yʜwʜ. . . ." (*wayyihyû yĕrēʾîm ʾet-yhwh*, 17:32)
B.   "Yʜwʜ they were fearing" (*ʾet-yhwh hāyû yĕrēʾîm*, 17:33aα)
B'.   "and their gods they were serving. . . ." (*wĕ-ʾet-ʾĕlōhêhem hāyû ʿōbĕdîm*, 17:33aβ).

The chiastic epitome, on the other hand, involves verbal repetition, and in particular the terms for the divinities concerned:

A. "and the nations were each making <u>their gods</u>"
B.   "<u>and they were fearing</u> Y<small>HWH</small>"
b'.   "Y<small>HWH</small> <u>were they fearing</u>"
a'. "and <u>their gods</u> were they serving"

Since the last two subunits are noticeably shorter than the first two and since they add little to what is said in 17:29-32 they are better treated as an epitome than as a full ABB'A' chiasm. The subunit thus reproduces on a smaller scale the overall structure of the whole of 17:6-41, which also involves a concluding epitome, though in parallel rather than chiastic order: ABa'b'.

In interpretation too these patterns give further support to our earlier discussion of the whole passage. The principal dynamic is intensification, signaled by the pattern of immediate repetition, rather than contrast of corresponding subunits in the chiasm. The syncretism of the foreign immigrants is not contrasted with Israelite worship and condemned as something improper. It is presented as something surprising, exceeding what was expected of them: "they worshiped their gods, and they worshiped Y<small>HWH</small> too!"

3. 2 Kings 21:19-26

Our final example of multiple symmetry presents a rich variety of patterns, including compound symmetry. The brief account of the reign of King Amon involves four subunits. The introductory and concluding regnal formulas that structure most of 1–2 Kings surround a brief report of Amon's idolatry (21:21-22) and his assassination (21:23-24).[13] Since the regnal formulas are as long as the surrounded subunits they carry more weight than a complex inclusion would ordinarily do. This points to a basically chiastic reading of the whole passage.

A. Formulaic introduction (21:19-20)
B.   Amon's idolatry (21:21-22)
B'.   Amon's assassination (21:23-24)
A'. Formulaic conclusion (21:25-26)

The formulaic character of the "A" subunits lessens the opportunity for contrast. The principal item in this regard is the mention of Amon's

---

[13] There is a grammatical indicator in the Hebrew text that marks the dividing point between these two subunits, but it does not survive translation. The word order of the last clause of 21:22 breaks the flow of the narrative. The techniques Hebrew narrative uses to mark boundaries between literary units will be our topic in Part II, "Structures of Disjunction."

father, Manasseh, at the end of subunit A, which balances the mention of Amon's son, Josiah, at the end of subunit A'. The first is not a standard part of the regnal formula, and therefore it stands out. In the larger context of 2 Kings it points to the contrast between the evil Manasseh and the good Josiah, a contrast that will be invoked again as the fundamental reason for the Babylonian exile (see 23:26-27).

The correspondence of subunits B and B' is implicit. The text does not present either the palace coup[14] in which Amon dies nor the popular retaliation against the assassins as a result of or response to Amon's idolatry. Nevertheless the juxtaposition of the two suggests a theological causality: Amon abandoned YHWH, and (so) he was killed. The connection is hinted at by an ironic correspondence in vocabulary: Amon "served" (*'bd*) other gods; he was killed by his own "servants" (*'bdym*).[15] The point is talion law: the punishment fits the crime.

Each of the internal subunits has its own symmetry. The description of Amon's crime is presented concentrically. The following translation is literal, with repeated words underlined and terms that correspond as opposites in boldface type.

a.   He <u>walked in</u> every <u>road</u> that his father walked
b.   and he **served the idols** that <u>his father</u> served
c.   and he bowed down to them
b'.   and he **abandoned YHWH**, <u>his fathers</u>' God
a'. and did not <u>walk in</u> YHWH's <u>road</u>.

Here there is contrast: the roads that Amon does, or does not, walk in; the gods of his father versus the God of his fathers; serving the ones, abandoning the other. Centered is Amon's ultimate sin: bowing down to foreign gods, a direct and verbatim violation of Exod 20:5, "You shall not bow down to them."

The report of the conspiracy displays compound symmetry. A literal translation:

21:23a. Amon's servants conspired against him.
21:23b. And they killed the king in his house.
21:24a. And the people of the land struck down all the conspirators against King Amon.
21:24b. And the people of the land made Josiah his son king in his place.

---

[14] "Servants of the king" does not mean slaves but royal officials of the court and the government.

[15] On keywords as a means of linking separate literary units see Part III, "Structures of Conjunction." In this passage "his father" links subunits A and B, "serve / servants" link B and B', and "Josiah his son" links B' and A'.

Three different patterns can be discerned in these verses. First, there is an alternating repetition involving the party who is the main focus of interest, with some verbal repetition:

    a.   The servants, who <u>conspire against Amon</u> . . .
    b.   The <u>king</u>, who is killed . . .
    a'. The <u>conspirators against Amon</u>, who are struck down . . .
    b'.   Josiah, who is made <u>king</u> . . .

Second, there is also a chiastic pattern involving the action of each subunit, though there are no verbal repetitions that support the pattern:

    a.   Agreement to assassinate Amon
    b.   Servants kill the king
    b'.   People of the land kill the conspirators
    a'. Agreement to install Josiah.

Finally, there is a symmetry of immediate repetition (aa'bb'). This involves the grammatical subjects of each sentence, and to that extent is a secondary aspect of plot development, but it is reinforced in this case by a notable difference in sentence length:

    a.   Amon's servants conspired . . . (21:23a, 4 words in Hebrew)
    a'. They [i.e., Amon's servants] killed . . . (21:23b, 4 words in Hebrew)
    b.   The people of the land . . . (21:24a, 9 words in Hebrew)
    b'.   The people of the land . . . (21:24b, 7 words in Hebrew).

Interpretation of the passage involves dynamics of forward movement as well as reversal. The four subunits form a single causal chain: conspiracy leads to assassination, then to execution of the conspirators, and finally to installation of a new king. Moreover, despite the violence and death the overall result of the action is the assurance of dynastic continuity; yet there is reversal at the center, where the killing of the killers echoes the law of talion. And there is a contrast between "inside" and "outside": the conspirators are palace personnel, and they kill the king "in his house," whereas the "people of the land" are the leading citizenry, especially from the towns and villages outside Jerusalem. Those "inside," associated with the palace and with idolatrous Amon himself, threaten to destabilize the political realm by overthrowing the Davidic line; this is analogous to Amon's own crime of destabilizing the religious life of Judah by infidelity to YHWH. Those "outside," associated with "the land" that was YHWH's gift to the people, restore the Davidic line, just as their chosen king, Josiah, will restore faithful adherence to YHWH.

6. ASYMMETRY

Asymmetry can be one of the most forceful stylistic devices in biblical Hebrew narrative. It is not to be confused with absence of symmetry; it refers rather to deviation within an otherwise clear symmetry. In other words, both a symmetrically patterned context and the anomaly of a deviation must be evident for asymmetry to have an impact on a reader. It is the tension between pattern and deviation that affords asymmetry its expressive power. For this reason multiple asymmetries in a single pattern, while theoretically possible, are in practice unlikely to be effective: they weaken the overall symmetry and thereby lessen the tension that foregrounds the deviation. Deviation from symmetry can be achieved in a variety of ways. In principle that variety permits classifying asymmetry into different forms; in practice, however, a single example of asymmetry will sometimes involve more than one deviation and therefore fall into more than one type. The descriptions that follow, therefore, are categories of convenience, not mutually exclusive species of a genus.

The most noticeable variety of asymmetry occurs when a subunit in one sequence lacks a corresponding subunit in the other. (This does not apply, of course, to the central subunit of a concentric symmetry.) The extra subunit may be in either sequence (e.g., AB+CDD'C'B'A' or ABCDD'C'B'+A', where "+" is the extra subunit), and it may occur in forward or reverse patterns. A related case involves a substantial difference in length between corresponding subunits, for example when a subunit of a verse or two in one sequence corresponds to a passage of several verses in another. It is sometimes impossible to determine whether the extra material constitutes a separate, unmatched subunit in itself or is simply an extreme lengthening of one corresponding subunit. (In the schemas above, for instance, the "+" material might be considered part of the "B" subunit that precedes it.) In our examples we will call this form of asymmetry "unmatched subunit."

Another variety of asymmetry involves lack of correspondence in two subunits that occupy corresponding positions in the pattern: for example, they may have no repeated elements in common of a sort that are otherwise numerous in the pattern. This might be schematized ABXCDD'C'YB'A', where "X" and "Y" correspond in position but share no common elements. We will call this "non-correspondence." This form of asymmetry is easily overlooked and will be an effective literary device only to the extent that the lack of correspondence obtrudes itself.

Finally, there is asymmetry of transposition, where the order of subunits in one sequence does not correspond exactly to that of the other (e.g., ABCDEFF'E'D'C'A'B'). Transposition of this sort can seriously obscure a symmetrical pattern, particularly if the sequences are short or if the transposition is complicated. For example, without strong correspondence in repeated elements the single transposition in patterns like ABCB'A'C' and ABCDEE'A'C'B'D' will disrupt the clear encompassing symmetry necessary to sustain the effect of the deviation. Moreover, it is quite often difficult to distinguish between a true transposition and complex symmetry. In ABCDEFF'E'D'C'A'B', if the "B" subunits are not clearly distinct from the "A" subunits it might be better to analyze the passage as a complex symmetry, with the "A" subunits each comprising two parts in parallel: $A_1A_2BCDEE'D'C'B'A_1'A_2'$ (compare, for example, subunits A and A' of 2 Kings 18–20 above, pp. 85–87). For these reasons, clear and convincing examples of asymmetry by transposition are less common than other forms of asymmetry.

Interpretation of asymmetry begins from the principle that the anomaly draws attention to itself. It is therefore a focal point in understanding a passage. Unlike unbroken symmetry, however, asymmetry does not point to a characteristic interpretive dynamic such as reversal, intensification, or the like. Each case must be approached on its own terms. The interpreter will often benefit from contrasting the text as it stands to a hypothetical text with undisturbed symmetry; this will point up the effect of the asymmetry on the construal of the whole passage. A second important interpretive principle is that, like symmetry itself, asymmetry invites intratextual readings as well as linear ones. Asymmetry only becomes evident when an established pattern is violated, that is, when a linear reading first recognizes the pattern, then encounters the deviation. So a linear reading offers a first, indispensable interpretive approach, but an intratextual reading that compares the two sequences can afford additional possibilities. For example, in a pattern like ABCDA'B'C'+D' a linear reading will perceive the asymmetry as an extra subunit "+" in the second sequence and will concentrate on "+" as crucial for interpretation. An intratextual reading, on the other hand, can also read the *first* sequence as *lacking* a subunit "D" (thus: ABC–EA'B'C'D'E') and focus on the *absence* of material at that point as significant.

A. UNMATCHED SUBUNIT

1. 1 Kings 2:39

We examined above the concentric structure of 1 Kings 2:38-41 (see pp. 48–49, and the layout of the text there). There is no material in the second half of the passage that corresponds to the sentence "At the end of three years, two slaves of Shimei fled to Achish, son of Maakah, king of Gath" (2:39a). The words are best construed as a separate, un-matched subunit in the otherwise symmetrical structure.[1]

In this instance the unmatched material is a narrative device de-signed to add detail to the plot[2] and retard its development. Preced-ed by the notice that Shimei stayed in Jerusalem in obedience to Solomon's commands for "many days," 2:39a spells out that the "many days" lasted a full three years. Further, the sentence is much longer than the narrative requires: the narrator could have said simply, "Later, two of his slaves fled to Achish, king of Gath." The unnecessary wordi-ness slows the pace of the narrative considerably, and thereby affords the reader an *experience* of a delay analogous to that the plot undergoes.

2. 1 Kings 18:9-14

When YHWH sends Elijah from Zarephath back to Israel to confront the Baalist King Ahab and to end the drought, Elijah first encounters Obadiah, who, though he is Ahab's major-domo, is also secretly a wor-shiper of YHWH and protector of YHWH's prophets from royal persecu-tion. Elijah orders Obadiah to tell Ahab, "Elijah is here!" *(hinnēh ʾēlîyāhû)*, a phrase that in Hebrew is aurally indistinguishable from "Behold! YHWH is my God!" *(hinnēh ʾēlî yāhû)*. Either message will put Obadiah in jeopardy. First, Ahab has been sedulously searching for Elijah for years with hostile intent, and if Obadiah now appears to have known his whereabouts all along (which he has not), he may be suspected of

---

[1] On this see below, pp. 138–39.

[2] The details are part of a larger narrative agenda. The slaves' flight to Achish, king of Gath, is an allusion to David's flight from Saul (1 Sam 21:10-15; 27:1–28:2). The effect is irony: David's journey to Gath saved him from death at Saul's hands; the same journey costs Shimei, a relative of Saul (2 Sam 16:5), his life at the hands of David's son.

shielding other Yнwн prophets as well (which he has). Second, Ahab's wife, Jezebel, has been killing worshipers of Yнwн with impunity; for Obadiah to announce his loyalty to Yнwн would be to invite martyrdom. Obadiah is understandably reluctant to carry out Elijah's command, and objects strenuously and asymmetrically:

A. "How have I sinned, that you put your servant in Ahab's hand, to make me die?" (18:9)
B.   First argument begun: Ahab has looked everywhere for you. (18:10)
C.   "Now you say, 'Go, tell your master, *hinnēh ʾēlîyāhû.'*" (18:11)
B'.   First argument concluded: you'll disappear again. (18:12a)
A'. "He will kill me." (18:12b)
B".   Second argument: I have been faithful to Yнwн. (18:12c-13)
C'.   "Now you say, 'Go, tell your master, *hinnēh ʾēlîyāhû.'*" (18:14a)
A". "He will kill me." (18:14b)

The "A" subunits are linked by Obadiah's claim that Elijah's command is tantamount to a death sentence. Subunits A' and A" are identical; subunit A uses a synonymous though different verb form. The "C" subunits are identical, and cite verbatim Elijah's original words to Obadiah. The "B" subunits contain Obadiah's arguments against the course of action Elijah requires.

The structure of Obadiah's speech, however, wavers between reverse and forward symmetry because the first argument is presented in two parts while the second is presented all at once. In effect either subunit B' intrudes to disrupt a perfect forward symmetry (ABC+A'B'C'A"), or the lack of a subunit between C' and A" disrupts a perfect reverse symmetry (ABCB'A'B"C'–A"). It is important to note that the narrator could easily have made the symmetry perfect following either pattern. The two parts of the first argument could have been stated together:

> "As Yнwн your God lives, there is no nation or dominion where my master has not sent seeking you. And when they said, 'He is not here,' he would make that dominion or nation take an oath that they had not found you. Now when I leave you, a divine wind will take you I don't know where, I'll come and tell Ahab, he won't find you and he'll kill me."

This would eliminate B' and produce perfect forward symmetry. Conversely, the two parts of the second argument could have been separated by subunit C':

> "Your servant has been a worshiper of Yнwн from childhood. But now you say, 'Go tell your master, *hinnēh ʾēlîyāhû.'* Haven't you heard what I did when Jezebel was killing the prophets of Yнwн—how I hid a hundred prophets of Yнwн . . . ."

This would add a subunit between C' and A" and produce perfect reverse symmetry.

However one analyzes the asymmetry, it involves an unmatched subunit, yet in neither analysis does the unmatched subunit seem important enough to warrant the emphasis given it by the asymmetry. What, then, is the effect? In this case it is the fact of disruption rather than the content of the disruptive element that is most telling. It contributes much to the characterization of Obadiah. Obadiah is a highly placed royal official, perhaps second only to the king in power and clearly closest to the king in the effort to relieve the current crisis (18:5-6). One would expect him to be gifted in all the ways that distinguish responsible courtiers, including polished rhetoric and apt expression (see, for example, Prov 16:13, 21, 23; 22:11; 25:11, among many other passages in the wisdom literature that extol the values of skilled speech). The near-perfect symmetry of Obadiah's speech reflects his rhetorical capabilities; the flaws in the pattern betray his panicked distraction.

3. Genesis 1:26-28

Among the symmetrically organized passages we considered above is the story of the six days of creation in Genesis 1 (see pp. 21–23). The forward symmetry is broken by the inclusion of an extra act of creation on the sixth day, namely the creation of humankind. Since the fundamental effect of asymmetry is to call attention to the anomalous element, the creation of humankind stands out emphatically as especially important within the account of the coming-to-be of the cosmos. Conversely, considered intratextually the absence of a subunit in the first three days of creation to correspond to the creation of humankind is also highlighted. In the first three days environments are established: heavens, firmament, seas, dry land; in the last three days they are populated: celestial bodies, birds, fish, animals. The absence of an environment proper to humanity implies that humans are not restricted to a single realm and correlates with the dominion they are granted over "fish of the sea, birds of the air, cattle, all wild animals, and all creeping things"—in other words, over all creation except the heavens, whose dominion has already been awarded to the celestial bodies (1:16-18).

The same passage is also an example of asymmetry of non-correspondence, since it lacks several of the phrases that characterize the other eight acts of creation (see p. 74). Instead, the importance of the passage is emphasized by poetic language. Commentators have long recognized three lines of poetry here. In fact, there are four.[3] Genesis

---

[3] I am indebted to K. Tishler for this insight.

1:27-28a is a chiastically organized quatrain that uses word order and wordplay to establish its pattern and express its theology:

A.   And God created *(wybrʾ)* humankind in his image.
B.   In the image of God he created *(brʾ)* it;
B'.   Male and female he created *(brʾ)* them.
A'. And God blessed *(wybrk)* them.

In Hebrew the "A" subunits begin with the verb of the sentence, which is the normal Hebrew word order. The paronomasia of *wybrʾ*, "he created" and *wybrk*, "he blessed" suggests that the creation of humankind is not to be understood as a simple, neutral cosmogonic event, but as salvific.[4] The "B" subunits use unusual word order to emphasize the first phrases in each line: "in the image of God" and "male and female" are coordinated. Neither gender is the image of God alone, but in their diversity and complementarity they are.

4. Genesis 21:1-7

The unifying factor throughout the Abraham story is suspense about the fulfillment of YHWH's promises, particularly the promise of an heir. This is the overarching concern when Abram sells Sarai to Pharaoh; when Abram separates from his nephew (and therefore potential heir) Lot, then later rescues him from the coalition of kings that conquered Sodom; when Sarai proves to be barren; when pregnant Hagar flees her abusive mistress; when YHWH promises Abraham a child by Sarah herself; when Sarah is taken into the harem of Abimelech of Gerar; when God instructs Abraham to send away Ishmael, his firstborn; and, finally, when YHWH orders Abraham to sacrifice Isaac. One climax of this dramatic plot is the birth of Isaac, the child of the promise, in 21:1-7, which is emphasized by having no corresponding subunit in the Abraham story (see the layout on pp. 89–90).

This asymmetry can also be read intratextually, as a lack in the first sequence rather than a surplus in the second. The principal counterpart to Isaac in the Abraham story is Ishmael: their birth announcements are structurally parallel, and Ishmael is the potential rival for Isaac's role as heir of the promise (see, for instance, Gen 17:18-21; 21:10-11). Ishmael's birth is recounted very briefly at the end of the subunit announcing his destiny (16:15-16). Isaac's could have been narrated similarly, for example with an editorial aside following Sarah's words in 18:15, something like "But Sarah conceived and bore a son in due season, according

---

[4] It is important to note, however, that this paronomasia occurs in 1:21-23 as well. The presence of other living creatures in the cosmos is likewise a blessing.

to the word of Yʜwʜ." By deferring the notice of Isaac's birth for three chapters the narrator prolongs dramatic tension about the promised heir; and by expanding the account to a full scene, complete with dialogue, he demonstrates Isaac's preeminence over Ishmael, whose birth warrants no comparable scene.

B. Non-correspondence

1. 2 Kings 2:25

Second Kings 2 recounts the assumption of Elijah into heaven in the whirlwind and the transfer of prophetic power and authority from him to Elisha. To this story are attached three brief narratives about the beginning of Elisha's ministry. The entire chapter has a concentric structure:

A. From Gilgal (2:1)
B.   Bethel (2:2-3)
C.   Jericho (2:4-5)
D.   At the Jordan (2:6-7)
E.   Crossing the Jordan (2:8)
F.   Elijah's departure; Elisha's succession (2:9-13)
E'.   Crossing the Jordan (2:14)
D'.   At the Jordan (2:15-18)[5]
C'.   Jericho (2:19-22; 2:18 puts Elisha "in Jericho")
B'.   Bethel (2:23-24)
A'. To Carmel and Samaria (2:25)

The symmetry is clear, but the "A" subunits involve a double asymmetry, both aspects of which function to connect the stories of Elijah with those of Elisha and to emphasize the continuity between the two prophets.

The first asymmetry involves a change of location. In the other corresponding pairs of subunits in the chapter the location is the same (Bethel, Jericho, the Jordan). In the "A" subunits, however, Gilgal is paralleled with Carmel. The effect of the change is to link Elijah to a place that will later be associated with Elisha (Elisha will "return to Gilgal" in 2 Kings 4:38), and to link Elisha to a place already associated with Elijah (see 1 Kings 18, where Elijah bests the prophets of Baal on Mount Carmel).

The second asymmetry is the addition of a second place name in 2:25, Samaria. This effects a transition to ch. 3, which begins in Samaria.

---

[5] The "D" subunits are also linked by the Hebrew word *minneged*, which is not always translated the same in both places. The NRSV renders it "at some distance" in 2:7 and "at a distance" in 2:15.

It thereby points to an extension of the concentric structure of ch. 2 to incorporate the stories that precede and follow, since both are set in Samaria (1:2; 3:1). In 2 Kings 1 Elijah is antagonistic to King Ahaziah of Israel because of the king's patronage of foreign gods (1:16). In 2 Kings 3 Elisha is antagonistic to King Joram of Israel, Ahaziah's brother and successor, because of royal patronage of foreign gods (3:13-14). In this way the larger concentric pattern, which "Samaria" in 2:25 highlights, emphasizes the continuity between Elijah's ministry and Elisha's as well as the change in prophetic leadership from one to the other.

2. 1 Kings 1:33-35

We have seen the concentric structure of David's speech scripting the ceremony that inaugurates Solomon as king (above, pp. 15–16). We noted there one unusual feature of the speech, namely the displacement of the most important event, Solomon's anointing, from its expected emphatic position at the center of the structure.

However, the lack is compensated by an asymmetry of non-correspondence. Subunit C, which describes the anointing, differs from other subunits in the pattern, and especially from its corresponding subunit C', in two ways. First, it is the longest subunit in the pattern and is more than twice as long as C'. The extra length is especially noteworthy because it is unnecessary. "There" is superfluous, and the mention of "Nathan the prophet" is out of place, since only Zadok will in fact anoint Solomon (see v. 39). Second, subunit C also stands out by not being in the second person ("you"), as are most of David's other directives in the speech. These factors set subunit C apart from the rest of the speech and afford it the emphasis due it as the climax of the dramatic movement of the whole chapter.

3. 1 Kings 11:31-39

Ahijah of Shiloh delivers an oracle to Jeroboam announcing to him YHWH's plans to give much of the kingdom of Solomon to Jeroboam himself because of Solomon's idolatry. We saw above that very frequent verbal repetition organizes the oracle in detailed parallel symmetry (see pp. 41–43). There we schematized the text to highlight the repeated elements and display clearly the strong parallel symmetry that organizes the speech. However, the sections where there is little or no repeated vocabulary are similar in length to sections where the repetitions are more frequent, and a layout that more accurately reflects the proportions of the passage highlights the asymmetries more:

A. [31]I am tearing the <u>kingdom from</u> Solomon's <u>hand</u>
 <u>and I will give you the ten tribes.</u>
 [32]The <u>one tribe</u> will be his
 <u>for the sake of my servant David</u>
 and for the sake of <u>Jerusalem, the city I have chosen</u> from all the tribes of Israel.

B. [33]For they[6] have forsaken me
  and bowed down to Astarte the deity of Sidon,
  and to Chemosh the deity of Moab,
  and to Milcom the deity of the children of Ammon.

C.   They did not <u>walk in my ways</u>
   <u>by doing what is right in my sight,</u>
   <u>my statutes and my</u> decrees,
   like <u>David</u> his father.

D.   [34]But I will <u>not</u> take the whole kingdom from his hand
   but will make him ruler <u>all the days</u> of his life,
   <u>for the sake</u> of my servant <u>David</u> whom I chose
   and who did keep my commandments and my statutes.

A'. [35]I will take the <u>kingship from the hand</u> of his son,
 <u>and I will give</u> it to <u>you, the ten tribes.</u>
 [36]To his son I will give <u>one tribe.</u>
 <u>for the sake of</u> a lamp[7] for <u>my servant David</u> all days before me
 in <u>Jerusalem, the city I have chosen</u> for myself to put my name there.

B'. [37]You I will take
  and you shall be king over all your heart desires;
  you shall be king over Israel.

C'.   [38]If you heed all I command you and <u>walk in my ways</u>
  and <u>do what is right in my sight</u>
  by keeping <u>my statutes and my</u> commandments
  as did <u>David</u> my servant

(+)   I will be with you
   and I will build you a sure house
   as I built for David
   and I will give you Israel.

D'.   [39]I shall punish <u>David's</u> line <u>for</u> this <u>sake</u> [i.e., "for this reason"], but <u>not</u> for <u>all the days.</u>

The symmetrical pattern is so strongly established in subunits A/A' and C/C' that it is able to support two instances of asymmetry, the

---

[6] The Hebrew text has plural forms in subunits B and C: "*they* have forsaken . . . bowed down . . . did not walk." Most English versions follow the ancient Greek translation in reading singulars here: "*he* has forsaken . . . ," etc.

[7] The meaning of the word traditionally translated "lamp" *(nîr)* is disputed. It may mean a "fief" or small possession remaining under the control of the Davidic house.

absence of repeated vocabulary in subunits B/B' and the unmatched subunit (+) between C' and D'.

Subunits B and B' correspond in position and approximate length, but they differ in subject matter and purview. Both sequences start with a declaration of YHWH's decision to transfer ten tribes from the house of David to Jeroboam (subunits A and A'). Subunit B looks to the past to explain the motivation behind YHWH's decision: the Israelites' idolatry following the lead of Solomon. Subunit B', on the other hand, looks to the future and spells out more clearly the implications of YHWH's decision: Jeroboam will be "king over Israel" (this is the first time the phrase is applied to him). In both sequences the next subunit (C/C') continues the temporal perspective and invokes the Davidic model. Subunit C measures past Israelite idolatry against David's faithfulness; subunit C' sets David as the standard for Jeroboam's future behavior. The shift from past to future is adumbrated in subunits A and A' ("Solomon's hand," v. 31; "the hand of his son," v. 35), but it is accomplished and brought into clear focus in subunits B and B'. There is a further contrast between subunits B and B' in terms of divine and human loyalties. Where subunit B describes Israel's rejection of YHWH, subunit B' announces YHWH's election of Jeroboam.

The contrast between past and future illuminates the other asymmetry in the passage as well. There is nothing in the first sequence that corresponds to the last words of v. 38. The sentence uses covenant language and promises Jeroboam a dynastic descendance comparable to David's. In a linear reading the presence of such a promise here, in an unmatched subunit, gives strong emphasis both to the promise and to its echoes with the similar promise made to David in 2 Samuel 7: Jeroboam has the potential to be a new David. In an intratextual reading the absence of any reference to the Davidic covenant between subunits C and D is ominous. Israel's idolatry has brought the Davidic house into serious jeopardy: the potential for dissolution of the covenant is real. Only in subunits D and D' does YHWH draw back from that extreme measure and set limits to the punishment of the house of David.

C. TRANSPOSITION

1. Exodus 6:10-13, 26-30

We examined above the multiple external inclusions surrounding the genealogy of Aaron and Moses in Exod 6:14-25. The outermost inclusion (6:10-12, 28-30) has several repeated elements in parallel, with the exception of the last two (ABCDEF/A'B'C'D'F'E'; see the discussion on pp. 71–73). The transposition of these two elements effects a subtle change in the characterization of Moses and a slight redirection of the narrative. In 6:12 Moses' speech begins with two parallel clauses,

> But the Israelites did not listen to me.
> How will Pharaoh listen to me?

The poetic parallelism of the two clauses isolates and thereby emphasizes the third clause, whose final position already affords it some emphasis:

> I am unrefined of lips.

Literally, Moses says he is "uncircumcised of lips"; compare Isaiah's similar protest in Isa 6:5 that he is "unclean of lips." This portrays Moses' concern for the success of his mission as focused on himself and his own personal inadequacy, and it invites the reader to expect YHWH to address that condition (as, in Isaiah, the saraph purifies the prophet's lips with a coal from the holy altar of incense).

In 6:30, however, the parallelism is missing, and the mission comes in the last, emphatic position:

> I am unrefined of lips.
> How will Pharaoh listen to me?

The effect of the transposition is to focus attention less on Moses, or on his earlier failure with the Israelites, and more on the mission itself. When YHWH finally responds to Moses' objection, the response is to its second form. YHWH's decision provides for the success of the mission, but not by lessening Moses' verbal clumsiness. Rather YHWH assigns Aaron to "speak to Pharaoh that he should send the Israelites from his land" (7:2).

The change reflects the impact of the intervening genealogy. Moses and Aaron are a team, and the mission will be entrusted to them together. By changing his focus from himself (6:12) to the mission (6:30) Moses shows himself open to accepting his brother as his divinely appointed collaborator even before YHWH makes the appointment.[8]

2. Genesis 1–11[9]

The so-called "Primeval History" (Genesis 1–11) has a structure that uses forward symmetry with one transposition:

---

[8] In the larger context, of course, YHWH appointed Aaron as Moses' spokesman in Exod 4:14-16. In the more limited context of 6:10-30 the earlier passage does not seem to be remembered.

[9] Based on Gary A. Rendsburg, *The Redaction of Genesis* (Winona Lake: Eisenbrauns, 1986) 7–25, with some modifications.

A. Narrative: creation (1:1–3:24)
B.   Narrative: sin and curse of the son (4:1-16)
C.   Genealogy: the origins of culture (4:17-26)
D.   Genealogy: from Adam to Noah and Shem (5:1-32)
E.   Narrative: blurring the divine-human boundaries (6:1-4)
A'. Narrative: re-creation (the flood story: 6:5–9:19)
B'.   Narrative: sin and curse of the son (9:20-29)
C'.   Genealogy: the origins of nations (10:1-32)
E'.   Narrative: blurring the divine-human boundaries (11:1-9)
D'.   Genealogy: from Shem to Terah and Abram (11:10-26)

The echoes of the creation story, particularly in Genesis 1, have long been noted in the flood account. Both stories begin with a brief statement of the lack of due order (1:1-2; 6:5-6). The separation of waters above and waters below, the separation of sea and dry land, the creation of birds, land animals, and human beings—all accomplished in Genesis 1—are systematically undone and then reestablished in Genesis 6–9. The blessing conferred on human beings in 1:28 is renewed in 9:1-2. In these ways, and in many others as well, the flood story announces a negation of the first creation account and a new beginning. The "B" subunits depict the continuing presence of sin in the generation following the founding parents. The "C" subunits are genealogies, but neither has a familial focus. The "D" subunits together trace the entire familial genealogy from Adam to Abram: 5:1-32 lists the ten generations from Adam to Noah, ending with Noah and his three sons; 11:10-26 traces the ten generations from Noah to Terah, ending with Terah and his three sons. The "E" subunits are both brief narratives, and both depict how the boundaries that separate the divine realm from the human are endangered: in 6:1-4 miscegenation between the "divine sons" and the "human daughters" threatens to impart to human beings the gift of divine immortality that was forbidden to humans from the beginning (see 3:22); in 11:1-9 human hubris presumes to encroach on heaven itself.

The transposition of subunits D' and E' has several effects on the way we read the primeval history. The first and most significant effect arises from a linear reading. In the sequence ABCDE forward progress (evoked in particular by the genealogy of subunit D) is thwarted by the transgressions of subunit E. The result is a return to the pre-creational chaos and a new start from the original point: re-creation, a new originating ancestor, a repeated blessing of fertility, etc. By putting E' before D' the second sequence preserves the forward momentum of the genealogy and suggests that the divine response to this new transgression will not require wiping the slate clean to return to the starting point. It will be different, and will allow the human story to enter a new era.

A lesser but still real effect can be discerned by an intertextual reading. The genealogy of subunit C is not exhaustive, since it merely traces the descendants of Cain; only when it is combined with the Sethite genealogy in subunit D do we have a complete genealogy of humankind. Subunit E then leads immediately into the statement of lack that initiates the flood story. Divine-human intermarriage, this suggests, contributes to the lack of due order (violence: 6:5-6) the flood is intended to rectify. By contrast the genealogy of subunit C' is exhaustive: it traces the descendance of all Noah's sons. This allows subunit E' to come between the two genealogies and thereby strengthen its links to both. It relates to the ethnic genealogy of 10:1-32 because God's dispersion of the peoples from the Tower of Babel explains the existence and distribution of the diversified nations of the world, and it relates to the genealogy of Terah since it is one of Terah's sons, Abram, in whom the dispersed nations of the earth will ultimately find their blessing (12:3).

3. 1 Kings 3:16–4:34; 9:26–10:29

A complicated and interesting transposition occurs in the complex symmetry that links 1 Kings 3:16–4:34 with 1 Kings 9:26–10:29 (subunits D and D' on pp. 92–93). Both passages use as their organizing principle the three gifts YHWH granted Solomon in 1 Kings 3:11-13, namely discernment, riches, and honor.[10] In 1 Kings 3:16–4:34 the three gifts are illustrated sequentially: Solomon's discernment allows him to resolve the case of the two harlots' children (3:16-28); his wealth derives from wise administration of internal affairs (4:1-20), external affairs (4:21-25), and chariot forces (4:26-28); and his reputation for wisdom was universal (4:29-34). In 1 Kings 9:26–10:29 the organization is less clear. Solomon's discernment enables him to answer and impress the Queen of Sheba (10:1-10, 13). His reputation for wisdom remains universal (10:23-25). But the discussion of his riches is dispersed throughout the passage: internal display (10:14-21), maritime enterprises (9:26-28; 10:11-12; 10:22, corresponding to the "external affairs" of 4:21-25), and commerce in chariots and horses (10:26-29).

There are two transpositions relative to 3:16–4:34, both involving the material that describes Solomon's riches. First, the section dealing with "external affairs" (specifically, in the later passage, maritime enterprises) has been broken up into three separate components, only one of which is in the expected place. Second, the paragraph dealing with

---

[10] See my *1 Kings* (Collegeville: The Liturgical Press, 1996) 130–32 for a more detailed discussion.

chariots and horses has been transposed to follow that dealing with honor. The following comparison shows the differences:

1 Kings 3:16–4:34		*1 Kings 9:26–10:29*
	(2b.)	9:26-28
3:16-28	1. discernment	10:1-10, 13
	(2b.)	10:11-12
4:1-20	2a. riches: internal affairs	10:14-21
4:21-25	2b. riches: external affairs	10:22
4:26-28	2c. riches: chariots and horses	10:26-29
4:29-34	3. honor	10:23-25

These transpositions have several effects. Parceling out the information about Solomon's ocean-going fleets into three separate passages highlights the differences as well as the progression among the three. There are at least two different fleets in view, one belonging to Solomon (9:26), one to Hiram (10:11), though they seem to work together (10:22). On one auspicious occasion they brought an immense quantity of gold to Solomon (9:28), along with other wealth (10:12); but their triennial circuit was also a significant source of luxuries (10:22). Furthermore, distributing the three passages throughout the whole account cleverly emblematizes the worldwide peregrinations of the fleets themselves.

The placement of the transposed materials underscores the dominant economic note of the whole literary unit. In 3:16–4:34 Solomon's "wisdom" was the keynote in all parts of the passage. His discernment was an exercise of wisdom that produced justice (3:28); his wise administration of the kingdom and the empire produced prosperity (4:20) and security (4:25) throughout Israel and Judah; his worldwide reputation for wisdom led people to him to learn from his sayings and songs (4:34). By contrast, all parts of 9:26–10:29 focus on Solomon's wealth. His discernment produces not justice but more riches (10:10[11]); his worldwide reputation for wisdom no longer issues in songs and sayings but simply serves to amass tribute (10:25). The transposition of the "riches" motif to 9:26-28 and of 10:26-29 from its expected position between "discernment" and "honor" means that the whole passage begins and ends with commercial profit.

---

[11] The mercenary character of the exchange is highlighted by parallel formulation: "gold, a great quantity of spices, and precious stones; never again . . ." (10:10) and "gold, a great quantity of almug wood, and precious stones; . . . never again . . ." (10:11-12).

PART II

STRUCTURES OF DISJUNCTION

In Part I we examined the ways in which single literary units can be organized symmetrically. In Parts II and III we turn to the relationships between contiguous literary units. Part II will consider the ways in which Hebrew narrative marks boundaries between units, and Part III will study the ways in which successive units are linked across those boundaries. The topics of Parts II and III are complementary since in a large narrative that encompasses many subunits both their borders and their continuities contribute to the organization of the whole.

Literary units exist on every level from the smallest phonetic units to complexes of biblical books. In theory, then, boundaries between units can be studied on any of those levels. In practice only the mid-range is of more than passing interest for the understanding of narrative. Ways of marking the boundaries between syllables or words, for instance, are interesting linguistically, but not narratively, and the major topical shifts that mark the boundaries between large narrative complexes, such as the shift from Edomite genealogies in Genesis 36 to stories of Jacob's sons in 37:1-2, are too obvious to warrant much comment. What remain are literary units comparable to the English terms paragraph, episode, scene, and the like—in other words, narrative units that function as subunits of larger, connected narratives or closely woven narrative complexes. In Part II we will examine how these subunits are divided from one another; in Part III we will consider the techniques that preserve narrative coherence across those divides.

In recent years some analysts of language and literature have pursued this sort of textual study in many languages. The discipline of "text linguistics" attempts to define the syntax, so to speak, of units larger than the sentence (e.g., "paragraphs" and "discourses"), just as traditional grammar describes the rules for well-formed phrases, clauses, and sentences. Some few studies have concentrated on biblical Hebrew, and some have specifically targeted biblical Hebrew narrative.[1] Much of what follows is based on those works, though I have inevitably

---

[1] See, in the bibliography, the works of Robert D. Bergen, David Allan Dawson, Robert Longacre, Samuel A. Meier, Alviero Niccacci, and E. J. Revell.

(over)simplified their technical expertise and blunted their nuances. I hope that in so doing I have not unduly compromised the advances their contributions make to our understanding of biblical Hebrew narrative.

The ability to discern the boundaries between literary units and subunits is not a luxury. The articulation of a text into structural units and subunits mirrors and reinforces its thematic organization.[2] While the latter is usually clear enough for the careful reader to follow, at times it is not, and the former can supply crucial clues to reveal it. Unfortunately, studying the elements that mark textual boundaries requires some understanding of Hebrew grammar and the unique resources available in Hebrew, since these resources are often quite different from those of English. For this reason each of the sections that follow will have to include some explanation in non-technical language of features of Hebrew grammar that underlie the narrative techniques being illustrated.

The first section will examine how changes in some of the basic components of a narrative—characters, setting in time and space, and narrative voice—can signal the opening of a new narrative unit or subunit. This part of our study will hold few surprises, since similar changes are standard ways of marking scene boundaries in most literatures. The second section will look at repetition. This is a powerful weapon in any stylist's arsenal, and can serve a wide variety of purposes in different literatures. In the first part of our study we saw how repetition forges links and establishes connections between different parts of a narrative. Another of repetition's several uses in biblical Hebrew narrative is to mark unit boundaries. Finally, in the last section we will look at particular linguistic conventions in biblical Hebrew, above all the device known as "narrative sequence." Here we tread on very important but difficult terrain: these conventions include the most common and unmistakable signals of unit boundaries, but they rarely survive translation intact. Among other questions, we will find it necessary to ask what means exist in English to capture their boundary-marking function.

---

[2] Text linguists point out that the thematic organization of a text is itself many-leveled, and they will use terms like "topic" and "focus" to distinguish different sorts of thematic highlighting.

7. NARRATIVE COMPONENTS

The most obvious way in which a narrative is divided into subunits is by a shift in one of the primary constituents of scenic unity: participants, spatial context, or temporal framework. If the shift is prominent it needs no other textual indicators to establish a break. Nevertheless, shifts of place, time, and characters are often accompanied by identifiable textual markers that, simply by being unnecessary, serve to underscore the unit boundary.

Whereas changes in setting, time, or characters usually indicate a comparatively major division of units, analogous to a change of scene in a dramatic work, subunits *within* a scene are often divided by changes in what might be called the "narrative voice." On the simplest level this term refers to the difference between a character's speech (where the "voice" we hear is that of the character) and the narration proper (where the "voice" we hear is that of the narrator).[1] That difference, however, is merely the most basic distinction in a complex series of ways in which the narrative voice can be realized. We will have occasion to consider some of these below.

As we shall see, several of the boundary-markers to be considered in this and the following sections can converge to reinforce one another. For example, place, time, and characters may all change from one scene to the next. This redundancy does not necessarily mean that the boundary is more important than others, but can make the separation of

---

[1] Recognizing the narrator as a "voice" in a story is easiest when the story is narrated by one of the characters. When *Moby Dick,* for instance, begins with the words "Call me Ishmael," we realize that the voice telling us the story is that of a participant. (In the Hebrew Bible the principal example of this sort of narration by character is the book of Nehemiah.) But even when the narration comes to us unattached to a named character it is still a "voice" that recounts the events of the tale.

units very clear. Conversely, when boundary-markers are few, and especially when they can be used for other narrative functions as well, the structure of the narrative may be less easily discerned.

Characters

Ancient literature, both dramatic and narrative, tended to restrict scenes to relatively straightforward interaction between a very limited number of characters. This is true of biblical narrative as well as of classical (and, we might add, of much contemporary popular literature). The reason is not hard to fathom. The more complex the interaction in a scene, the more difficult it becomes for the reader to construct the scene in imagination. To keep track of four mutually interacting characters taxes the average reader's imagination severely. (Detective stories take full advantage of this by requiring the reader to picture the simultaneous whereabouts and movements of several different suspects at once.)

In the Hebrew Bible some scenes feature only one main character. Frequently such scenes are long speeches, such as the "farewell" speeches that major characters conventionally deliver (often in poetry) at the end of their lives. See, for instance, the farewell speeches of Jacob (Genesis 49), of Moses (Deuteronomy 32–33), of Joshua (Joshua 24), of Samuel (1 Samuel 12)[2], or of David (2 Samuel 22–23; David has another, shorter farewell speech in 1 Kings 2). Other single-character scenes can be internal monologues, though these are comparatively uncommon in the Hebrew Bible. Finally, there are single-character action scenes (Gen 41:46-57, for example). From an author's point of view scenes with only one main character are difficult to achieve effectively: conflict is essential to compelling narrative, and it is difficult to embody conflict with only one character.[3] As a consequence such scenes generally occur only as subunits within larger stories that include conflict. One-character scenes will themselves often have subunits, of course, but

---

[2] Although Samuel does not die until 1 Samuel 25 he plays little part in the intervening chapters, and the "farewell" quality of this speech is clear in 12:2.

[3] The passage just mentioned, Gen 41:46-57, is a good example of the difficulty of injecting interest into such a scene; surely it is the most forgettable passage in the Joseph story! On the other hand, Genesis 1 is a strikingly successful example that awakens a reader's interest by skillful use of a variety of narrative techniques: formalized language with just enough variation to please, rhythmic cadence, and a structure that combines forward dynamism with gradually increasing suspense. See the discussions of this passage above on pp. 37–38 and 74.

those subunits will have to be separated by means other than character change.

More commonly two main characters are central to a scene, and while other figures may be present their presence is clearly secondary. Generally only the two main characters interact; secondary characters do little more than supply whatever is needed to keep the scene running. The "young men" who accompany Abraham and Isaac in Genesis 22 are necessary (somebody has to watch the donkey!—22:5), but only Abraham and Isaac are truly principal actors in the scene. The departure of one of the main characters, or the appearance of a new character, can signal a unit boundary in such cases, even when the departure or arrival is not explicitly mentioned in the text. Within the scene subunits can be distinguished by the narrative voice (narrator, character A, character B), or by shifting the focus from one character to the other.

A more complex scenic structure involves three main characters, but in such scenes usually only one character will interact with the other two. That is, A will interact with B and with C, but B and C will not interact with each other. Here too the departure of a character can signal a unit boundary. (Arrival of a fourth main character would be untypical of classical Hebrew narrative unless one of the others departed first.) As in two-character scenes, internal subunits can be marked by changes in narrative voice and shifts in focus.

In all the above it would probably be more proper to speak of "parties" than of "characters," since a character role can be filled by a group. For example, in 2 Kings 2:15-24 Elisha interacts successively with the "sons of the prophets,"[4] the "people of the city," and the "small children" of Bethel. Often the group's character role will become embodied in a single representative. In 2 Kings 6:1-7, for instance, the "sons of the prophets" speak in vv. 1-2, but this awkward plural voice is reduced to a single representative from that point on. Similarly in Gen 3:1 the snake is identified as "the most crafty of all the animals YHWH God had made" and thereby becomes the representative of the character role that "the animals" held in ch. 2. The same technique appears in the New Testament gospels when one of the disciples—generally Peter—speaks as representative of the rest.

---

[4] The phrase is a technical one. It does not refer to prophets' offspring, but to a group of people who, as a group, engaged in prophetic activity. (See, for instance, the "four hundred fifty prophets of Baal" in 1 Kings 18:20-29, or the "four hundred prophets" of 1 Kings 22:6-12.) In English we would be more likely to call it a "prophetic guild" or a "company of prophets."

Setting: locale

Most narrative scenes take place in a single locale, and a change in that locale signals the end of one scene and the beginning of another. The transition from one scene to the next is frequently marked by an explicit notice of movement: a statement of departure for one or both main characters of the preceding scene or a statement of arrival for one of the main characters of the following scene. The former is usually called a "departure notice"; by analogy we might call the latter an "arrival notice." Structurally these statements may form part of either scene or they may constitute a brief transitional subunit between the two scenes (often forming framing verses with other statements of movement). Naturally locale can shift without any such explicit signals, but their appearance is common enough to warrant treating them as a conventional narrative device. At times the device is used to mark a scene boundary even when the locale does *not* change. In some of the examples below, for instance, we will see two scenes that are separated by statements of the movement or location of characters even though the following scene takes place in the same locale as the preceding one.

Setting: time

Time, like space, is one of the narrative components that can unify a scene. And like locale, a change in temporal setting can signal a change in scene.

Biblical Hebrew has a standard narrative device for indicating a change of time. At the beginning of a new unit—or at least at the beginning of the action, following background information that may need to be supplied—the temporal setting is specified by a set grammatical construction. First comes the verb "to be" in the narrative tense.[5] This is followed by a word, phrase, or clause that gives a temporal reference. The reference may be as short as a single word (for example, "in-the-evening" is one word in Gen 29:23); and it may be absolute ("at the end of forty days," Gen 8:6) or relative to an event ("when they were in the field," Gen 4:8) or to a character in the story ("in the six-hundred-first year [of Noah's life]," Gen 8:13). Finally comes the next action verb, usually in the narrative tense, although it

---

[5] "Narrative tense" and "simple past" refer to two different grammatical forms in Hebrew. For a fuller discussion see below, pp. 155–56. We will see in a later section that the verb "to be" in the narrative tense can, all by itself, mark a boundary between units or subunits.

appears frequently in the simple past as well.[6] The whole sequence looks something like this, in an extremely literal rendering: "and-it-was at-the-end of-days and-he-brought . . ." (Gen 4:3; NRSV: "In the course of time, Cain brought . . ."). Since this construction almost always appears at or near the beginning of a new unit or subunit it is a very reliable boundary indicator. Unfortunately, as our example makes clear, it cannot survive identifiably in any smooth translation. It is up to the translator to recognize the boundary-marking function of the construction and to reflect it in the translation in some way. Paragraph indentations and section headings are typical ways of accomplishing this in English translations.[7]

A shorter variant of the full temporal construction just described occurs much less commonly, but with similar effect as a boundary marker. In this form the first element ("to be" in the narrative tense) is lacking. The construction begins immediately with the temporal reference, followed by the action verb, which can be in either the narrative tense or the simple past. It is difficult to discern any significant difference between this abbreviated form of the temporal construction and the full form that includes the first element.

Time can change temporarily *within* a literary unit as well. Often in the course of narrating a scene the narrator will insert background information that the reader must have in order to follow the story. At times this background information will take the form of a secondary narrative about things that happened even before the scene actually being recounted. Technically this is called a "flashback," and it entails a change of time backwards—grammatically from past tense ("X happened") to past perfect tense ("Y had already happened"). Similarly,

---

[6] The occurrence of a simple past (technically a *qatal*) rather than a narrative tense (technically a *wayyiqtol*) for the action verb is attested frequently enough that this sequence probably represents a recognized alternative to the commoner one. The difference in nuance between the two sequences is not entirely clear, but it is clear that both function similarly as boundary markers for units and subunits.

[7] Those who are following this discussion using the NRSV will have noted that there is no paragraph indentation or section heading at Gen 4:3. The reason is that in this passage the construction marks the beginning of the *action* of the scene and is preceded by two verses of information (4:1-2) that supply background for the action. Both background and action are part of the literary unit, which the NRSV properly locates as beginning at 4:1. The narrative tense of "to be" with its following temporal reference separates the subunit of background information from the subunit that recounts the action proper. The main change one might suggest to increase the NRSV's precision in this passage is to treat 4:1-2 as background rather than narrative and render it in the past perfect: "Now the man had known his wife Eve, and she had conceived . . ." etc.

though less often, the narrator may also interrupt the course of the primary narrative to point forward to something that will happen later—technically a "foreshadowing" or a "prolepsis." This entails a change of time forward—grammatically from past tense ("X happened") to a conditional future ("Y would happen later" or "Y was to happen later"). Since both of these time changes are interruptions of the primary narrative rather than new stages in it, they generally mark subunits *within* a scene or episode rather than boundaries between scenes or episodes. Flashbacks and prolepses are usually signalled in the Hebrew text by special verb forms and grammatical constructions. We could also treat them as changes in narrative voice, since the narrator suspends the primary storytelling to recount what is in effect a brief narrative-within-the-narrative. We will see some examples below, and others in the later section on "Narrative Sequence."

Narrative voice

The simplest changes of narrative voice occur when one character stops speaking and another begins, or when character speech gives way to narrative and vice versa. Even in modern English fiction the speeches of the different characters in a dialogue are usually separated by paragraph indentations. In biblical Hebrew narrative, however, unlike modern English narrative, one character's speech does not generally touch directly upon another's. There is almost always a brief narrative transition of the "and he said" sort; this is required to separate the speeches since Hebrew has nothing comparable to quotation marks. Without the narrative separator it would not always be clear where one speaker stops and the other begins.[8]

The same holds true when the narrative voice shifts from character to narrator. It is not always clear where to locate the shift. The potential for ambiguity is great, both negatively and positively: a careless author can produce a confusing text; a gifted one can create layered alternative readings and thereby evoke multiple (and not always compatible!) possibilities in a reader's mind.

Narrative voice, however, can be much more complex than the simple distinction between character and narrator. One character, for instance, can quote another (or even quote him- or herself); this introduces a sort of voice-within-the-voice and can indicate a separate sub-

---

[8] A good example of the potential for ambiguity is 1 Kings 20:34. There is no indicator in the Hebrew that the speaker changes before the sentence "I will let you go on those terms," yet it must. So the NRSV adds "The king of Israel responded" to insure clarity.

unit within the character's speech.[9] The narrator's voice, too, can vary. Sometimes the narrator will, so to speak, step out of the flow of the narrative to address the reader directly; the technical term for this is "breaking frame," and it changes the narrator's voice from that of a storyteller to that of a commentator on the story. The narrator will "break frame" to relate some event he has just described to something contemporary to his audience; see, for example, the last words of Josh 7:26 and 8:29. As we mentioned above under "Setting: time," a similarly subtle change of voice occurs when the narrator temporarily suspends storytelling to supply the audience with important background information. This change is usually signalled grammatically (we will examine the technique in a later section), but it is also an instance of a change in narrative voice. Any such shift within the narrator's own voice can indicate a separate subunit within the structure of the narrative.

A. CHANGE IN CHARACTERS

1. 1 Kings 2:1-10

This is an example of a one-character unit. It is David's farewell speech, though it is shorter than the others mentioned above. Solomon is said to be present (2:1), but only David is active in the scene, and his only activity is speaking. The scene is distinguished from what precedes by a complete change of main characters (Solomon and Adonijah in 1 Kings 1:51-53; David alone in 2:1-10), and from what follows by the death of the main character (2:10), a variation on the conventional formula for the end of a regnal account (2:11), and the introduction of a different active main character (2:12). The unity of the scene is shown not only by its being a single speech but also by the inclusion that marks its beginning and end: David is about to die (2:1); David dies (2:10).

Recognizing the speech as an independent unit within the narrative of Solomon's accession to the throne allows us a richer appreciation of its structural effect in the literary context. It points both backward (David's death culminates the theme of his terminal illness established in 1:1-4[10]) and forward (the enemies David tells Solomon to eliminate are eliminated in 2:28-46). More precisely, the narrative inclusion (2:1, 10) points

---

[9] On the phenomenon of quotation in biblical Hebrew narrative see George W. Savran, *Telling and Retelling: Quotation in Biblical Narrative* (Bloomington, Ind.: Indiana University Press, 1988).

[10] See the symmetrical structure on pp. 25–26.

backward, and the second half of David's speech (2:5-9) points forward. The unit, then, acts as a sort of structural hinge linking the story of Solomon's emergence as David's successor and the story of his purge of threats to his power. (We will examine this technique more closely in the third part of our study; see below, pp. 186–90.)

It is clear even to a casual reader that the speech has internal subunits. The thematic contrast between the pious platitudes of 2:2-4 and the unscrupulous pragmatism of 2:5-9 is unmistakable. In the second part the further subdivision into sections dealing with Joab, Barzillai's sons, and Shimei is equally clear. Since our primary focus in this book is narrative, to study the verbal indicators that mark subdivisions in speeches would take us too far afield. Suffice it to say that text linguists have made contributions here, too; we may point to a single example. The opening word of 2:5, *wĕgam*, is recognized as an indicator of a new subunit in a character's speech. The NRSV rendering, "Moreover," is accurate, and its choice to begin a new paragraph here reflects the fact that the term marks the beginning of a new thematic subunit.[11]

2. 2 Kings 7:3-11

Ben-Hadad of Aram has Samaria, the capital city of Israel, under siege; as a result the city is in the grip of dire famine (6:24–7:2). Suddenly the scene shifts to a spot outside the city, with four "lepers"[12] acting as a group character. Their group will be the only active character for the next several verses. The scene boundary at 7:3 is marked not only by the change of locale and of characters but also by a grammatical construction that interrupts the narrative flow. (On this technique see the section below on "Narrative Sequence.") The lepers' first scene consists of a monologue with forward symmetry:

A. Why should we stay here . . . ? (7:3b)
B.   If we . . . (7:4a)
C.   But if we . . . (7:4b)
A'. Now[13] let us go to . . . (7:4c)

---

[11] Since we have in English no obvious way of indicating units smaller than paragraphs but larger than sentences the NRSV quite correctly marks the lesser thematic subunits dealing with Barzillai's sons and Shimei with verbal boundary markers ("however" in 2:7; "also" in 2:8) which correspond not to individual words in the Hebrew but to syntactic constructions that indicate new subunits.

[12] See n. 4 on p. 15.

[13] Text linguists point to the word translated "now" *(wĕʿattāh)* as one of the standard boundary markers between subunits of a character's speech.

B'.   If they . . . (7:4d)
C'.   But if they . . . (7:4e).

The scene ends with a departure notice in two parts: "they got up to go" and "they came to the camp's edge."

The men's next scene begins with a subunit of background information. This subunit is marked by another break in the narrative flow comparable to the one at the beginning of 7:3; in this case the break establishes a shift in time as well, a flashback to a series of past perfect events, and a shift to a new character, "the LORD," who did these things in the past. In other words, the subunit of background information constitutes a secondary narrative within the narrative. The boundaries of the subunit are marked by an external inclusion with the words "and they/these lepers came to the edge of the camp" (7:5b, 8).

The second subunit in this scene returns to the four men. It comprises an unbroken series of narrative verbs that describe the men's behavior in plundering the Aramean tents. The verbs form two series in parallel, with two unmatched components and an unusual central element:[14]

A. They entered one tent
+.   and they ate
+.   and they drank
B.   and they took from there silver and gold
C.   and they went
D.   and they concealed
X. and they repeated:
A'. They entered another tent
B'.   and they took from there
C'.   and they went
D'.   and they concealed.

The reason for not repeating "and they ate and they drank," of course, is simply common sense: the starving lepers would eat and drink their fill in the first tent and not need to do it over again in the next one. The central line (marked "X" above) is unusual in parallel symmetry, and therefore its effect is worth analyzing. It acts as a sort of pivot verse that

---

[14] In Hebrew the scene is extremely laconic. Direct objects are eliminated wherever possible: "they concealed" [that is, the silver, the gold, the clothing]; from the second tent "they took" [that is, similar plunder] and "they concealed" [that plunder too]. The result of this is an intensely active scene: the subunit, less than one verse long, contains eleven complete verbal clauses, of which seven are only a single word, the action verb. "They entered . . . ate, drank, took . . . went, hid, repeated, entered . . . took . . . went, hid." The rapid-fire assault by action verbs gives the scene a frenetic quality that expresses the anxiety of the four lepers trying to grab everything they can before their luck runs out.

calls the reader's attention to the verbatim repetition of the lepers' actions. (It could, in fact, imply that the sequence was repeated not just once but several times.)

The scene ends with another monologue of the lepers, though it lacks the symmetrical structure of their first monologue. The first word of 7:10, "they came," announces a change of locale to the next scene, which will also involve the addition of a second main character, the gatekeepers.

The two-character scene (the lepers and the gatekeepers, 7:10-11) has a concentric symmetry:

A$_1$. and they called out *(wayyiqrĕʾû)* . . .
A$_2$. and they told *(wayyaggîdû)* . . .
B.   [the speech announcing the good news]
A$_1$'. and they called out *(wayyiqrĕʾû)* . . .
A$_2$'. and they told *(wayyaggîdû)* . . .

The scene, in effect, moves the locale of the larger story from the Aramean camp to the Israelite palace in two stages. The four come to the gate and announce the news to the gatekeepers (being "lepers," they could not enter the city themselves); the gatekeepers then announce the news to the palace.

3. 1 Kings 1:15-37

The four scenes that take place in David's chambers each involve two characters, as even the most casual reading makes plain. (The second character in the fourth scene is a group of three people whose representative spokesman is Benaiah.) What is interesting about this passage is the effect of the way the narrator handles the characters' entrances and exits. In the course of examining the symmetry of the passage we mentioned that it is difficult to decide whether to treat these four scenes as a single unit or as two units of two scenes each (see above, pp. 25–26). The way the changes of characters are presented is one of the factors that create this difficulty.

There is no problem in identifying the boundaries between the scenes. The first begins with Bathsheba's entrance to the king's room (1:15), the second with Nathan's entrance (1:22), the third with David's change from passive to active and Bathsheba's return (1:28), and the last with David's summons of Nathan and his companions and their arrival (1:32). What is noteworthy is that no one is ever said to *leave* the room! In other words, there are no departure notices. It is not until 1:28 that we realize that Bathsheba must have left at 1:22; similarly it is not until 1:32 that we deduce Nathan's departure in 1:28; and we have no way of knowing whether Bathsheba remains in the room to hear 1:32-

37 or not. The effect of this is to link scenes 1 and 2, and scenes 2 and 3, and scenes 3 and 4 much more closely than might otherwise be the case. (Contrast, for instance, the effect if 1:22 read: "And when she had finished speaking she went out from the presence of the king. And the prophet Nathan came in.") Were all the exits as explicit as all the entrances the four scenes would be clearly separate, and the shift of David from passive in scenes 1 and 2 to active in scenes 3 and 4 would be the dominant structural feature: thus, two units of two scenes each. But with the exits unmarked and the scenes seeming to blend into one another by virtue of the overlapping characters (notice 1:22's "while she was still speaking"), the sense of continuity counterbalances the effect of David's transformation.

4. Ruth 2:1–3:18

In the section above on "Complex Symmetry" we examined the multileveled symmetry of the book of Ruth (see pp. 88–89). The two longest subunits of the book are the two central sections, 2:1-23 and 3:1-18, both of which concern themselves principally with the interaction between Ruth and Boaz. As we saw, internal chiastic symmetries further structure each central section and relate the two sections to one another as well. It is instructive to see how changes in character combine with other boundary markers to differentiate the subunits of these two chapters.

Ruth 2 begins with background information in a brief narrative prologue (2:1). The action proper of the chapter then opens with a dialogue between Ruth and Naomi (2:2); the presence of Ruth (Naomi was mentioned in 2:1) and the change in narrative voice (narrator to characters) mark the boundary. Another change in narrative voice (characters' dialogue to narrative) and change of characters (Naomi disappears) mark the boundary to the next subunit, Ruth's actions (2:3). There is strong textual emphasis on both changes, since 2:3 begins with three narrative verbs in the feminine singular: "and-she-went, and-she-came, and-she-gleaned . . . ." The next subunit (2:4-7) begins with a brief sentence that breaks the narrative sequence[15] to supply necessary background information: "(Boaz was just then arriving from Bethlehem)." The new subunit involves a complete change of characters (Ruth, though spoken about and perhaps even present, has no active role in this scene; only

---

[15] A "break in the narrative sequence" is the commonest technique for marking the boundaries between units and subunits in biblical Hebrew narrative. We will examine it in greater detail in a later section.

Boaz and his reapers, eventually represented by their foreman, speak), and by another shift in narrative voice back to dialogue.

The next subunit (2:8-16) continues as a dialogue, and the narrative sequence is unbroken, but there is a character change: Boaz now converses with Ruth, and his servants fade into the background. There is a temporal shift at 2:14 from earlier in the day to mealtime, but the NRSV misreads it by starting a new paragraph. In fact, the Hebrew does not use the standard narrative device described above for indicating a change in temporal setting, but carefully *avoids* breaking the narrative sequence, even at the expense of some ambiguity.[16] In other words the text minimizes the boundary-marking effect of the time change in order to let the continuity of characters (Boaz and Ruth) and of narrative voice (dialogue between them) weld the two separate dialogues into a single literary unit. The integrity of the literary unit is threatened also at the end of the verse, where the narrative voice shifts briefly to a string of narrative verbs about Ruth ("and-she-ate, and-she-was-sated, and-she-had-left-over, and-she-arose to-glean"), followed by a speech Boaz addresses to his servants. But here too the text strives in two ways to emphasize continuity rather than discontinuity. It avoids introducing a change of place: to say "and-she-gleaned"—or even more "and-she-went, and-she-gleaned"—would have been a departure notice, but to say that she "got up to glean" implies that she did not yet leave the scene. It also avoids introducing a change of characters, because the servants to whom Boaz speaks do not become active characters by responding. (Their presence in the scene had already been established in 2:10.) The chapter continues with two more subunits marked by changes of narrative voice and characters: 2:17-18a is a narrative about Ruth's actions, ending with a notice of a change of place ("she entered the city"); 2:18b-22 is a combination of narrative and dialogue between Ruth and Naomi. The chapter ends with a brief narrative epilogue (2:23).

The structure of Ruth 3 is similar. The chapter begins with a dialogue between Naomi and Ruth. The next subunit (3:6-7) begins with a notice of change of place ("she went down to the threshing floor," 3:6a), and continues with a change of narrative voice (narrative rather than dialogue) and of characters (Ruth and Boaz). The next subunit (3:8-9) begins with a temporal indicator that breaks the narrative sequence. This boundary marker is important because the characters do not change and at first the narrative voice remains the narrator's as well. The action of 3:8, however, clearly belongs with the ensuing dialogue that it occa-

---

[16] The Hebrew could be read either "Boaz said to her at mealtime, 'Come here and eat . . .'" or "Boaz said to her, 'At mealtime, come here and eat . . . .'" Only the narrative verbs that continue the verse make the first reading more likely.

sions rather than with the series of actions described in the preceding verses. The case is quite different at 3:10, however. There is no conventional textual indicator of a new subunit: place and time are unchanged, the characters are the same, the narrative sequence continues unbroken, and the narrative voice remains Boaz's. The only differences between 3:8-9 and 3:10-15 are that dialogue becomes monologue (only Boaz speaks in 3:10-15) and Ruth's role is reduced to a few silent acts of obedience (3:14-15). The lack of boundary markers strengthens the connection between 3:8-9 (Ruth's initiative) and 3:10-15 (Boaz's response).

The next subunit is textually uncertain; some ancient sources read "and *he* [that is, Boaz] went to the city," while others read "and *she* [that is, Ruth] went to the city." (The difference is only a single letter in Hebrew.) In either case the change of place marks the boundary, and the next subunit is the extremely brief narrative that Ruth "went to her mother-in-law" (3:16a). Finally, the chapter ends with a dialogue between Naomi and Ruth (3:16b-18).

5. 1 Kings 18:21-40

The scene of the contest on Mount Carmel between YHWH, represented by his prophet Elijah, and Baal, represented by his four hundred fifty prophets, is a good example of a scene with three active characters. Two of them—the "people" and the "prophets of Baal"—are groups that fill character roles. Though there are three roles, the entire scene is composed of two-character subunits. Elijah speaks with the people, who at first do not, then do, respond (18:21-24); then he speaks to the prophets of Baal, who do not speak but who comply with Elijah's directives to them (18:25-29); then he again addresses the people (18:30-35), who also do as Elijah has told them (18:30a, 33b-34);[17] then he addresses God (18:36-37). YHWH's entrance onto the scene in 18:38 introduces a fourth character and sets off a flurry of character actions: YHWH acts (18:38), the people speak (18:39), Elijah speaks (18:40a), the people act (18:40b), Elijah acts (18:40c). The conventional maximum of three active characters is preserved by reducing the prophets of Baal to passive victims of the actions of the people and of Elijah. In this way theological meaning and literary structure correspond: YHWH's active appearance reduces Baal (theologically) and his representatives (literarily) to impotence.

---

[17] This thread of Elijah's commands and the people's compliance unifies the paragraph, despite the fact that the interior focuses exclusively on Elijah's actions (vv. 30b-33a).

B. Change in setting: locale

1. 2 Kings 10:12-17

The use of notices of departure and arrival to separate literary sub-units is seen clearly in the account of Jehu's journey from Jezreel to Samaria. (We discussed the larger context of this passage above, pp. 43–45; 2 Kings 10:12-17 is the central subunit of that larger unit.) The narrative material in these verses comprises two parallel subunits framed by inclusive statements of movement:

frame: "And he arose and <u>he came</u> and <u>he went to Samaria</u>."
A. Jehu "found" the brothers of Ahaziah
B. He questions them.
C.   They reply.
D.   Jehu responds.
E.   Jehu kills them.
frame: "And <u>he went</u> from there."
A'. He "found" Jehonadab.
B'. He questions him.
C'.   He replies.
D'.   Jehu responds (twice).
E'.   Jehu honors him (twice).
frame: "And <u>he came to Samaria</u>."

Once we recognize that the changes of place mark the encounter with Jehonadab as a distinct subunit we can see several things that highlight that subunit within the whole larger passage. First, it is part of the central subunit of 9:14–11:20. Second, it is the only scene from 9:14 to 11:20 that does not deal with death (thematic non-correspondence). Third, it contains asymmetries (unmatched subunits) that emphasize it over against the encounter with Ahaziah's brothers. Elements D' and E' are doubled: Jehu speaks to Jehonadab, brings him up into his chariot, speaks to him again, and has him ride with him in the chariot. All of these factors point up the importance of Jehonadab, not as an individual (he is not mentioned again in 2 Kings), but as a representative of the intransigent Yahwism Jehu intends to champion.[18]

2. 2 Kings 18–20

The account of Sennacherib's invasion of Judah during the reign of Hezekiah also uses departure notices to subdivide the unit into sub-

---

[18] Jehonadab and the Rechabites were well known for their religious absolutism; see Jeremiah 35.

units. In our earlier discussion of composite symmetry we examined this passage in detail (see pp. 85–87). Here we will only call attention to how the three statements of movement (the return of Hezekiah's representatives to him, 18:37; the return of Sennacherib's envoys to him, 19:8; and Sennacherib's own return to Assyria, 19:35-37) reinforce the changes of character that separate the three main scenes (B, B', and B'' in our earlier discussion).

3. Genesis 18

The scenes in this chapter reveal some of the flexibility that the conventional "departure notice" can exhibit. The boundary between the scene of Abraham's hospitality to the three men in 18:1-16 and the next scene involves a change of locale, signaled by a double departure notice about "the men" and Abraham, and by a change of characters. Usually when a double departure notice occurs it is appropriate because the two main characters depart in different directions. Here the usage seems paradoxical, since the departure notice for Abraham simply says that he accompanied the guests. In this way, however, the text establishes an external inclusion around the next scene, 18:17-21, which ends with another double departure notice about "the men" and Abraham.

The change of characters is clear insofar as only YHWH is active in 18:17-21. He had been announced already in 18:1, and he appeared as an active character first in 18:13, where he became the singular representative filling the group character role held by the "three men." In 18:17-21 Abraham is presumably present, since he accompanied "the men" in 18:16 and he "remains standing before" YHWH in 18:22; YHWH, however, does not address him directly but instead speaks *about* him. It seems that we are to understand YHWH's speech as self-directed, and to take the verb "said" in 18:17 as meaning "said to himself"—a usage well attested in Hebrew elsewhere. This is then a rare example of a complete scene of internal monologue. Most often such monologue is only one element within an action scene (as it is, for example, in Gen 3:22), but here it constitutes a scene in itself.

The effect of presenting YHWH's internal monologue as a scene unto itself is essentially transitional, but it is transitional on several levels. In terms of character it deepens the process of individuation of YHWH. In 18:13-15 YHWH emerges from the "three men" as their representative spokesperson. In 18:17-21 YHWH develops an identity and personality distinct from the other "men," and in 18:22 that distinction becomes complete: YHWH remains while "the men" continue on their way. In the Sodom episode of ch. 19 "the men," now reduced to two, will be revealed as "angels" (19:1). YHWH never does arrive at Sodom in person, and is thus never exposed to the threat of sexual violence that menaces the angels.

Thematically, 18:17-21 functions as a hinge. It connects the theme of the preceding scene, the promise that Abraham will have offspring, with that of the following scene, the doing of righteousness and justice (compare 18:19 with 18:25). In this way it has the profound theological significance of introducing "justice"—a virtue noticeably lacking elsewhere in Abraham's treatment of Sarah, of Hagar and Ishmael, and even of Isaac—into the story of the Abrahamic promise, and even of situating the interdependence of promise and justice at the heart of YHWH's own intentions for Abraham.

The boundary between the scene of YHWH's internal monologue and the ensuing dialogue between YHWH and Abraham is signaled by the double departure notice of 18:22, but, ironically, because Abraham's "departure" is not a departure but a "remaining," the locale does not in fact change. What changes is the characters: from being an unmentioned bystander in 18:17-21 Abraham becomes an active participant in 18:22-33. The scene is a typical two-character dialogue, and ends with a classic example of a double departure notice (18:33): YHWH goes one way and Abraham another.

4. 1 Kings 18:6-16

In 1 Kings 18:1 YHWH commands Elijah to "Go, present yourself to Ahab." Elijah carries out the command, but in a rather roundabout fashion that affords us an illustration of two sorts of boundary markers: the tendency to restrict scenes to two characters, and the use of departure notices.

After YHWH's opening command, Elijah departs to obey (18:2). The scene shifts abruptly to Samaria, with a complete change of characters. Ahab and his majordomo Obadiah undertake a desperate search for water. The scene ends with a classic double departure notice (18:6), with Ahab and Obadiah heading in different directions (symbolizing their contrary religious commitments). On his way Obadiah encounters Elijah, and the two of them engage in a long dialogue.[19] This scene too ends with a double notice of movement (18:16), but it is not a typical double departure notice: instead of describing a departure of Elijah and introducing a change of locale it tells of the arrival of Ahab at the place where Elijah has awaited him. The echoes with 18:6 are striking: in both Ahab and Obadiah are spoken of; in both they are spoken of in identical words; and in both the two figures are going in opposite directions. Finally, in the ensuing scene, Elijah "presents himself to Ahab."

---

[19] On the asymmetries of this dialogue see above, pp. 103–105.

5. Numbers 20:22–21:20

In Exodus and Numbers, which narrate the journeys of the people of Israel from Egypt to the Promised Land, there is a special type of notice of movement called an "itinerary notice." It is likely that these notices were originally independent of the stories that are now strung along the itinerary like beads on a string,[20] but now they serve to mark boundaries between episodes along the journey. Occasionally, when there are no intervening episodes, a string of itinerary notices makes a sort of journey episode in itself.

Numbers 20:22 is a departure notice and an arrival notice that separates the preceding scene of failed negotiations with the king of Edom from the scene of Aaron's death on Mount Hor (20:23-29). Since the people do not depart from Mount Hor until Num 21:4 there is no itinerary notice to separate the death of Aaron from the next episode (21:1-3). There is nonetheless a change of locale, since 21:1 begins by introducing a new place name, Arad, as well as a new character, Arad's king. Another itinerary notice separates the war against Arad and destruction of Hormah from the episode of the bronze serpent (21:4-9). From 21:10 to 21:20 there is virtually no narrative material other than the itinerary notices; only the two brief snatches of poetry (21:14-15 and 21:17-18a) interrupt the progress of the journey.[21]

C. CHANGE IN SETTING: TIME

1. Genesis 24

The long, well-crafted story that introduces Rebekah into the biblical drama has several scenes and subscenes and uses a variety of boundary markers to separate them. Among those boundary markers are several examples of the standard construction for changing the temporal setting.

The story begins with a dialogue between Abraham and his oldest and most trusted servant. The boundaries of the scene are marked by an inclusion with the words "put your/his hand under my/his thigh" and "swear [an oath]," phrases that feature in Abraham's opening words (24:2) and the servant's compliance (24:9).

The next scene depicts the servant's journey. Its beginning is marked by the unnecessary repetition of the subject "the servant" in

---

[20] See Jerome T. Walsh, "From Egypt to Moab: A Source Critical Analysis of the Wilderness Itinerary," *CBQ* 39 (1977) 20–33.

[21] A much longer example of unbroken itinerary is found in Numbers 33.

24:10. (See the next section for this technique for marking boundaries.) The scene is divided between two narrative voices: the narrator's (24:10-11) and the servant's (24:12-14). The first subscene depicts the servant's doings (he is the subject of each of the five narrative verbs) and is marked by an inclusion with "camels"—the servant "takes" them to begin the journey and "makes them kneel" when the journey reaches its end. The second subscene is the servant's prayer. The two are separated by a simple time reference (that is, the reference lacks the full construction described above): "at evening time, at the time when the women who draw water go out."

The following scene begins with a full temporal construction, though somewhat paradoxically it specifies that the time did *not* change: "While he was not yet finished speaking . . ." (24:15a). Before the third element of the construction (the first action verb) the narrative is interrupted by a series of clauses that introduce a new character, Rebekah, to the reader. The clauses supply us with two sorts of background information: things the servant is also aware of because he sees them (she comes out, she carries a waterjar on her shoulder, she is very beautiful), and things he cannot know (she is of Abraham's kindred, and a virgin). The remainder of the scene is an unbroken series of narrative verbs, almost all of them with Rebekah as subject (the servant is subject only in 24:17, "the servant ran to meet her and he said"). The scene ends, as it began, with a series of clauses describing what the servant is seeing (24:21).

The next scene too begins with the full temporal construction (24:22). Like the previous scene it involves only two characters, Rebekah and the servant, but now the servant is the active one and Rebekah's role is limited to two short speeches. Each of her speeches is introduced by "she said," but since the two speeches are continuous the repetition of "she said" is superfluous for the second speech. In the next section we will see that unnecessary repetition can be used to mark boundaries, but here the use is different: it is an asymmetry. The entire scene has a symmetrical structure:

A. The servant's actions (24:22b)
B₁.   The servant's first question to Rebekah (24:23a)
B₂.   The servant's second question to Rebekah (24:23b)
B₁'.   Rebekah answers the first question (24:24)
B₂'.   Rebekah answers the second question (24:25)
A'. The servant's prayer (24:26-27)

The servant's questions are presented under a single introduction; Rebekah's answers each have a separate introduction. This asymmetry calls attention to Rebekah's second answer and points up that it goes beyond what the servant asked. He asked about lodging; she responds that there is food for the animals as well as lodging. The effect is to foreshadow something portentous about Rebekah's character: she is the sort of woman who anticipates situations and their consequences, and plans ahead (see Genesis 27).

There follows a brief and essentially transitional scene. It affords the narrator an opportunity to change characters without changing place: Rebekah "runs" home and tells her family about her adventure, we are introduced in an aside to her brother Laban, and Laban "runs" back to where the servant is waiting (24:28-29).[22]

The subsequent scene begins with a very lengthy example of the full temporal construction (24:30a), including a double time reference to what Laban saw and what he heard. It is essentially a two-character scene (with Laban as representative of Rebekah's family), divided into two major subscenes. The first part involves actions and dialogue (24:30-33); the second is a long monologue by Abraham's servant that repeats the whole story for the benefit of Rebekah's family (24:34-49), and the family's response (24:50-51). Except for the change of narrative voice there are no boundary markers between the two parts.

The next scene also begins with the full temporal construction (24:52), even though neither time, place, nor characters change. The character roles expand, however: the servant's companions (mentioned passively already in 24:32) are now associated with him in plural verbs of action (24:54a), and the family now includes the mother as an actively participating member (24:55). The entrance of Rebekah as a third active character in 24:58 does not begin a new scene. The narrator emphasizes continuity rather than discontinuity by eschewing all boundary markers: the narrative sequence is not interrupted, there is no unnecessary repetition, there are no departure or arrival notices, no temporal references, etc.[23] The scene comes to a gradual close with a shift into poetry (common in moments of intense climax in biblical Hebrew narrative), and a double departure notice (Rebekah and her maids, 24:61a; the servant, 24:61b).

---

[22] There is a stock scene in biblical Hebrew narrative that describes how a hero meets his future wife at a well; Gen 29:1-12 and Exod 2:15-21 present other examples. (See Robert Alter, *The Art of Biblical Narrative* [New York: Basic Books, 1981] 51–62.) The hero never returns to the woman's home with her immediately; someone must always invite him. This may reflect a cultural constraint (perhaps an unchaperoned woman should not travel with a man who is not a member of her family?), or it may be a literary convention, or both.

[23] Had the narrator wished, he could easily have marked the boundary much more forcefully, for example with a temporal reference: "They called Rebekah. And when she heard all the words of the servant, she said . . . ."

The final scene begins with several indications of a boundary. There is an interruption of the narrative sequence and the introduction of a new character, Isaac. In addition, two place names indicate that the locale has shifted from Rebekah's home city. Following a subunit of background information that introduces the new character (24:62), the scene is divided into three subscenes. First, Isaac alone (24:63), marked by the unnecessary repetition of his name as subject of the first action verb. Second, Rebekah and the servant (24:64-65), separated from Isaac's subscene by a break in the narrative sequence.[24] A brief transitional verse (24:66) allows the servant to bring Rebekah and Isaac together for the final subscene (24:67). The end of the scene, and of the whole story, is marked by the unnecessary repetition of Isaac's name ("and Isaac was comforted after his mother"[25]) and the reintroduction of the character of Abraham in 25:1.[26]

2. 1 Kings 2:39

The full temporal construction most commonly marks the beginning of a new scene or comparable unit. In particular circumstances, however, it can mark a subunit boundary *within* a scene. Earlier we examined both the symmetry and the asymmetry of the story of Shimei's search for his runaway slaves (1 Kings 2:38b-41; see pp. 48–49, 60, and 103). The unmatched subunit, 2:39a, begins with the full temporal construction, although the concentric symmetry marks the whole unit as beginning at 2:38b. (The NRSV has overlooked the symmetry and reckoned the temporal construction as beginning a new unit, so it uses a paragraph indentation at 2:39.)

---

[24] This is not clear in the NRSV. A literal translation of 24:63-64 would run: "Isaac went out in the evening to walk in the field, and he looked up, and he saw: Camels are coming! And Rebekah looked up, and she saw Isaac, and she dismounted from the camel . . . ." The clause describing what Isaac saw breaks the string of narrative verbs.

[25] The NRSV's "after his mother's death" is interpretive, since the word "death" is not in the Hebrew; but in the context of ch. 23 this understanding is inescapable.

[26] It is noteworthy that the boundary markers are so few here. Narrative sequence is not broken from 24:67 to 25:1, and there are no indications of change of place or locale, though either or both would have been perfectly appropriate in biblical Hebrew narrative. The effect is to establish a degree of continuity between Isaac's marriage in 24:67 and Abraham's in 25:1, and thereby to create overarching thematic links that connect chs. 23–25 of Genesis. After Sarah's death and burial (ch. 23) her bereaved son and husband both find consolation in marriage, Isaac explicitly in his love for Rebekah, Abraham implicitly in Keturah's fecundity.

The effect of the full temporal construction is to mark strongly the boundary between 2:38b and 2:39, but not in this case for the purpose of beginning a new literary unit. It rather underscores 2:39a as a sub-unit independent of 2:38b. This highlights its status as an asymmetrical element (unmatched subunit) and in that way emphasizes its significance (see p. 103).

3. Genesis 22:4

The scene of Abraham's preparation for his sacrificial journey with Isaac ends with a departure notice (22:3b). The next scene, the arrival at the place of sacrifice and Abraham's separation from his servants, begins with an abbreviated temporal construction (temporal reference followed by the action verb in the narrative tense): literally, "on the third day, and Abraham lifted his eyes . . . ." This scene, like the preceding one, will end with a departure notice (22:6b).

4. 2 Kings 18:13

The narrative of Shalmaneser's invasion of Judah during the reign of Hezekiah (2 Kings 18:9-12) ends with a bit of theological commentary by the narrator. The next narrative unit is the account of Sennacherib's invasion ten years later. It begins with an abbreviated temporal construction (temporal reference followed by the action verb in the simple past): literally, "and in the fourteenth year of King Hezekiah, Sennacherib, King of Assyria, came up against . . . ." In this case the omission of the first element ("to be" in the narrative tense) and the use of "and" to introduce the unit may be intended to strengthen the connection between the two invasion accounts ("It was in the fourth year that . . . and in the fourteenth year that . . .") and thereby to suggest that the theological comment attached to Shalmaneser's aggression was still valid at the time of Sennacherib's.

5. 1 Kings 18:3-4

In general, flashbacks and foreshadowings constitute interruptive subunits within a literary unit like a scene, not independent units themselves. For this reason they need not be introduced by the full temporal construction we have been illustrating, though they sometimes are. Often the temporal shift is indicated only by the breaking of narrative sequence (which we will examine more closely in a later section) and the use of verbal forms that point backward (for a flashback) or forward (for a foreshadowing).

When YHWH sends Elijah from Zarephath to confront Ahab (1 Kings 18:1-2a) the scene ends with a break in the narrative sequence: 18:2b is a bit of background information that shifts our attention from Elijah's journey to his destination, Samaria. The next scene begins with a complete change of characters: Ahab (whom we know from earlier chapters as the king of Israel) and Obadiah (whom we don't know at all) take the stage. Since we know nothing of Obadiah, the narrator interrupts the story to fill us in on this character. First, his present position is described in a subordinate clause: he was, literally, "over the house"—that is, overseer of the royal palace and properties. Second, the narrator speaks of Obadiah's faithfulness to YHWH (18:3b); the sentence is marked by unusual word order that breaks the narrative sequence. Finally comes a lengthy flashback introduced by the full temporal construction followed by three clauses (18:4), the whole verse constituting a short secondary narrative embedded within the primary narrative. The story returns to the time of the main narrative line with 18:5.

D. Change in narrative voice

The commonest changes in narrative voice are found when narrative alternates with direct speech. The boundary-marking function of such changes is evident, since speeches are almost by definition literary units (although a speech may of course have a lengthy and complex internal structure). Our examples will comprise three less obvious cases of changes of narrative voice, for instance within a character's speech, or within the narrator's account.

1. 1 Kings 18:12c-13

In an earlier section we noticed the asymmetry of Obadiah's speech to Elijah (see above, pp. 103–105). One of the subunits of his speech (labelled B" on p. 104) has no strong boundary markers to separate it from what precedes it. (Note how the NRSV includes 18:12c as part of the preceding sentence.) Nonetheless, there is a change of narrative voice. Obadiah is repeating almost verbatim information that we, the audience, have already learned from the narrator in 18:3-4.[27] That makes Obadiah's words at this point a citation (though of course Obadiah is unaware of it) and sets them apart as a separate subunit within his speech.

---

[27] Obadiah's fidelity to the narrator's wording reflects his truthfulness. His few variations (for example, "from my youth" in place of the narrator's "greatly") allow some insight into his character. The techniques biblical Hebrew narrative uses to achieve characterization lie beyond the scope of this work.

In fact, change in narrative voice is a major factor in structuring Obadiah's whole speech. Units C and C' are citations of Elijah's command, and unit A" could easily be read as a citation of Obadiah's own words in the identical unit A'.

2. 1 Kings 21:20-26

The first half of the story of the royal murder of Naboth and seizure of his vineyard has a chiastic structure we have already examined (see above, pp. 28–29). The second half shows the same symmetry:

A.   "The word of YHWH came to Elijah the Tishbite . . ." (21:17-19)
B.   Elijah announces YHWH's message to Ahab (21:20-22)
C.   The punishment of Ahab's wife and household (21:23-24)
C'.   Summary condemnation of Ahab (21:25-26)
B'.   Ahab's reaction to YHWH's message (21:27)
A'. "The word of YHWH came to Elijah the Tishbite . . ." (21:28-29).

Subunit "C" is sometimes treated as a continuation of Elijah's speech (for example, by the NRSV); more commonly 21:24 is treated as a continuation of the speech, and 21:23 as a parenthetical interruption,[28] but the situation is rather more complex than either of those approaches would suggest. Elijah is clearly the speaker in 21:20-22, and the narrator's voice is equally clear in 21:25-26. What is far from clear is where one voice stops and the other starts. Since there are no indicators in the text of a change of speaker at 21:23 our first inclination is to assume that Elijah continues speaking in 21:23-24. (This is what the NRSV does.) But the narrator's appearance in 21:25, also with no indicator of a change of speaker, invites us to consider the possibility that 21:23-24 are the narrator's words. We realize then that either reading is possible. And so, in effect, we hear *both* voices in those verses, and this sets them apart as a separate subunit.[29]

3. 1 Kings 3:16-28

The riveting story of Solomon and the two harlots (1 Kings 3:16-28) owes at least some of its narrative power to the unusually complex interaction of the characters. Although there are only three main characters,

---

[28] The reasons for this more common reading derive from theories about the process of formation of the story from hypothetically earlier, shorter versions to the present hypothetically expanded account.

[29] For a more extended analysis of the whole Naboth story see Jerome T. Walsh, "Methods and Meanings: Multiple Studies of 1 Kings 21," *JBL* 111 (1992) 193–211.

they speak in at least five roles: Solomon the king, who addresses an unnamed audience (the court?) but never the two women; the "first
woman," who addresses the king in 3:17-21 and argues with the "second
woman" in 3:23; the "second woman," who argues with the first in the
same verse; the "true mother" (the text does not tell us whether she is the
"first woman" or the "second"[30]), who speaks to the king in 3:26a; and
the "other woman" (that is, not the true mother), who responds to the
true mother in 3:26b. Even the king's role is complex, since his "narrative
voices" include his own words to others (3:24-25, 27), an internal monologue (3:23) that consists in him quoting the words of "first woman" and
"second woman" from 3:22, and in 3:27 a citation of the "true mother's"
words in 3:26.

The story's structure is intricate but basically chiastic,[31] with units
and subunits marked by changes in the narrative voice:

A$_1$. Narrative introduction (3:16; ending "<u>they stood before him</u>")
B$_1$.   Dialogue of the two women (3:17-22a)
A$_2$. Narrative (3:22b; ending "<u>they spoke before the king</u>")
C$_1$.   The king speaks (3:23, repeating the women's words)
C$_2$.   The king speaks (3:24a, in his own voice)
A$_3$. Narrative (3:24b; ending "<u>before the king</u>")
C$_3$.   The king speaks (3:25, in his own voice)
B$_2$.   Dialogue of the two women (3:26)[32]
C$_4$.   The king speaks (3:27, repeating the true mother's words)
A$_4$. Narrative conclusion (3:28; "<u>from before the king</u>")

The structural importance of narrative voice appears most clearly in
the king's various speeches. Difference in voice distinguishes subunits
C$_1$ and C$_2$, and their separation is reinforced by the gratuitous repetition of "and the king said" in 3:24a. The shift to the king's own voice at
3:24a marks the pivotal point in the episode, where the king, essentially
passive to that moment, begins to take the initiative. Note too that each
of the king's speeches following the women's dialogues repeats something from the preceding dialogue. This gives the four royal speeches a
chiastic pattern of their own:

---

[30] This view is common among commentators. In "The Guilty Party in
1 Kings iii 16-28," *VT* 48 (1998) 534–41 Gary Rendsburg has argued otherwise, but I
do not find his argument compelling.

[31] Units C$_3$ and C$_4$ disturb the chiasm, which without them would run smoothly:
ABACCABA. The disruptive units, therefore, have an asymmetric character ("un-
matched subunits") while at the same time they form part of the chiastic series of
"C" units.

[32] Subunits B$_1$ and B$_2$ are parallel in structure. Each begins with "and (one)
woman said" and ends with "while this one was saying."

a. The king repeats the two women's words (3:23)
b.   The king speaks in his own voice (3:24a)
b'.   The king speaks in his own voice (3:25)
a'. The king repeats the true mother's words (3:27).

The chiastic structures reflect the problem/solution dynamic that energizes the whole story. The first half of the story presents the judicial problem, how to find out the truth (3:16-23); the second half describes its resolution, the discovery of the true mother (3:24-28). The chiasm of the king's speeches reflects a second problem/solution dynamic. Where the story as a whole represents the juridical dilemma the king faces, the chiasm of the king's speeches represents the bewilderment of the women about the king's intentions: his call for a sword is as unexpected as it is ominous; what does he want a sword for? His command in 3:25 answers their question with gruesome clarity.

8. REPETITION

In general, biblical Hebrew narrative tends to be spare rather than prolix. Repetition will stand out for the experienced and sensitive reader, and thus it affords the ancient author a flexible tool apt for achieving a variety of effects.[1] In the first part of this book we looked at how repeated elements can link subunits of a narrative unit to produce a symmetrical pattern. Another common function of repetition is emphasis; see, for example, David's poignant repetition of "Absalom, my son" in 2 Sam 18:33 (19:1 in the Hebrew text). It can also enhance and further characterization. In this last usage the repetition usually involves a change in the narrative voice: characterization emerges from the similarities and differences between the narrator's choice of words and a character's, or between one character's and another's.[2]

Occasionally repetition seems to have no significant effect other than to mark the beginning of a new subunit. Repetition of this sort takes three forms: gratuitous repetition of information the reader already knows, unnecessary repetition of subject nouns, and unnecessary interruptions of direct speech by an introductory "and [so-and-so] said" when the speaker has in fact not changed. The key word in the first phrase is "gratuitous"; by this I mean repetition that does not seem to serve any other literary function. Information whose repetition serves plot development, for instance, is not gratuitous: in Gen 6:7

---

[1] Numerous scholars have studied repetition in biblical Hebrew style; see the references above on p. 7, n. 2. As valuable and helpful as those discussions are, we still lack a full, detailed, systematic treatment of the subject.

[2] For instance, Elijah's meticulous obedience to YHWH is revealed when the narrator repeats the words of YHWH's command in describing Elijah's compliance (1 Kings 17:3-6); Obadiah's veracity is shown when he describes himself in the same words the narrator has already used (1 Kings 18:3-4, 12-13; see above, p. 140); Ahab reveals something about himself and his opinion of Jezebel by *not* repeating accurately the conversation he had with Naboth (1 Kings 21:2-3, 6).

YHWH utters the intention to "blot out from the ground humankind that I have created—human and beast and creeping thing and bird of the heavens"; when, in 7:4, YHWH announces a plan to "blot out every extant thing that I have made from the face of the ground" the repetition advances the plot by communicating the divine plan to Noah.

The second type of repetition involves a violation of stylistic convention. Both Hebrew and English regularly use pronouns to avoid repetition of nouns, unless the pronoun would be ambiguous. Usually the pronoun follows the noun it refers to ("When Janet got the news, she said . . ."), but in certain circumstances, both in Hebrew and in English, the pronoun may come first ("When the news reached her, Janet said . . ."). Unnecessary repetition of the noun ("When Janet got the news, Janet said . . .") is generally avoided in both languages, although it seems to occur slightly more frequently in biblical Hebrew narrative than in English.[3] In some cases at least the main function of the repetition seems to be to mark a subunit boundary. Unless a translation is striving for one-to-one verbal correspondence such repetitions will often be suppressed in translation to conform to the stylistic constraints of English.

The third type of repetition appears when a single character's direct discourse is interrupted with a narrative line such as "and he said." In 1 Kings 22:28, for instance: "Micaiah said, 'If you indeed return safely, then YHWH did not speak through me.' And he said, 'Hear, all the peoples!'" Since the speaker has not changed, the repeated narrative line is unnecessary and in fact breaks what one would expect to flow smoothly. This case must be carefully distinguished from dialogue, where two characters speak in turn. In that case their respective, alternating speeches are generally separated by narrative lines of the "and he said" sort as well, and clearly constitute separate subunits of the narrative. The situation under consideration here occurs when two consecutive speeches (or parts of the same speech) by the *same* speaker are separated by such a line.[4]

The device may have other functions as well,[5] but certainly its disruptive force has the effect of dividing the speech into narrative sub-

---

[3] The converse is also true: biblical Hebrew is often content with a pronoun where English would require a noun in order to avoid ambiguity. Repeated naming of a character may be one technique biblical Hebrew narrative uses to establish the character as the principal one in a scene.

[4] The line may sometimes be elaborated by a subject term or a reference to the addressee (which must be the same as in the preceding speech as well) or the like.

[5] Some study has been devoted to this device in biblical Hebrew narrative. Shimon Bar-Efrat proposes that the repeated "and he said" indicates a point where the speaker paused to allow for a reply or a reaction (*Narrative Art in the Bible* [Sheffield:

units. While it is outside this book's scope to explore the markers used *within* a speech to divide its subunits, the interruptive line "and he said" belongs to the narrator, not to the character's direct discourse, and therefore marks a boundary between two subunits of the *narrative* as well. The examples below are chosen to illustrate passages where the text-structuring function seems to be the primary, if not the exclusive effect of the device.

A. REPETITION OF INFORMATION

1. Genesis 5:32; 6:9-10

The repetition of the names of Noah's three sons in Gen 6:10 is redundant, since those names were already given at the end of the genealogy in Genesis 5. In some ways the repetition resembles an external inclusion (see above, pp. 58–59), but close examination reveals important differences. First, the material between the repeated elements is not itself a single unit, as is normally the case with external inclusion, but falls into two relatively autonomous blocks: 6:1-4 about the commingling of the divine and human lines, and 6:5-8 about YHWH's grief over human wickedness. Second, the material surrounded by an external inclusion is usually relatively independent of the surrounding material; here, however, 6:11-13 picks up not from the genealogy of Genesis 5 but from the divine observations in 6:5-7. It is better, then, not to treat this repetition as an example of inclusion.

The boundary markers point to 6:9-12 as a literary unit. The statement in 6:8 uses unusual word order (we shall examine this way of marking a unit boundary in the next section), and 6:13 involves a

---

Almond, 1989] 43). While this may be true in some cases, the illustration Bar-Efrat himself uses is poorly chosen: in 1 Kings 2:42 the force of the unnecessary "and the king said" is quite different from the pause Bar-Efrat conjectures (see the discussion above, pp. 48–49); a more convincing example of the use of a repeated introduction to indicate a pause would be Gen 15:5. In *Speaking of Speaking: Marking Direct Discourse in the Hebrew Bible* (Leiden: E. J. Brill, 1992) 73–81, Samuel A. Meier recognizes that the phenomenon is more complex than Bar-Efrat's analysis allows, but does not attempt to analyze the literary functions it can achieve. A valuable and more nuanced recent treatment is E. J. Revell, "The Repetition of Introductions to Speech as a Feature of Biblical Hebrew," *VT* 47 (1997) 91–110. Revell recognizes that a repeated introduction both structures the narrative by dividing the discourse into two speeches and structures the discourse itself by dividing it topically. "The second speech may not be directly related to the first; it may be dependent on the first, complementing it in some way; it may reconfirm the first by some form of repetition" (p. 102).

change in narrative voice from narrator to God. Contrary to the NRSV, there is no indication in the Hebrew text of a unit boundary at 6:11: there is nothing corresponding either to the paragraph indentation or to the NRSV's introductory "now." How are we to understand the coherence of this literary unit?

Genesis 6:9 and 6:10 must be considered together, since the phrase "these are the descendants of" regularly introduces a genealogical table (5:1; 10:1; 11:10; 11:27; etc.); it also regularly begins a new unit that may comprise more than a bare genealogy (5:1; 11:27-32). Here 6:9 marks the beginning of a literary unit, and the unnecessary repetition of the sons' names in 6:10 reinforces its introductory character. These first two verses establish that Noah is righteous (6:9) and implicitly associate his sons with him in that righteousness; the last two verses contrast to the righteousness of Noah's line the otherwise universal corruption and violence of the earth. The entire unit coheres, then, as an explication of the laconic statement of 6:8 that "Noah found favor in YHWH's eyes": he alone, with his sons, was righteous on the earth.

2. 2 Kings 8:28–9:2; 9:14-16

The last part of 2 Kings 8 is the regnal account of King Ahaziah of Judah. It recounts how he joined King Joram of Israel in warring against Hazael of Aram at Ramoth-gilead, how Joram was wounded there and retreated to Jezreel for healing, and how Ahaziah visited him there. The scene shifts abruptly at the beginning of 2 Kings 9 to the prophet Elisha. In 9:1-2 he commissions one of his associates to anoint "Jehu, son of Jehoshaphat, son of Nimshi" as king of the northern kingdom, Israel.[6] The remainder of 9:1-13 describes the anointing of Jehu and the immediate support his military comrades lend to his ambitions.

The unusual naming of Jehu's ancestry back two generations has a double purpose. First and foremost, it marks him as a crucially important figure in Israel's history. Kings, even kings who found new dynasties, have only their fathers named, not their grandfathers. Second, it eliminates the possibility that an inattentive reader would think Jehu to be the son of the recently deceased King Jehoshaphat of the southern kingdom, Judah, since the latter's father was named Asa.[7]

The long, bloody story of Jehu's *coup d'état* begins in 9:14. The beginning of the account is marked by a repetition of Jehu's full patronymic

---

[6] The anointing is an act of treason, of course, since Joram, though wounded, is still alive, and Jehu, an army general, has no claim on the succession.

[7] Note how a later reference to Jehu's lineage leaves out the ambiguous Jehoshaphat altogether (2 Kings 9:20).

as well as of many of the details from 8:28-29. See the more complete remarks above, pp. 43–45. The identification of 9:14 as the beginning of a major new literary unit is confirmed when we recognize the symmetrical structures of the units that precede and follow that boundary marker (see pp. 29–30 and 43–44).

3. 1 Samuel 17:12a

Repetition of information need not entail verbal repetition. In the account of Samuel's anointing of David (1 Sam 16:1-13) we learn that Jesse of Bethlehem has seven sons older than David, his youngest (16:10-11). So when we are told in 17:12a and 14a that "David was the son of an Ephratite man; the man was from Bethlehem of Judah, he was named Jesse, and he had seven sons . . . and David was the youngest," the information is redundant. The repetition, along with the change of characters and setting, has the effect of marking 17:12 as the start of a new literary unit.

The structure of the whole passage, however, is not so simple. The first part of the story of David and Goliath is an example of alternating repetition similar to 1 Sam 1:12-13 and 1 Kings 20:16-21 (see above, pp. 50–52). The author attempts to depict events happening simultaneously in two different settings; we could liken this device to the "split-screen" technique of cinema and television. The "A" subunits depict the military camps of the contending armies, with the Philistine Goliath as their focal point. The "B" subunits focus on David, first in Bethlehem, then at the Israelite camp. Once David encounters Goliath (17:23b), the alternation of subunits ceases.

A_1. The military camps; Goliath appears (17:1-11)
B_1.   Introduction of David (17:12-15)
A_2. The military camps; Goliath appears "early in the morning *(haškēm)*" (17:16)
B_2.   David sent to the camps (17:17-18)
A_3. The military camps (17:19)
B_3.   David goes to the camp "early in the morning *(yaškēm)*" (17:20-22)
A_4. Goliath appears (17:23a)
B_4.   David hears Goliath's boast (17:23b).

The alternating structure is not entirely successful in this passage because the brevity of subunits A_2, A_3, and A_4 makes it easy to overlook their place in the pattern. (Note, for instance, how the NRSV subsumes them all into paragraphs concerned with David.)

The gratuitous repetition of information in 17:12a marks the boundary between subunits A_1 and B_1, and it thereby also establishes the basis for distinguishing a series of "Philistine" subunits from a series of "David" subunits.

B. Repetition of Subject Nouns

1. Genesis 21:25

Genesis 21:22-24 recounts a request from Abimelech to Abraham for an oath of solidarity; in Gen 21:25-26 Abraham complains to Abimelech about mistreatment by the latter's servants in the matter of a well. There is little to mark a unit boundary other than the change of topic. Characters, setting, and time are all unchanged; no unusual word forms or word order are present. The only marker is the unnecessary repetition of the subject noun "Abraham" in 21:25. A literal translation of 21:24-25 shows the effect:

> And Abraham said, "I do swear." And Abraham complained . . . .

Repeating the subject noun imparts a sense that what follows is a new issue. (Something similar occurs in English for large literary units. It would be unusual, for instance, to begin a new chapter in a novel with a pronoun simply because that person was the last individual mentioned in the previous chapter.) The NRSV recognizes this by beginning a new paragraph at this point.

2. 1 Kings 12:26

After Rehoboam's bungled attempt to win the support of the elders of the northern tribes he is forced to flee from Shechem to Jerusalem, abandoning to fate the minion he has sent to quell the uprising (1 Kings 12:18). From that time on the federation of northern and southern tribes that David had forged disintegrated, and the two power blocs became two separate kingdoms (12:19-20), Israel in the north and Judah in the south. Rehoboam immediately made plans to regain the lost territory militarily, but he was dissuaded by a prophet (12:21-24). Jeroboam, new king of the northern kingdom, fortified and then moved his capital (12:25), and then undertook extensive religious innovations to assure that his citizenry would not continue to frequent the Temple in Jerusalem, where they would be subject to Judahite influence and be expected to pray for the Judahite king (12:26-29).

The common reading of events following the withdrawal of the Israelites from the federation places a paragraph break between 12:24 and 12:25, using the change of character and setting (from Rehoboam in Jerusalem to Jeroboam in Israel) as marking the boundary. This is the reading of the NRSV, and indeed it is the reading of the medieval Jewish tradition reflected in the standard Hebrew text. But that reading neglects the awkward repeated subject noun "Jeroboam" in 12:26. When that is recognized as marking the beginning of a new unit the topical difference between units is highlighted, and the symmetry of each subunit falls into place.

> 1. MILITARY PREPARATIONS (12:21-25)
> a.   Rehoboam's offensive military preparations (12:21)
> b.   Divine oracle rebuking Rehoboam (12:22-24)
> a'.   Jeroboam's defensive military preparations (12:25)
> 2. JEROBOAM'S RELIGIOUS INNOVATIONS (12:26-29)
> a.   Jeroboam speaks about the people (12:26-27)
> b.   Jeroboam makes the two calves (12:28a)
> a'.   Jeroboam speaks to the people (12:28b)
> b'.   Jeroboam places the two calves (12:29)
> 3. THE DEDICATION CEREMONY AT BETHEL (12:30–13:34)[8]

3. 1 Chronicles 14:3b

The organization of a long, complex literary work entails not only marks of disjunction to identify the boundaries between units and subunits but also techniques of conjunction to link and unify the component parts of a whole. The third part of our study will explore techniques of conjunction, but this passage is a good example of how a single verse can act as mortar, both holding apart and binding together the materials it touches. In 1 Chronicles 14 David has established his seat at Jerusalem. The first verses have a political purview: acknowledgment of David's kingship by Hiram of Tyre assures David that he has established himself internationally.

Verse 3 appears to shift the horizon from the political to the domestic, David's wives and children.

> And David took more wives in Jerusalem;
> And David fathered more sons and daughters.

The repeated subject noun in 14:3b invites a different reading. Since 14:4-5 name David's children, but not his wives, it is likely that the second subunit of the whole is 14:3b-5, David's children, rather than 14:3-5, David's domestic life, and that David's acquisition of more wives is to be read with what precedes, namely the recognition of his political establishment on an international scale—perhaps implying that at least some of the wives were foreigners, married for the sake of political alliance.

---

[8] On the structure of this literary unit see above, pp. 67–68.

Yet we cannot overlook that the verse is a syntactically and rhythmically balanced couplet. This means that it forms a literary subunit in its own right as well, each half of which is simultaneously linked to what precedes or follows. Thus there is an overlapping structure:

> David's political establishment
>> "And David took more wives in Jerusalem.
>> And David fathered more sons and daughters."
> David's children

This sort of intermediate subunit that connects the two units contiguous to it is called, appropriately enough, a "hinge." We will examine the device in more detail in the third part of our study.

C. Interruptions of discourse

1. Exodus 5:4-5

Pharaoh's angry speech to Moses and Aaron uses alternating symmetry; the repeated elements that structure the symmetry are single words. (The pattern is lost in the NRSV, whose terms do not correspond one-for-one to the Hebrew terms.)

> The king of Egypt said to them:
> A. "Why, Moses and Aaron, do you separate <u>the people</u> from their works?
> B.   Go to your <u>labors</u>."

> And Pharaoh said:

> A'. "Look! <u>The people</u> of the land[9] are now many,
> B'.   and you are giving them rest from their <u>labors</u>."

The repeated introduction is unnecessary, since "the king of Egypt" and "Pharaoh" are the same person and the discourse is clearly a single speech. But it divides the discourse structurally, between the two pairs of corresponding subunits, and thematically, between a relatively stronger focus on Moses and Aaron and a relatively stronger focus on the people.

2. Exodus 3:14-15

A similar though slightly more complex example occurs in Exod 3:14-15, a text we have studied before as an example of concluding epitome (see pp. 78–79).

---

[9] Since the scene is Egypt the phrase "the people of the land" seems like it ought to mean the Egyptians rather than the Israelites. As a term for the Israelites it is an anachronism, since they have not yet settled on their land. But it is a conventional phrase in biblical Hebrew for the Israelites, and is so used here.

A. ¹⁴ᵃ<u>And God said to Moses</u>, "I AM THAT I AM."

B.   ¹⁴ᵇ<u>And he said</u>, "Thus you shall say to the Israelites:
'I AM has sent me to you.'"

B'.   ¹⁵ᵃ<u>And God said</u> further <u>to Moses</u>, Thus you shall say to the Israelites:
'YHWH, your fathers' god . . . has sent me to you.'

A'. ¹⁵ᵇThis is my name forever, and this is my remembering for the ages."

There are two unnecessary introductions, the words beginning 3:14b (unit B) and those beginning 3:15a (unit B'), but the repeated phrases are not identical. The fuller repetition at 3:15a, almost identical to the introduction to the whole speech, marks the major division in the passage between the two pairs of corresponding units. The more succinct repetition at 3:14b marks the lesser division between the two subunits of the first pair. The absence of an introduction at 3:15b injects an asymmetry into the passage and signals the different character of unit A': it does not correspond completely to unit A (words addressed privately to Moses) as the chiasm might suggest, but is rather a concluding epitome whose two clauses point back to units A and B+B' respectively.

3. 1 Kings 22:28b

This chapter tells the story of Ahab of Israel's final battle and death, and of the court prophet Micaiah ben Imlah who prophesied it. At the end of the scene where Micaiah appears before the kings of Israel and Judah and the four hundred assembled prophets of the king of Israel, there is an unnecessary repeated introduction before the words, "Hear, all the peoples!" The scene does not have symmetrical structure, so the separation of Micaiah's words into two speeches is not for the sake of establishing symmetry. On the surface of things, too, there seems to be no topical change that would account for a break here. There is, however, a subtle intertextual allusion that only one extremely familiar with the Bible will recognize. The separate unit, "Hear, all the peoples," is a quotation of the opening words of the prophet Micah (Mic 1:2). The author (or perhaps a later editor or glossator) is using the similarity of the names of the two prophets, Micaiah (*mî-kâ-yāh*, "Who is like Yahweh?") and Micah (*mî-kâ*, "Who is like?"—with the divine name elided)[10] to direct the reader's attention to another biblical book as if it were by the same person. In other words, in this instance the unnecessary repeated introduction is analogous to a modern scholarly footnote reference!

---

[10] Compare the name Michael: *mî-kâ-ēl*, "Who is like El?" El was a Canaanite god often treated in the Hebrew Bible as identical to YHWH.

9. NARRATIVE SEQUENCE

Biblical Hebrew narrative has a grammatical way to indicate the main line of a narrative's action; this is called the "narrative sequence." As I shall explain in more detail below, the narrative sequence is marked by a characteristic verb form and a required word order. Any disruption of that sequence is immediately obvious to the reader. Authors can use such disruptions for many purposes: to subordinate material, to insert background information or parenthetical comments, to direct an aside to the reader, and so forth. One of the common uses is to mark boundaries between units that we might call "scenes" or "episodes." Before turning to examples, we need to understand in more detail exactly how this device works in biblical Hebrew.

Narrative tense and simple past

In English our basic narrative tense is the simple past tense: "I came, I saw, I conquered." We do not usually advert to the fact that, even in narrative, we use that tense in two different ways. First, we use it to describe a *sequential series* of past actions and to imply that those actions occurred in chronological succession: "Mary entered the room, sat down, and opened her book." But we also use it to describe several past actions with no implication of sequence or succession: "Mary ate, drank, and danced at the party." Hebrew has two different verb forms to express these two ideas. One form conveys succession as well as pastness; for our purposes we will call it the "narrative past" or the "narrative tense." The other form conveys pastness without implying succession; we will call it the "simple past." The skeletal structure, so to speak, of Hebrew narrative is a string of clauses that use narrative past tense forms. These clauses constitute the main line of the action; clauses that do not use narrative past forms are "off" the line, that is, in some way removed from the main flow of the narrative.[1]

For the English reader of the Bible this structural signal is almost inevitably lost. The conventions of acceptable English style prohibit a direct one-to-one rendering of Hebrew prose into English. For example, a slavishly literal rendering of Gen 3:6-7, with the narrative past forms underlined, would run:

> And the woman <u>saw</u> that good [was] the tree for eating and that attractive [was] it to the eyes and desirable [was] the tree for succeeding and she <u>took</u> from its fruit and she <u>ate</u> and she <u>gave</u> also to her man with her and he <u>ate</u> and the eyes of the two <u>were opened</u> and they <u>knew</u> that naked [were] they and they <u>sewed</u> leaves of fig and they <u>made</u> themselves aprons.

English style requires variation of word order, alternate forms of coordination ("also," "but," "then," punctuation without "and"), subordination with a variety of conjunctions, etc. This means, however, that mapping the "on-line" and "off-line" forms exactly onto the English translation is next to impossible, and that other means must be used to mark boundaries of units and subunits. English translations have available typographic devices like punctuation (commas separating phrases, semicolons between clauses, periods ending sentences, etc.), paragraph indentations, blank lines between paragraphs, section headings of various levels, and other such things to accomplish this. However, scholarly attention to Hebrew structuring devices is relatively recent, and the structuring devices Hebrew uses have not been adequately studied. Consequently the paragraphing of most English translations is often more reflective of the translator's subjective appreciation

---

[1] For the more technically minded, our "simple past" is the *qatal* or perfect tense; the "narrative past" is the *wayyiqtol*, or imperfect tense with *waw* consecutive. Traditional Hebrew grammar theorized that the series of narrative past tense forms had to begin with an explicit or implicit simple past tense, which was then *continued* by the narrative forms (hence the term "*waw* consecutive"). Contemporary text linguistics has demonstrated that in ordinary narrative this is not the case. Narrative past forms constitute the whole of the main narrative line; simple past forms, even when they appear to start a narrative sequence, are in fact "off-line." On the other hand, the fact that the main line of the narrative consists of narrative past forms does not preclude the occurrence of such forms off-line as well. For instance, a paragraph of background information (therefore "off-line") may use narrative past forms to recount a sequence of actions that took place prior to the present scene—a sort of secondary narrative embedded in the primary one. In rare cases this can lead to ambiguity about the main story line, at least to the modern reader.

of the text than of the usages inherent in Hebrew narrative prose. The reader of an English version, therefore, must be aware that even the typographical layout of his or her translation embodies interpretive judgments about the structure as well as the meaning of the original Hebrew.

Breaks in narrative sequence

Since the narrative sequence comprises a series of clauses that use narrative tense verbs, any clause that does not use such a form disrupts the sequence.[2] It is an invariable rule of Hebrew grammar that a narrative past form *must* be the first word in its clause. Any clause, then, that begins with a word other than the verb *cannot* use a narrative form and therefore breaks the sequence.[3] Several factors can affect the word order of a clause. Certain clauses contain no verb at all in Hebrew. In Gen 3:6-7, above, for instance, there are four verbless clauses, though English grammar requires a form of "to be" [inserted in square brackets above] for correctness. Other clauses, such as relative clauses (English: "the man *who* . . . ," "the thing *that* . . ."), causal or result clauses (English: "he did this *in order that* . . ." or "she was so successful *that* . . ."), negative clauses (English: "he did *not* go . . ." or "*before*[4] she

---

[2] Contemporary text linguists are endeavoring to define the various functions and nuances of "off-line" clauses in biblical Hebrew narrative. For example, E. J. Revell has investigated the book of Judges in detail. He categorized all clauses in the book (excepting poetry and speech) into narrative clauses and three non-narrative types (descriptive, contextualizing, and incidental), on the basis of their function in the story. He then correlated these four categories with the verb forms they use and applied his findings to the battle passage in Judg 20:29-48 to show its narrative structure. See "The Battle with Benjamin (Judges xx 29-48) and Hebrew Narrative Techniques," *VT* 35 (1985) 417–33. In the same vein Robert E. Longacre's study of Joseph (*Joseph: A Story of Divine Providence: A Text Theoretical and Textlinguistic Analysis of Genesis 37 and 39–48* [Winona Lake: Eisenbrauns, 1989]) devotes a whole chapter to "Verb Rank in the Story," in which he attempts to determine the precise functions of different types of clauses based on their initial word form. More theoretical approaches appear in the works of Alviero Niccacci.

[3] In theory any clause that begins with a verb in a form other than the narrative tense also breaks the sequence, but examples of this are so rare in biblical Hebrew narrative that linguists are as yet unable to formulate convincing systematic conclusions about the function of such clauses. For one recent attempt see Robert E. Longacre, "*Weqatal* Forms in Biblical Hebrew Prose: A Discourse-modular Approach," in Robert D. Bergen, ed., *Biblical Hebrew and Discourse Linguistics* (Dallas: Summer Institute of Linguistics, 1994) 50–98.

[4] In Hebrew this can be expressed as a negative clause: "when she had *not yet* gone . . . ."

went . . ."), and many others require a conjunction to begin the clause or a negative to precede the verb. None of these types of clauses, then, can contain a narrative past form, and they always effect a break in the narrative sequence. However, because the construction is unavoidable in the language the break is often felt as just a minor interruption of the sequence and not as a boundary marker between units or subunits.

On the other hand, since word order is more flexible in biblical Hebrew prose than in English, a narrator may freely choose to use a word order that puts something before the verb. In Hebrew narrative prose, for instance, the subject of the verb will usually follow the verb. (The first three words of Gen 3:6, quoted above, actually run in Hebrew: "and-saw the-woman that . . . .") Reversing the word order, that is, putting the subject first requires using a verb form other than the narrative past.[5] This produces a break in the narrative sequence that is evident in Hebrew but often overlooked in translation. Genesis 4:1 and 4:17, for example, are quite different; 4:1 breaks the narrative sequence while 4:17 does not:

> 4:1
> *wĕhāʾādām yādaʿ ʾet-ḥawwāh ʾištô*
> And-the-Human knew Eve his-wife . . .
> 4:17
> *wayyēdaʿ qayin ʾet-ʾištô*
> And-knew Cain his-wife . . .

The difference is that 4:17 portrays Cain's intercourse as part of a narrative sequence (the genealogy of Cain), whereas 4:1 portrays *hāʾādām*'s intercourse with Eve not as part of the sequence but as background information to a new episode whose action proper begins in 4:3 (Cain's fratricide). A more precise translation would put 4:1-2 in the past perfect: "The Human had known his wife Eve, and she had conceived and borne Cain . . ." but, as the NRSV shows, translators can easily disregard the nuance. (See below for a more detailed discussion of this example.)

The same effect is achieved when the narrator freely precedes the verb with some other element. In Gen 3:14-19, for instance, each of YHWH's speeches to the three characters has its own introduction, but only the first is in the narrative sequence:

> 3:14
> *wayyōʾmer yhwh ʾĕlōhîm ʾel-hannāḥāš*
> And-said YHWH God to-the-snake . . .

---

[5] See Ziony Zevit, *The Anterior Construction in Classical Hebrew* (Atlanta: Scholars, 1998).

3:16
ʾel-hāʾiššāh ʾāmar
To-the-woman he-said . . .

3:17
ûlĕʾādām ʾāmar
And-to-Human he-said . . .

The NRSV reflects the Hebrew word order accurately, but the nuance that the Hebrew conveys cannot be captured in English simply by word order. By breaking the narrative sequence at the second and third speeches the narrator *avoids* implying that the three speeches are successive, and thereby gives them a timeless quality that is difficult to capture in English.[6]

When the narrator breaks the sequence freely, unconstrained by syntax, the disruption is much more salient to the reader. Among other effects, an unnecessary break in the narrative sequence often marks a unit or subunit boundary. It may indicate the end of one unit, or the beginning of the next, or it may mark the beginning of a subunit (for example of background information) within a larger, encompassing unit.

The verb "to be" and verbless clauses

The verb "to be" poses special problems. Despite the fact that it is a verb it is not essentially an action word but a word that describes a state or condition of being. For that reason clauses that use the verb "to be" are more closely akin to verbless clauses than to verbal ones. (Look once more at the translation of Gen 3:6-7 above: the four verbless clauses are all equivalent to "to be" clauses in English.) As we might expect, clauses that use "to be" in the simple past break narrative sequence. But even clauses that use the narrative tense of "to be" are usually "off-line" and often function as unit boundaries. We have seen this in our earlier discussion of the "full temporal construction" (see pp. 122–24).

Because of their utility in describing continuing states or conditions verbless clauses and clauses that use "to be" are particularly apt for conveying background information. They will often be found, therefore, at the beginning of a narrative unit, either alone or as part of a complex subunit that sets the background for a scene.

---

[6] We might come close in English by omitting the verb in the second and third introductions: "Yhwh God said to the snake: . . ." "To the woman: . . ." "And to Human: . . . ."

A. BROKEN NARRATIVE SEQUENCE BEGINNING A UNIT

1. Genesis 3:1

The group character "animals" was introduced in 2:19-20, but they were entirely passive in that scene. Now the snake, not previously mentioned, steps forward as an active character. In order to establish and justify his role as representative of the animals the narrator begins the scene with a bit of background information: the snake was the cleverest of all of them. The sentence breaks the narrative sequence (subject followed by "to be" in the simple past) and reinforces the boundary that is already evident from the change in characters. (The end of the previous scene is also marked: 2:25a is a "to be" clause, and 2:25b is a negative clause that breaks narrative sequence.)

2. Genesis 18:17

The previous scene ended with a double departure notice about "the men" and Abraham (see above, pp. 133–34). The scene that begins in 18:17 is a divine interior monologue introduced by the words "And YHWH said," but the word order breaks the narrative sequence: the subject precedes the verb, which is in the simple past. If 18:17 began with normal narrative sequence the boundary between the scenes would be marked only by the departure notice. But since the departure notice states that Abraham accompanied the men, the natural understanding of the opening phrase of 18:17 would be "And YHWH said [to Abraham]." By breaking the sequence the narrator emphasizes the unit boundary and the beginning of a new scene in 18:17. This makes room for an alternative (and equally possible) understanding of the Hebrew verb: "And YHWH thought" (or "And YHWH said [to himself]").

3. Exodus 3:1

Narrative units often begin with background information that is necessary in order to understand the story. Sometimes this information is brief, one or two clauses; sometimes it can develop into a lengthy passage comprising verbless clauses and even secondary narrative sequences (see the following examples). In Exod 3:1 we are told that Moses was working as a shepherd for Jethro, his father-in-law. The word order breaks the narrative sequence (subject, followed by the verb "to be" in the simple past). This supplies background information for the action of the episode, which is Moses' encounter with YHWH at

Horeb in the course of shepherding the sheep in the wilderness. The action of the scene begins with the narrative tense verb in 3:1b, "he led the flock."

4. Genesis 4:1-2

The story of Cain and Abel begins with a genealogical note that introduces the two main characters and relates them to the characters of the preceding scene. The word order of the first clause ("And the Human knew his wife Eve") breaks the narrative sequence, but then a secondary narrative develops. It uses a series of four narrative tense verbs to recount the conception, birth, and naming of Cain and the birth of Abel. Finally, two descriptive statements using the verb "to be," one in the narrative tense and one in the simple past, conclude the subunit of background information. The main action of the scene begins with a full temporal construction (4:3; see p. 123).

The use of two different verb forms in the two final clauses is worth considering in more detail. In literal translation the clauses run:

> *wayĕhî hebel rō'ēh ṣō'n*
> and-was Abel a-shepherd-of flocks
> *wĕqayin hāyāh 'ōbēd 'ădāmāh*
> and-Cain was a-tiller-of soil.

The first clause uses the narrative tense of "to be" *(wayĕhî)*, while the second uses the simple past *(hāyāh)*. The first thereby acts as a sort of transition between the secondary narrative sequence about the births and the final clause of the subunit, whose simple past form breaks that secondary narrative sequence and brings the subunit to a conclusion. The clauses also demonstrate the stylistic elegance of which Hebrew is capable even on this small scale. Overall, they have alternating symmetry:

> A. And-was Abel
> B.   a-shepherd-of flocks
> A'. And-Cain was
> B'.   a-tiller-of soil.

But the "A" elements form a chiasm:

> a. And-was
> b.   Abel . . .
> b'.   And-Cain
> a'. was . . .

This use of broken narrative sequence simultaneously to mark a boundary and to create a chiasm is very common in biblical Hebrew narrative. Unfortunately it rarely survives translation.

5. Jonah 1:4

We saw the concentric structure of Jonah 1 above (pp. 18–20). The entire first subunit of that structure (1:4) supplies background information; all three clauses are "off-line." The first clause breaks narrative sequence (subject followed by simple past tense); the second is a "to be" clause that describes a condition ("there was a great storm on the sea"); the third clause is another subject plus simple past tense. This subunit separates the introductory narrative (1:1-3, which is an unbroken narrative sequence after an initial "to be" clause) from the main, symmetrically structured episode of the chapter, namely, Jonah's experiences in the ship.

6. Genesis 39:1-6

The story of Joseph is interrupted at the point where he is taken down to Egypt by the Midianites and sold to Potiphar (37:36). After the story of Judah and Tamar (ch. 38) the Joseph story resumes in ch. 39. The first six verses of the resumed story are a long, complex unit of background information that includes a recapitulation of earlier material (compare 39:1 with 37:28 and 37:36), "to be" clauses that describe conditions (for example, there are three such clauses in 39:2), secondary narrative sequences that recount earlier (past perfect) events necessary for understanding the ensuing episode (39:3-4), narrative and "to be" clauses that spell out the results of those events (39:5-6a). The subunit ends with a negative clause that breaks narrative sequence ("he paid no attention to anything . . ." 39:6b). The next subunit, which is the episode itself, begins with a single "to be" clause that reveals background immediately pertinent to the episode, namely how handsome Joseph was (39:6c), and the action is introduced with a full temporal construction (39:7a).

B. BROKEN NARRATIVE SEQUENCE ENDING A UNIT

Clauses that mark the end of units and subunits are less likely to contain background information. More commonly these are simple boundary markers, often with the sort of stylistic flair we noted above in Gen 4:2. An additional function is to point forward to later developments (foreshadowing or prolepsis).

1. Genesis 1

Each of the six days of creation ends with a double "to be" clause, "and it was *(wayĕhî)* evening and it was *(wayĕhî)* morning, the nth day."

The verbs are in the narrative tense, which, by not breaking the narrative sequence formally, gives the whole a forward momentum. The effect of counting the days is also proleptic: interest increases as one approaches the symbolic seventh day.

2. Genesis 2:25

We saw above, in looking at Gen 3:1, how the end of the previous scene is doubly marked by a "to be" clause and a negative clause. These two clauses are proleptic. They introduce a theme that will be strangely obtrusive in the remainder of the story: nakedness and embarrassment. The theme is absent from the next scene, the dialogue of the woman and the snake,[7] and will not reappear until 3:7. But it pervades the story from that point on (3:10-11, 21) and seems to replace—or perhaps substitute for—the theme of death that we expect to encounter.

3. 1 Samuel 15:34

The use of double departure notices affords the narrator an opportunity for stylistic elegance. Reversing the word order of the second notice produces a chiasm as well as a break in the narrative sequence. After Samuel has announced to Saul that Yhwh has rejected him because of his mercy to Agag the Amalekite, the two principal characters go their separate ways:

> *wayyēlēk šĕmûʾēl hārāmātāh*
> and-went Samuel to-Ramah
> *wĕšāʾûl ʿālāh ʾel-bêtô . . .*
> and-Saul went-up to-his-house . . .

The narrative unit continues with four more clauses (15:35), but none of them contains narrative tense verbs, thus producing a sort of "epilogue" subunit that spells out the long-term results of the episode that has just ended.

4. 1 Kings 18:6b

The chiastic pattern in the previous example may be intended to emphasize the contrast between Samuel and Saul: they not only go

---

[7] Except by a wordplay that is lost in translation. The human couple in 2:25 are "nude" *(ʿărûmmîm);* the snake is "shrewd" *(ʿārôm).*

their separate ways geographically, but Saul's rejection by Y H W H means that all relations between the two men are henceforth broken off ("Samuel never again saw Saul," 15:35). Sometimes, however, similar contrast is emphasized, paradoxically, by using parallel rather than reverse symmetry. The scene in which Ahab (Baalist king of Israel) and Obadiah (his secretly Yahwist major-domo) are desperately seeking water to save the lives of the royal herds ends with a double departure notice where both clauses break narrative sequence:

> *ʾaḥʾāb hālak bĕderek ʾeḥād lĕbaddô*
> Ahab went in-one direction by-himself
> *wĕʾōbadyāhû hālak bĕderek-ʾeḥād lĕbaddô*
> and-Obadiah went in-one-direction by-himself.

The parallel symmetry of the two clauses emphasizes the final word of each, "by himself," ending the scene with a graphic reminder of the contrary religious commitments of the two characters.

5. 1 Kings 17

The first chapter of the story of Elijah comprises four scenes. The first is very brief: Elijah's confrontation with Ahab (17:1). The second, Elijah's stay at the Wadi Kerith in compliance with a command from Y H W H, begins with a departure notice ("and he went," 17:5). The third, Elijah's stay at Zarephath, again in compliance with a command from Y H W H, also begins with a departure notice ("and he arose and he went," 17:10). The fourth is the resuscitation of the widow's son (17:18-24). Each of these scenes is separated from the others by clauses that use the narrative tense of the verb "to be" *(wayĕhî)*. In this way the clauses simultaneously mark the boundary between scenes and continue, at least formally, the narrative sequence that connects the scenes, and thereby serve as smooth transitions between them.

Between scenes one and two is a single "to be" clause (17:2) that introduces a divine word (17:3-4):

> *wayĕhî dĕbar-yhwh ʾēlāyw lēʾmōr*
> and-was[8] the-word-of-Y H W H to-him saying . . .

The word Elijah receives connects the two scenes causally. The only reason he needs to "hide" is because his word to Ahab has endangered him; his journey to the Wadi Kerith is his compliance with the divine command.

---

[8] This is a standard construction in prophetic texts. English translations usually render the verb "came": "The word of the L O R D came to him" [NRSV].

Between the stay at Wadi Kerith and the departure notice of 17:10a are two more "to be" clauses. The first (17:7) is a full temporal construction that establishes Elijah's need to move somewhere else; the second (17:8) is identical to 17:2 and introduces the divine word (17:9) that tells him where to move.

Between the scene of 17:10-16 and the resuscitation of the widow's son are two more "to be" clauses. The first (17:17a) is a full temporal construction that establishes the situation of need and connects it with the preceding scene. The second (17:17b) describes a condition, the severity of the boy's illness.

The next chapter begins with two more "to be" clauses that, together, form a full temporal construction. The first introduces the construction in the usual way, "to be" in the narrative tense *(wayĕhî)* followed by a temporal reference ("after many days," 18:1a). However, the expected third element, the action verb, is replaced by another "to be" clause. This clause, like 17:2 and 17:8, introduces a divine command, but uses the simple past instead of the narrative tense:

> *ûdĕbar-yhwh hāyāh ʾel-ʾēlîyāhû baššānāh haššĕlîšît lēʾmōr*
> and-the-word-of-Yʜᴡʜ was to-Elijah in-the-third year saying . . .

The combination of full temporal construction plus a simple past verb form plus an additional temporal reference marks this boundary much more strongly than the boundaries at 17:7-8 and 17:17 and in that way sets ch. 17 apart as a narrative unit in itself, separate from ch. 18.

6. 2 Samuel 18:18

Absalom rebelled against his father David and seized the throne. In the course of attempting to capture his father, Absalom is killed by Joab, David's general. The scene of his death ends with a departure notice that also effects a break in the narrative sequence (subject followed by simple past verb) in 18:17b, "All Israel fled, each one to his own tent." This is followed by a subunit that comprises both a flashback and a narrator's aside to the reader. The first clause of 18:18 breaks narrative sequence (subject plus simple past verb) to give background information ("Absalom had taken"). This is followed by a secondary narrative sequence that describes how and why Absalom set up his monument, and what he named it. The verse ends with an aside to the reader (still in narrative sequence) that calls the reader's attention to the contemporary existence of the monument. The next scene, Joab's dialogue with Ahimaaz, begins (18:19a) with a break in narrative sequence.

C. BROKEN NARRATIVE SEQUENCE INTERRUPTING A UNIT

When narrative sequence is broken *within* a narrative unit—that is, when the break does not mark the beginning or the end of the unit that contains it—it can serve several purposes other than structural ones. It can supply background information that is given more appropriately in the course of a scene than at its beginning, or it may be a narrator's parenthetical aside to the reader. Often this sort of interruption relates something in the scene to the reader's own day; this is called "breaking frame" and can give the present-day scholar an invaluable clue about the setting in which the text was composed. Such breaks are often structurally important as well. They may constitute short subunits in themselves within the structure of the whole unit, or they may mark the beginning of a longer subunit (of background, for instance, or of secondary narrative), or they may simply mark structural divisions within the organization of the larger unit.

1. Ruth 1:14b

The last clause of the verse ("Ruth clung to her") is off-line (subject followed by simple past verb). This produces a chiastic pattern that contrasts the behaviors of Orpah and Ruth (and in this way reveals that Orpah's kiss is a farewell):

A. And-kissed
B.   Orpah . . .
B'.   And Ruth
A'. clung . . .

But the verse also functions somewhat like a double departure notice to separate a scene where Naomi is in dialogue with both her daughters-in-law from one where she is alone with Ruth.

2. Jonah 1:10b

Subordinate clauses that begin with a word other than the verb are necessarily "off-line." Because they are syntactically constrained they are less likely to be structurally significant. Nevertheless, sometimes they have structural impact. In the concentric structure of Jonah 1 (see pp. 18–20 above) 1:10b constitutes a complete subunit. That subunit comprises three subordinate clauses, each introduced by the conjunction *kî* (the English equivalents vary: "*for* the men knew *that* he was fleeing from Yhwh, *because* he had told them"). The entire subunit is a flashback, since it can only refer to something that had happened prior to the question of 1:10a. The co-occurrence of three successive off-line clauses reinforces the parallelism occasioned by their identical conjunctions to set the three clauses apart as a subunit unto itself.

3. Genesis 23:10a

The symmetry of Genesis 23 is straightforward. It begins with a "to be" clause (23:1a) that separates this episode from the story of Isaac's near-sacrifice and introduces a short narrative subunit (23:1-2). The beginning of the next subunit is marked by the unnecessarily repeated subject "Abraham" in 23:3. The scene continues with three dialogic subunits, 23:3-6, 7-11, 12-15, each of which comprises a speech by Abraham and a reply either by the Hittites as a group or by Ephron individually. This is followed by an unmatched narrative subunit that spells out in detail the terms of the contract (23:16-18),[9] and a narrative conclusion (23:19-20) that corresponds to the introduction. The boundary between the last two narrative subunits is marked by the break in narrative sequence (time reference followed by simple past tense) that begins 23:19.

A. Narrative introduction (23:1-2)
    (inclusive vocabulary: "Sarah"; "that is, Hebron, in the land of Canaan")
B.   First dialogue (23:3-6)
B'.   Second dialogue (23:7-11)
B".   Third dialogue (23:12-15)
+. Land contract (23:16-18)[10]
A'. Narrative conclusion (23:19-20)
    (inclusive vocabulary: "Sarah"; "that is, Hebron, in the land of Canaan")

The second dialogue, however, is interrupted by a verbless clause that breaks the narrative sequence: "Ephron [was] sitting among the Hittites" (23:10a). This affords an alternative analysis of the dialogue. Rather than consider it as three questions and answers, we may read it

---

[9] The first clause of 23:16 concludes the third dialogue. The terms of the land contract begin with the unnecessarily repeated subject "Abraham" in "Abraham weighed out . . . ."

[10] The asymmetry of this unmatched subunit underscores its formalized language with its details about the weights used for weighing the silver and about the specific features (cave, trees, extent of the surrounding ground) whose ownership is being transferred. All highlights the binding legal force of the agreement reached "in the ears of all the Hittites" and "in the eyes of all the Hittites." The importance of this legal contract, of course, is that it marks Abraham's first step in coming into possession of the land that God has promised him. The cave at Machpelah is the gage of the divine promise.

as two conversations: before the interruption Abraham addresses the Hittites; afterward he is in dialogue with Ephron individually. When we see it from this angle we can understand that the two conversations have quite different points. Abraham's negotiation with the Hittites is political. He is an outsider; they are the "people of the land" (23:13). He must be accepted by the local authorities before he can entertain the possibility of becoming a "man of the land" himself. His dialogue with the Hittites achieves that political acceptance. Only then can he turn to Ephron and begin the economic negotiations.

4. 1 Kings 13:1-10

Jeroboam, chosen by YHWH to replace Solomon as king over the ten northern tribes of Israel, has turned quickly to idolatry. He builds a sanctuary at Bethel, where he sets up a golden calf.[11] An unnamed "man of God" (that is, a prophet) comes north from Judah (that is, the southern territory YHWH has left to Rehoboam, Solomon's son) and confronts Jeroboam on the occasion of his dedication of the new shrine at Bethel. The scene has complex symmetry: overall it is chiastic (ABC-C'B'A'), but the subunits of "B" and "C" are in parallel:

A.   Narrative introduction: the man of God arrives (13:1a)
B_1.   Jeroboam is standing at the altar (13:1b)
B_2.   Man of God delivers YHWH's oracle (13:2)
C_1.   Parenthesis (13:3)
C_2.   King's response and punishment (13:4)
C_1'.   Parenthesis (13:5)
C_2'.   King's response and healing (13:6)
B_1'.   Jeroboam invites the man of God (13:7)
B_2'.   Man of God tells of YHWH's command (13:8-9)
A'.   Narrative conclusion: the man of God departs (13:10).

The two "C_1" elements, both described above as "parenthesis," are marked by breaks in the narrative sequence. In each case the break marks the whole of a subunit, not just its beginning. The two breaks are achieved with different syntax, though the net effect is the same: both involve a change in temporal framework and a change in the narrator's voice from storytelling to an aside to the reader. The first parenthesis does not use reverse word order to break narrative sequence; the sen-

---

[11] Jeroboam set up a similar shrine at Dan in the north as well. The narrator of 1 Kings considers the calf-shrines idolatrous. Historically this was probably not the case—the calves were most likely intended as pedestals upon which YHWH would stand. But in the narrative world constructed by the author of 1 Kings they are idols.

tence begins with the verb, but in a non-sequential tense form. This unusual syntax points to an unusual sense. The verb form could be translated as a simple past, as it is, for instance, in the NRSV: "He *gave* a sign . . . ." More commonly, however, the form indicates a time that is *future* relative to its context; it is therefore a form of foreshadowing or prolepsis. This is probably the best reading here: the narrator directs an aside to the readers to inform us of something that happened *after* the current scene of condemnation. He specifies that it happened on the same day, but the verb form implies that it was later in the day. Translate, including the parentheses: "(He was to give a sign that same day . . .)."[12] The second parenthesis breaks narrative sequence in the more usual fashion, by reversed word order (subject followed by simple past verb). It is a prolepsis of a different sort, situating itself in the future time of the reader and looking backward from there to an event, namely the fulfillment of the man of God's sign from 13:3, something that happened *after* the man of God's prophecy but *before* the reader's own day. Translate, including the parentheses: "(And the altar has been torn down, and the ashes[13] poured out from the altar, in accordance with the sign the man of God gave . . .)."

The effects of inserting the two parenthetical asides at precisely these points in the scene are several. First, symmetry is preserved by positioning the two asides to balance one another structurally. Second, the scene's tension is prolonged. We must wait before we learn the king's reaction to condemnation of the altar, and we must wait again before we learn of his reaction to his own maiming. The delay softens the intensity of the mood shifts in the scene, which would be otherwise starkly juxtaposed: a gruesome prediction of human sacrifice, a paroxysm of royal rage, a bathos of royal begging.

5. Genesis 41:47–42:5

After Pharaoh gives Joseph ascendancy in Egypt so that he might prepare the land for the coming years of famine, but before the intense family drama of Joseph's encounter with his brothers, there is a short

---

[12] The parenthetical character of the remark is shown too by the wording of 13:4. Jeroboam's reaction is to "what the man of God cried out against the altar," but those are the words of 13:2a, introducing the prophecy of 13:2b. The "sign" of 13:3 is different, and there is no indication that Jeroboam is aware of it.

[13] The "ashes" are the mixed residue of ash and fat from burnt offerings. They are therefore holy, and to be disposed of respectfully (see Lev 6:8-11 [MT 6:1-4]). To have them spill on the ground as a result of the altar's cracking open would be a desecration.

passage that displays many of the ways in which breaks in narrative sequence organize and illuminate a passage. The ancient and traditional division into chapters obscures the unity of the passage. The overall structure of the passage presents alternating symmetry:

A. Transitional subunit (41:45b-46)
B.   Seven years of plenty: Joseph's administrative strategy (41:47-49)
C.   Seven years of plenty: Joseph's Egyptian family (41:50-52)
A'. Transitional subunit (41:53-54a)
B'.   Seven years of famine: Joseph's administrative strategy (41:54b-56)
C'.   Seven years of famine: Joseph's Israelite family (41:57–42:5).

In the course of this relatively short passage narrative sequence is disrupted many times, with a variety of effects.

The passage is introduced by a transitional subunit that comprises a verbless clause of background information framed by narrative clauses that change the scene from Pharaoh's palace to the wider stage of Joseph's national administration (41:45b-46):

"Joseph <u>went forth</u> over the <u>land of Egypt</u>.
"Joseph [was] thirty years old . . .
"Joseph <u>went forth</u> from before Pharaoh
    and traveled through the whole <u>land of Egypt</u>."

The next subunit (to 41:49) describes how Joseph managed the grain produced during the seven years of plenty. It begins with a change of subject ("the earth produced . . .") and a thematic focus on the seven years of plenty. Narrative sequence is broken only once, at 41:48b. The break does not mark a subunit boundary; the single clause that is not in narrative sequence is a kind of explanatory parenthesis:

"He stored food in their cities (the food of a city's surrounding fields he stored inside it)."

The next subunit (41:50–52) begins with a break in narrative sequence (the indirect object "Joseph" precedes the simple past verb). It is a flashback, describing Joseph's family life during the seven years of plenty whose administrative procedures were spelled out in the preceding subunit. The naming of Joseph's two sons (41:51-52) balances forward and reverse patterns to create a tightly unified structure. This rendering reflects the Hebrew word order as closely as possible:

A. "<u>And-called</u> Joseph **the-name-of the-firstborn** Manasseh
B.   because (God) has-made-me-forget . . ."
A'. "**And-the-name-of the-second** <u>he-called</u> Ephraim
B'.   because (God) has-made-me-fruitful . . ."

The strongly ironic note in the text here is worth noting. In order to celebrate the divine gift of forgetfulness Joseph names his first-born son in a way that will constantly remind him of what he has forgotten! There is a subtle foreshadowing here, since the subunit parallel to this one in the whole passage will reintroduce the "father's house" that Joseph is so glad to have left behind.

Between the accounts of what took place during the years of plenty and the events of the years of famine there is another transitional subunit (41:53-54a). It has forward symmetry and does not break narrative sequence. In this way it renews the momentum of the story after the break in narrative sequence at 41:52 and suggests the inevitability of the coming famine.

A. "And the seven years of plenty finished
B.   that *(ʾăšer)* had been in Egypt
A'. "And the seven years of famine began to come
B'.   just as *(kaʾăšer)* Joseph had said."

The second half of the passage begins with an introductory epitome[14] that forecasts the content of the whole. The epitome (41:54b) comprises two "to be" clauses; narrative tense forms begin again at 41:55. The epitome itself is chiastic, and it relates to the following material chiastically as well. (On both levels the chiastic structure highlights contrast between the situations in Egypt and elsewhere.)

a. "<u>There was</u> famine **in all the lands**
b.   but **in all the land of Egypt** <u>there was</u> food."
B'. The situation in Egypt (41:55-56)
A'. The situation in other lands, especially Israel (41:57–42:5).

The situation in Egypt is described in two narrative subunits that focus on Pharaoh and on Joseph. Framing verses separate the two (with a break in narrative sequence) and surround the whole:

a. "And-was-<u>famined all-the-land-of Egypt</u>" (41:55a)
B.   Appeal to Pharaoh and his response (41:55b)
a'. "And-the-<u>famine</u> was upon-<u>all</u>-the-face-of <u>the-land</u>" (41:56a)
B'.   Joseph's response (41:56b)
a''. "And-was-strong the-<u>famine</u> in-<u>the-land-of Egypt</u>" (41:56c).

The description of the situation in the whole world (and more specifically in the land of Israel) begins with a break in narrative sequence (subject followed by simple past tense verb) at 41:57. As in the case of the subunit about Joseph's sons, this subunit is a flashback. It recounts events simultaneous with the preceding subunit: at the same

---

[14] On "epitome" see above, pp. 59–60.

time that Egypt was in famine and getting grain from Joseph, peoples from other famine-stricken lands were likewise coming to where they heard food was available. From 42:1 on the clauses use narrative past forms, but the unnecessarily repeated subject in 42:1b[15] suggests that 42:1a should be read with 41:57 as background:

> All the earth had come to Egypt to get grain from Joseph, for the famine was strong in all the earth. But Jacob had seen that there was grain in Egypt (41:57–42:1a).

The action of the scene begins with the appearance of a new group character, the sons, and Jacob's ensuing speeches to them (42:1b). The action continues with a sequence of narrative tense verbs that is broken only at 42:4 (the verb is preceded not only by the negative but by a long direct object phrase). The break emphasizes the contrast between the ten brothers who went down to Egypt and Benjamin, who was kept at home:[16]

> "And Joseph's ten brothers went down . . ." (42:3)
> "But Benjamin, Joseph's brother, Jacob did not send with his brothers . . ." (42:4)

Finally, the subunit ends with two clauses that form an inclusion with the beginning of the subunit:

a.	"All the earth <u>had</u> <u>come</u> to Egypt <u>to get grain</u>
b.	for the <u>famine</u> was strong <u>in all the earth</u> *(ʾereṣ)*" (41:57).
a'.	"And the sons of Israel <u>came to get grain</u> among those who <u>came</u>,
b'.	for there was <u>famine in the land</u> *(ʾereṣ)* of Canaan" (42:5).

Just as the beginning of the entire passage is marked by a transitional subunit containing a verbless clause ("Joseph [was] thirty years old," 41:46a), so its end is also marked by a transitional subunit containing two verbless clauses ("Joseph [was] governor over the land; [he was] supplier-of-grain to all people of the land," 42:6a).

---

[15] "*Jacob* saw that there was grain in Egypt; and *Jacob* said to his sons"—the repetition of "Jacob" is not reflected in the NRSV.

[16] The Hebrew word order is not reflected in this translation.

PART III

STRUCTURES OF CONJUNCTION

In the preceding part of this study we examined devices that Hebrew narrative style uses to mark boundaries between literary units and subunits. In this part we shall focus on how Hebrew narrative establishes continuity and connection across such boundaries. The groundwork for this investigation was laid by H. Van Dyke Parunak in an article entitled "Transitional Techniques in the Bible,"[1] in which he proposed a useful taxonomy of transitional techniques based on the distribution of connective elements in the connected units. Although his categories form the basis of my analysis I shall expand his system and draw examples exclusively from biblical Hebrew narrative.

Transition from one unit to the next or, in our terms, connection between two successive units is accomplished by repeating an element in both units. Like the repeated elements that organize a single literary unit, elements that connect adjacent units can occur on any linguistic level. Phonetic connectors—that is, repetition of similar sounds—are more likely in poetry than in narrative prose, but they occur in the latter as well. Repetition of grammatical constructions can also effect a connection between units, though as in any case of repetition the effectiveness of the technique depends on the likelihood that it will be noticed. Unusual constructions are more effective in this regard than ordinary ones. Much more common, because more easily perceived by a reader or hearer, are repetitions of words or even whole phrases, or repetitions of verbal roots in a variety of forms. Similarly, semantic or thematic repetition—that is, use of similar ideas without repeated vocabulary—is a common device for connecting successive units.

In addition to repeated elements, symmetrical structure can function as a connective technique. We saw in Part I that such patterns can give a passage formal unity that reflects and underscores its thematic unity. They can also join successive units. That occurs when several different repeated elements connect the adjacent units, and those elements are arranged in a symmetrical pattern that overlaps the boundary between

---

[1] *JBL* 102 (1983) 525–48. Parunak's title reflects his concern for how connective techniques facilitate the transition from one unit to the next.

the units. This adds structural bonds to those forged by the repeated units themselves. Although this connective device has not been widely studied, and a thorough exploration of it lies beyond the scope of this work, we will see some instances of the device.

The distribution of a connective element in each unit can range from frequent and pervasive appearances to a single occurrence, usually close to the boundary between the connected units. The former can be called a "thread"[2] and the latter a "link." A thread's main function is to unify the literary unit in which it appears; connecting successive units is only secondary. Because of its pervasiveness a thread is regularly thematically important—and often essential—in a passage. The figure of Abram/Abraham, for instance, is an obvious thread that unifies all the stories of the Abraham cycle from Gen 11:27 to 22:24 (see above, pp. 89–92). Of course the unifying function also entails tying together most or all of the unit's component subunits, but that is not the sort of connective function we have in view here. Rather we are interested in cases where a thread that unifies one unit occurs also in an adjacent unit (whether as a thread or a link), but does not pervade the larger literary whole of which both units are components: as, for example, the theme of hospitality connects the stories in Genesis 18 and 19 (see below), though it is not a unifying theme for the whole Abraham cycle.

A "link," by contrast, is most often not thematically significant in its literary unit. Its connective potential derives from the strength of the echo it makes with its appearance in the adjacent unit; this is why a link generally falls near the unit boundary. Scholars often refer to links as "catchwords," "hook words," or the like.

Structural threads and links differ somewhat from others because they involve extended patterns rather than repeated elements. By analogy with other threads and links, we can define a structural thread as one in which the connective structure incorporates the whole of a literary unit, and a structural link as one in which it incorporates only part of it. In both cases the connective structure extends into an adjacent unit.

A connection, then, can consist of a pure thread that runs through two adjacent units, a pure link that appears in two adjacent units only at their common boundary, or a linked thread, where a thread in one unit is repeated once in the adjacent unit. The last is perhaps the commonest transitional or connective technique in biblical Hebrew narrative. Naturally these devices can be overlaid, and complex types of

---

[2] Parunak uses the term "keyword," but "thread" offers a better metaphor for the pervasive character of the connective element. It also avoids implying that the element must be a "word." Another common term for a verbal or thematic thread is "leitmotif."

connections can occur. Many of the examples below—even those chosen primarily to illustrate a single connective device—exhibit multiple overlaid connections.

A further issue merits attention. Two linked threads can occur such that each adjacent unit contains a thread that is repeated as a link in the other. Parunak schematizes this Ab/aB, where "A" and "B" represent the threads and "b" and "a" their repetition as links. This is a strong and not uncommon transitional device, but Hebrew style sometimes takes it a step further and organizes the part of the passage that contains the links so that it forms an integrated unit on its own. Parunak schematizes this A/ba/B, and calls the connective unit a "hinge."[3] In a hinge, then, there are three separate connective dynamics involved: the repetition of elements that connect each unit to the hinge (A/a and b/B) and the device (frequently symmetrical structure) that unifies the hinge unit itself (/ba/).

Perhaps the most subtle form of connective device is what might be called a "double-duty hinge." In this case there are not two different elements that connect the hinge to the two surrounding units. Rather one element—often the entire hinge unit itself—functions in two different ways (e.g., two different structural effects, two different construed meanings, etc.) respective to the two surrounding units. In such cases the hinge unit is not a discrete entity interposed between the two; on the contrary, it belongs simultaneously to both, and no clear dividing line can be drawn between them. The image of a hinge is still appropriate, however, if modified. The analogue for the double-duty hinge is not the whole of the hinge, with two plates that attach it to the two panels it joins; it is rather the central pin of the hinge, inextricably part of the whole mechanism, but indivisible.

A. THREADS

1. Genesis 2:4b–3:24; 4:1-16

The story of the human couple in the Garden of Eden and the story of Cain and Abel are connected by two interwoven devices. The first is

---

[3] As Parunak points out, the relative independence of the hinge unit permits also a direct ordering of linked threads (A/ab/B) as well as an inverted ordering (A/ba/B). This can only happen in a hinge, for if /ab/ does not constitute a relatively separate literary unit, a direct ordering of elements will have no connective effect: Aa/bB. Parunak does not reckon with hinges that use pure threads, or pure links, or combinations of connective devices, instead of two linked threads, but we will see such examples below.

a pure thread, verbal and thematic. Both stories focus on the disinte-
grating relationship between the protagonist and the soil *(ʾădāmâ)*. The
first human being is formed from the soil (2:7) but is finally condemned
to eke out a subsistence living from it only with great difficulty (3:17-
18). His son Cain begins in that situation, as a tiller of the soil (4:2), but
eventually is alienated from it completely (4:11-12). The connective effect of the theme is strengthened by the frequency of the term *ʾădāmâ*
(eight times in the first story, six times in the second) and its almost
complete absence elsewhere in Genesis 1–5.[4]

The second connective device is a linked thread. Throughout the
story of the Garden of Eden the male character is called *hāʾādām*, literally "the human being," not simply *ʾādām*, the proper name "Adam."[5]
The same is true at Gen 4:1. From that point on, however, the form
ʾādām appears without the article (Gen 4:25; 5:1-5).

2. 1 Kings 1–11

We saw the complex symmetry of the Solomon story above (pp.
92–94). Each of the "D" units of that story is unified by a thematic
thread that also connects the unit to adjacent units. The theme of "wisdom" pervades unit D and ties together all of its subunits: the king's
penetrating wisdom is exemplified in the story of the two harlots in
3:16-28; his clear and successful administration of the kingdom is the
subject of 4:1-28 (Hebrew 4:1–5:8); his erudition is praised in 4:29-34
(Hebrew 5:9-14). The same thread recurs in both adjacent units. In unit
C Solomon asks and YHWH grants the gift of discernment (3:9), and in
unit E Hiram calls Solomon "wise" (5:7; Hebrew 5:21).

The theme of "wealth" pervades unit D' and connects its various
subunits. Its main expression is the word "gold" (fifteen times in
9:26–10:29), but it is also carried by terms for "silver" (five times) and
rare luxuries. That theme, however, is also a thread in the preceding
unit E' (9:11-25), and several terms connect the two units: "gold" (9:11,
14); measurements of weight, especially "talents of gold" (9:14, 28;
10:10, 14); and the figure of King Hiram of Tyre (9:11-14, 27; 10:11, 22).

---

[4] The term appears elsewhere only twice in Genesis 1–5. Genesis 1:25 speaks of
"creeping things of the earth" *(remeś hāʾădāmâ)*, and is a link connecting the creation
account of Genesis 1 to the story of Genesis 2–3. At the end of the Adamite genealogy of Genesis 5 the term reappears (5:29) and forms a link to its frequent appearance in the Flood story of Genesis 6–9.

[5] To be more precise, this is true in every instance where the article "the" (Hebrew *ha-*) could appear. In Gen 2:20 and 3:17 the Hebrew consonantal text *lʾdm* can
be read either as "to the human being" or as "to Adam."

3. Judges 17–21

The connective thread here is essentially verbal and only superficially thematic. Judges 17–18 tells the story of Micah and the Bethlehemite Levite he hires, then loses, as his family priest. Judges 19–21 tells the story of the rape of a Levite's concubine at Gibeah and the consequent war against the tribe of Benjamin. The figure of a Levite is a prominent thread in both stories but, as 19:1 makes clear, it is not the same Levite. The threads in the two literary units, then, share common vocabulary although they do not have a common referent. Nevertheless, when we read the two stories together the common elements create an echo between the two stories and invite us to read them both in terms of their other common themes: violation of hospitality, seizure of personal property, and intertribal violence within the people of Israel.

4. 1 Kings 13

The chapter involves two stories, both of which feature the same man of God from Judah. In 1 Kings 13:1-10 the man of God confronts Jeroboam and condemns the altar Jeroboam erected at Bethel. In 13:11-32 the man of God is betrayed into disobedience by an old prophet of Bethel and dies as a result. The figure of the man of God is an obvious thread connecting the two stories. But there is another thread as well. An unusual phrase, "by the word of YHWH," *(bidbar yhwh)* occurs four times in the first story and three times in the second, yet it is otherwise extremely rare (only five other times in the whole Hebrew Bible).[6]

Furthermore, there is a structural thread that connects the two stories. The entire chapter shows composite symmetry: the first story is chiastic (see above, pp. 168–69), the second uses forward symmetry.[7] The symmetry is also compound: overlaid on both stories is a parallel pattern whose sequences are not coterminous with the two stories themselves:[8]

> A. Jeroboam "stands by the altar" (13:1)
> B. The man of God "calls" against the altar (13:2a)

---

[6] The inclusion of 12:30-31 and 13:33-34 also points to the unity of the two stories (see above, pp. 67–68).

[7] For an analysis of the symmetry of 1 Kings 13:11-32 see Jerome T. Walsh, "The Contexts of 1 Kings xiii," *VT* 39 (1989) 355–70, and idem, *1 Kings* (Collegeville: The Liturgical Press, 1996) 182–90.

[8] This analysis is based on the work of James K. Mead, "Kings and Prophets, Donkeys and Lions: Dramatic Shape and Deuteronomistic Rhetoric in 1 Kings xiii," *VT* 49 (1999) 191–205.

    C. "Thus says YHWH," followed by a quotation (13:2b)
      D. Sign: the altar will be torn down (13:4)
        E. The altar is "torn down" (13:5)
          F. Threefold repetition of "by the way" (13:9-10)
            G. "There lived an old prophet in Bethel" (13:11a)
              H. The old prophet hears about the man of God (13:11b)
                I. He has the donkey saddled (13:13)
                  J. He "went" and "found" the man of God (13:14)
                    K. He invites the man of God to return (13:15)
                      L. The old prophet claims a divine word (13:18).
A'. The old prophet and the man of God "sit at the table" (13:20)
  B'. The old prophet "calls" against the man of God (13:21a)
    C'. "Thus says YHWH," followed by a quotation (13:21b)
      D'. Sign: the man of God will not be buried in his own tomb (13:22)
        E'. The man of God is "thrown by the way" (13:24)
          F'. Threefold repetition of "by the way" (13:24-25a)
            G'. "In the town where the old prophet lived" (13:25b)
              H'. The old prophet hears about the man of God (13:26)
                I'. He has the donkey saddled (13:27)
                  J'. He "went" and "found" the man of God (13:28)
                    K'. The old prophet brings back the man of God's body (13:29)
                      L'. The old prophet speaks a divine word (13:31-32).

By incorporating the two stories into the same parallel pattern, and in particular by *not* making the boundary between the two stories fall between the two parallel sequences, the structure welds the two stories tightly together and reinforces other signs of unity we have mentioned.[9]

5. Genesis 18–19

The theme of hospitality is a thread running through two successive episodes of the Abraham cycle: ch. 18, where Abraham first hosts three unidentified visitors, then bargains with one of them (who is now identified as YHWH in person) for the fate of Sodom, and ch. 19, where Lot

---

[9] For a fuller discussion of the meaning effect of the unity of this whole chapter, see above, pp. 67–68.

hosts the remaining two visitors (now identified as angels or divine messengers), and then is rescued by them from the destruction of Sodom. The thematic continuity of these two chapters forges a close connection between them; the bond is strengthened by verbal and structural parallels between the two chapters, particularly at their beginnings. For example:

> *18:1*
> YHWH appeared to him [i.e., Abraham] at the oaks of Mamre,
>> while he was sitting at the entrance of the tent,
>>> in the heat of the day.
>
> *19:1a*
> The two messengers came to Sodom
>> in the evening
>> while Lot was sitting at the gate of Sodom.

and

> *18:2b*
> He saw
>> and he ran to meet them from the entrance of the tent
>>> and he bowed to the ground.
>
> *19:1b*
> Lot saw
>> and he rose to meet them
>>> and he bowed with his face to the ground.

Thematic, verbal, and structural connections like these—even if they do not manifest the full parallel symmetry we studied in Part I—invite a comparative reading of the two chapters.[10] The story of Lot is a distorted reproduction of the story of Abraham; the contrast redounds to the glory of Abraham and the slight disparagement of Lot. Abraham "runs" to meet the visitors, and they accept his invitation willingly; Lot "rises" to meet his visitors, and they decline his invitation at first (19:2-3). Both patriarchs host their supernatural visitors, but Abraham's hospitality exceeds Lot's: Abraham "hurries" to prepare milk, veal, and mealcakes for the guests; Lot provides a meal with unleavened bread. Abraham's guests offer him a gift that advances him: a new child; Lot's guests give him a gift that preserves his present situation: they rescue him and his daughters from predatory townsfolk. YHWH deals directly with Abraham; Lot deals only with God's messengers. Abraham is proactive in interceding for Sodom; Lot and his family resist their own rescue (19:14, 16, 18-20, 26), much as his guests had at first resisted his invitation.

---

[10] Gordon J. Wenham discerns a concentric rather than parallel symmetry in the two chapters ("Method in Pentateuchal Source Criticism," *VT* 41 [1991] 103–105).

B. LINKS

1. Genesis 2:25; 3:1

Even though they are scenes in a single narrative, the disjunction between Gen 2:18-25 and 3:1-5 is strong. Not only is there a break in narrative sequence, but a new character is introduced and an unexpected dialogue about a new topic begins. The text eases the transition from one scene to the next by a link based on wordplay. Genesis 2:25 describes the human couple as "naked" *('rwm)*, and the next verse describes the snake as "clever" (also *'rwm*, though from a completely different Hebrew root).

The wordplay is not gratuitous. It invites us to compare the humans' simplicity with the snake's duplicitous words, and even to contrast the humans' nudity with the snake's disposable coverings.[11]

2. 1 Kings 20:43; 21:4

A striking verbal link connects two quite different stories about King Ahab of Israel. The first, about Ahab's victory in war with Ben-Hadad of Aram, ends with an unexpected prophetic condemnation of Ahab. As a result of the prophet's words Ahab went "to his house upset and resentful" (*'al-bêtô sar wĕzā'ēp*, 20:43). In the next story, after Naboth has refused to sell Ahab his ancestral vineyard, Ahab came "to his house upset and resentful" (*'el bêtô sar wĕzā'ēp*, 21:4). The verbal link helps connect two stories whose tones are otherwise very different: the first about an Ahab favored by YHWH, obedient to him and on generally good terms with his prophets,[12] the other about a conniving and craven king guilty of idolatry and collusion in judicial murder and condemned by YHWH through Elijah the prophet.

3. 2 Kings 2:25; 3:1

In Part I we discussed the effects of the double asymmetry in 2 Kings 2:25 (see above, pp. 107–108), which contains two place names instead of one as in the corresponding subunit 2:1. One effect of the added name, Samaria, is to create a link with 3:1, and thereby to con-

---

[11] In the Epic of Gilgamesh, too, the snake's theft of immortality from humankind is symbolized in its shedding of its skin.

[12] See my *1 Kings* 293–315.

nect the beginnings of Elisha's prophetic ministry (2:15-25) to the large complex of stories about him in 3:1–9:13.

4. Judges 8:33; 9:4

The series of stories about Israel's judges is interrupted in Judges 9 by the story of Abimelech, son of the judge Gideon. Abimelech, though not a judge himself, murdered Gideon's other sons and laid claim to the kingship the Israelites had once, unsuccessfully, offered to his father. A verbal link helps bridge the disjunction: the divine name "Covenant Master" *(baʾal bĕrît)* occurs in 8:33 and 9:4, but nowhere else in the Hebrew Bible. The effect is ironic. The Israelites sinned against YHWH by taking up the worship of Covenant Master; in consequence, Covenant Master's temple subsidizes the seizure of power by Abimelech that deprives Israel of the leadership of a judge chosen by YHWH.

5. Ezra 3:13; 4:1

Another ironic verbal link joins the scene in Ezra 3:8-13, the celebration of laying the foundation for the new Temple, to that in 4:1-3, where the residents of the surrounding territories approach Zerubbabel asking to assist in the building.[13] We are told (3:13) that the celebration in Jerusalem was so loud that it was "heard" from far away. Then 4:1 says that the residents of Judah and Benjamin "heard" of the plan to rebuild the Temple. The constraints of Hebrew grammar bring the two occurrences of the verb "heard" into close proximity (only two words separate them), which makes the echo quite strong. At first the reader expects that the noise heard "from afar" is what the Judahites and Benjaminites "heard." Then it becomes clear that what the latter heard is not the noise, but the news that the noise portends.

6. Genesis 16:16; 17:1

There is a subtle link that bridges the midpoint of the Abraham cycle of stories. (See above, pp. 89–92, for the overall organization of the Abraham cycle.) At the very end of ch. 16, where Abraham's long hope for progeny has seemingly been fulfilled, and at the very beginning of ch. 17, where that seeming will be undone and a new fulfillment promised, the text calls our attention to Abraham's advanced age.

---

[13] Noticed by Gordon F. Davies, *Ezra and Nehemiah* (Collegeville: The Liturgical Press, 1999) 18.

The fact that thirteen years have passed in silence between the two chapters makes Yhwh's disillusionment of Abraham more poignant, since his presumed heir is now nearing maturity. The link is especially striking since Abraham's age has not been an issue prior to this point. It was previously mentioned in 12:4, at the beginning of the cycle, but not since then.

C. Linked threads

1. 1 Kings 12:25

We discussed above the significance of the repetition of "Jeroboam" in 1 Kings 12:26 for establishing the structure of the passage (see pp. 150–51). This means, though, that the mention of Jeroboam in 12:25 belongs to a literary unit that is otherwise entirely about Rehoboam. Since Jeroboam is the focus of the next unit (12:26-29) we have an instance of a linked thread connecting the two units.

2. Ruth 1:22

The mention of the barley harvest at the end of Ruth 1 is a link to the theme of the harvest that is central to ch. 2. This is in fact a literary device technically called "prolepsis" or foreshadowing: the mention of an element that is tangential where it is mentioned, but prepares the reader for later developments. The device is common throughout the Hebrew Bible. The foreshadowing need not be developed in the immediately succeeding material; see, for instance, the foreshadowing in Gen 2:25 of the "nakedness" theme, which does not reappear until 3:7, or the mention of Josiah in 1 Kings 13:2, which does not bear narrative fruit until 2 Kings 22. However, when foreshadowing is elaborated in the immediately succeeding literary unit the prolepsis also acts as a linked thread to connect the two units.

3. Regnal formulas[14]

The regnal formulas are examples of foreshadowing, and many of them qualify as linked threads. The formula that concludes the account of a king's reign regularly names his successor, whose story will unfold

---

[14] We discussed the regnal formulas as an example of complex inclusion above, pp. 74–75.

in a later passage. In cases where the account of that successor's reign follows immediately, the connective structure is a linked thread.

4. Between books

There are several places where the boundary between biblical books is bridged by a connective device, often a linked thread. In some cases we may be dealing with literary techniques of an original author, but in others (e.g., Ruth 1:1 and the division between 1 and 2 Kings, both examined below) it is clear that the connective device is the product of later editorial work.

Simple examples include the following linked threads. Exodus 1:1-7, which recapitulates the last several chapters of Genesis, and 1:8, which mentions Joseph for a final time; Lev 36:13, which points forward to the "commandments and ordinances" of Deuteronomy; Josh 1:1, which begins the book by evoking the death of Moses from the end of Deuteronomy; Judg 1:1, which does the same for Joshua; 1 Kings 1, where David, the main figure of 2 Samuel, remains alive long enough to see Solomon established on the throne; and so on.

Two examples call for more extended comment. In the Hebrew Bible the book of Ruth is numbered in the last part of the canon, the "Writings," but in the biblical tradition represented by the ancient Greek translation, the Septuagint (third to second centuries B.C.E.), it is numbered among the historical books and placed between Judges and 1 Samuel. (English bibles generally follow this custom.) The Septuagint compiler's decision to move the book turns the first words of Ruth into a linked thread—"In the days when the judges judged . . ."—since it sets Ruth into the immediate chronological context of the book that precedes it.

The second example also hinges on a difference between the Hebrew and Greek biblical traditions. In the Hebrew Bible 1 and 2 Kings are reckoned a single book; in the Greek Bible they are distinguished. (Again our English Bibles follow the lead of the Septuagint.) The point where the Greek tradition chose to separate the books, however, is quite telling. It produces two overlapping linked threads, thereby insisting on the unity rather than the distinction between the books. The first linked thread is the figure of Ahaziah of Israel. 1 Kings ends with the introductory formula for his reign; the rest of his regnal account is found in 2 Kings 1. The natural tendency to read the regnal account as a whole works against the division of the books. The second linked thread is the figure of Elijah, the main character in 1 Kings 17–19 and 21. He is also the main prophetic figure in 2 Kings 1.

5. 1 Kings 1–2

The first unit of the Solomon story is 1 Kings 1:1–2:12a, which narrates how Solomon came to succeed David; the second is 2:12b-46, which recounts how Solomon eliminated threats to his kingship in order to consolidate his power.[15] Two separate linked threads connect the two units.

The first linked thread is verbal, involving two phrases that occur as threads in the first unit and are repeated briefly at the beginning of the second. Throughout 1:1–2:12a the main theme of Davidic succession is carried by the phrases "shall reign after me" (1:13; see also vv. 17, 24, 30, 35 ["shall reign in place of me"]) and "sit upon my throne" (1:13; see also vv. 17, 20, 24, 27, 30, 35, 46, 48; 2:12a). The next section begins with the story of Adonijah's suicidal approach to Bathsheba and Solomon; the story contains a brief evocation of both threads from the previous chapter. Adonijah says that "all Israel expected me to reign" (2:15), and Solomon claims that Yhwh "seated me on the throne of David my father" (2:24).

The second linked thread is thematic. The last part of 1:1–2:12a is the final speech of the dying David to Solomon (2:1-12a), comprising a narrative inclusion (2:1, 10-12) surrounding David's words. Structurally it forms part of the first unit of the Solomon story, balancing 1 Kings 1:1-4 (see p. 92). Thematically, however, it is a prolepsis pointing forward to Solomon's execution of Joab and Shimei in 2:28-45.

D. Hinges

1. *Genesis 26:33-35; 27:1*

The two-verse subunit about Esau's marriages (Gen 26:34-35) does not figure in the overall chiastic structure of the Jacob cycle (see above, pp. 31–34). It functions as a hinge to connect the two surrounding stories with pure links. The connective elements are essentially phonemic, based on wordplays. The preceding episodes (Gen 26:17-33) are about wells (Hebrew *bĕʾēr*) and the naming of the city of Beer-Sheba (*bĕʾēr-šebaʿ*, interpreted in this passage as meaning "Well of the Oath"). In 26:34 Esau marries Judith, daughter of a man named Beeri *(bĕʾērî)*.

The next verse, Gen 26:35, reads literally "And they were bitterness of spirit for Isaac and Rebecca," referring to the grief of Esau's parents over his marriages to outsiders. The phrase "they were bitterness," with a feminine plural verb, is *wattihyênā mōrat*. In 27:1 Isaac's weak

---

[15] See above, pp. 92–94.

eyes (*ʿênāyw*, which also takes a feminine plural verb) are described with a very similar-sounding phrase: *wattikhênā ʿênāyw mērěʾōt*.

2. Genesis 2:4

The two accounts of creation that begin the book of Genesis are very different in tone and content. The first is cosmic, recounting the creation of the whole universe in formal, almost liturgical language. The second is humanist, portraying the origins of humankind with compelling narrative skill. Scholars who study the history of the text have long held that the two passages derive from different sources and that the division between them occurs in the middle of 2:4. The first half of that verse contains two strong connections with the cosmic account of creation. There is characteristic vocabulary: the verb "to create" *(bārāʾ)* occurs frequently in Gen 1:1–2:4a, but nowhere in 2:4b–3:24. And there is a chiastic inclusion around the first creation account formed by 1:1 and 2:4a:

> *1:1*
> a. In the beginning God <u>created</u>
>   b. <u>the heavens and the earth</u>.
> *2:4a*
>   b'. These are the generations of <u>the heavens and the earth</u>
> a'. when they were <u>created</u>.

The second half of the verse has equally strong connections with the following story. Grammatically it forms a single sentence with 2:5-6. The compound divine name "Yhwh God" occurs in 2:4b and throughout the following story. Elsewhere in the Hebrew Bible it is relatively rare.

However, Gen 2:4 is itself a highly structured unit. It is a poetic couplet, each line of which contains three matching ideas, organized chiastically:

> A. These are the generations of <u>the heavens</u>
>   B. and <u>the earth</u>
>   C. <u>when they were created</u>
>   C'. In the day <u>when Yhwh God made</u>
>   B'. <u>the earth</u>
> A'. and <u>the heavens</u>. . . .

This tight organization enables Gen 2:4 to act as a hinge between the two creation accounts.

3. Genesis 23:1–25:11

Between the large cycles of stories about Abraham (see pp. 89–92) and Jacob (see pp. 31–34), at the center of the book of Genesis, are four episodes that, though of quite disparate length, are chiastically organized:

    A. Sarah's death, and her burial at Machpelah (23:1-20)
      B. Isaac's marriage to Rebekah (24:1-67)
      B'. Abraham's marriage to Keturah (25:1-6)
    A'. Abraham's death, and his burial at Machpelah (25:7-11)

The figures of Abraham and Sarah, of course, connect this hinge unit with the preceding Abraham cycle, while the story of Isaac's marriage to Rebekah connects it to the first stories of the Jacob cycle.

E. DOUBLE-DUTY HINGES

1. 2 Kings 17:6

We examined the structure of 2 Kings 17:6-41 above (see pp. 52–54). Part of the basis for that analysis is the repetition of elements in 17:6 and 17:24. Both verses mention "the king of Assyria," both speak of occupying "Samaria," both list geographical names of places to or from which exiles were moved, and both speak of "cities" where the king eventually "settled" *(wayyōšeb)* the exiles. However, in that earlier discussion we did not attend to the equally notable repetitions that connect 17:6 with the preceding unit that begins in 17:1. Both 17:1 and 17:6 mention Hoshea by name, speak of his nine-year reign, and mention "Samaria." This makes 17:6 effectively part of an inclusion surrounding the regnal account of Hoshea, last king of Israel. Hoshea's regnal account lacks the customary, stereotyped concluding formula. No doubt this is because Hoshea had no successor; the end of his reign was the end of the existence of the kingdom of Israel. But 17:6 functions in the place of that stereotyped concluding formula and, as such, belongs to the series of complex inclusions that demarcate the reigns of Israelite and Judahite kings. The verse itself is a single grammatical sentence, and cannot be easily divided between the literary units. It is therefore a hinge, and belongs equally integrally to both of the larger units that surround it. In this way the account of the fall of Samaria leads inexorably into the Deuteronomist's theological reflection about the causes of that fall.

2. 2 Kings 2:15b

When Elijah and Elisha miraculously cross the Jordan river the guild prophets from Jericho witness the miracle, but remain on the western bank (2:7). When Elisha duplicates Elijah's deed on his return the prophets take it as a sign that "the spirit of Elijah rests upon Elisha" (2:15a)—in other words, they testify that Elisha is the legitimate prophetic successor of the master. In the next episode the prophets pressure a reluctant Elisha into allowing a search for Elijah's body—a search that ultimately fails, as Elisha told them it would. Between the two episodes appear the words: "they came to meet him and bowed to the ground before him." The prophets' obeisance has subtly different meanings when read in the context of the two episodes.

After their testimony to Elisha's new status, obeisance is an act of submission and an acknowledgment of the other's superiority. It need not lead to any speech or action: it is simply present readiness before the superior. Compare, for instance, Adonijah's silent obeisance to Solomon in 1 Kings 1:53: Solomon has won the struggle for the throne, and Adonijah knows it. He submits and departs.

On the other hand, as preparatory to a request that is potentially challenging or even accusatory to the superior, obeisance is a prevenient apology, an attempt to soften the negative impact one's words may have. Compare, for instance, Bathsheba's and Nathan's obeisances to David in 1 Kings 1:16, 23. Both are going to risk offending the king by accusing him of violation of an oath (Bathsheba) or by implying that he has lost control of the throne (Nathan). To placate him in advance, they bow before him.[16]

The obeisance of the guild prophets before Elisha, therefore, has different—and perfectly appropriate—significance, depending on whether one reads it with what precedes or what follows. It conjoins the two episodes indissolubly.

3. 1 Kings 11:26-43

This passage is an example of what might be called a "structural hinge." Both the preceding and following large literary units are organized symmetrically, and 1 Kings 11:26-43 belongs structurally to both patterns. We saw the complex symmetry of the Solomon account above (pp. 92–94); 1 Kings 11:26-43 is the last subunit of that structure and corresponds, in both its parts, to the first subunit, 1 Kings 1:1–2:12a:

A_1. Nathan the prophet gains the throne for Solomon (1:1–2:9)
A_2. Formulaic notice of David's death (2:10-12a)
A_1'. Ahijah the prophet prophesies the throne for Jeroboam (11:26-40)
A_2'. Formulaic notice of Solomon's death (11:41-43).

---

[16] Notice that they do *not* perform such an obeisance when they are summoned into his presence later: 1 Kings 1:28, 32-33.

However, this subunit also begins the story of the reign of Jeroboam, which has its own symmetrical structure:

A$_1$.   Ahijah the prophet prophesies the throne for Jeroboam (11:26-40)
A$_2$.   Formulaic notice of Solomon's death (11:41-43)
B.   Political disunity: Israelite rejection of Rehoboam of Judah (12:1-20)
C.   A Judahite man of God's approval of Jeroboam (12:21-25)
D.   Jeroboam's cultic innovations (12:26-31)
C'.   A Judahite man of God's disapproval of Jeroboam (12:32–13:10)
B'.   Prophetic disunity: Israelite prophet betrays Judahite man of God (13:11-32)
A$_1$'.   Ahijah the prophet prophesies Jeroboam's downfall (14:1-18)
A$_2$'.   Formulaic notice of Jeroboam's death (14:19-20).

The passage has another, less obtrusive connection. In the overall pattern of the Solomon story subunit B describes how Solomon eliminated three threats to his throne: Adonijah, Joab, and Shimei. The detailed correspondences of the subunits of the Solomon story can lead a reader to expect that subunit B' will tell of three threats that Solomon does not eliminate. In the text, however, only Hadad of Edom and Rezon of Damascus are named. The mention of Jeroboam's rebellion against Solomon (11:26-27) fills the gap and joins subunits B' and A' by means of a thematic linked thread.

CONCLUSION

We have examined several stylistic devices used by biblical Hebrew to delimit, link, and organize the literary units that make up a prose narrative, and we have analyzed numerous examples of these devices, some simple, some very complex, and considered the impact they can have on our understanding of the meaning of a text. Let us summarize the results of our study and the insights it can afford us for reading the narratives of the Hebrew Bible.

1. Biblical Hebrew style uses a variety of symmetrical patterns, including symmetries that incorporate obtrusive asymmetries, to organize prose narratives. Not all narratives or narrative complexes are organized in this fashion, but the device is found frequently enough to warrant the conclusion that it is native to biblical Hebrew prose. This observation is of fundamental relevance to readers, since structural arrangement can be an important pointer toward interpretation. The reader should be attentive to the sorts of repetition that provide the framework for symmetrical organization. Unfortunately the constraints of translation make it difficult, if not impossible, to preserve all such repetitions in the target language. This places additional responsibilities upon translators to identify structures and their interpretive dynamics and to devise ways to realize comparable effects in translation.

2. Symmetrical organization occurs in prose narratives that, in our present state of knowledge, appear to date from every period of biblical Hebrew. This supports the conclusion that the device is an inherent and enduring feature of biblical Hebrew style. It is not found in every text, certainly. But readers should be attentive to the possibility of its presence whenever they read.

3. Symmetry can occur on any linguistic level from small-scale phonetic patterns in phrases and sentences to large-scale verbal and thematic patterns comprising narrative complexes of many chapters. It is the smaller end of the scale that is most often lost in translation: wordplays,

subtle grammatical signals, repetition of single words in different contexts and meanings, and the like. Here too the English reader is at the mercy of the translator either to capture in translation or, more often, to indicate in comment or footnote the text's subtleties. At the larger end of the scale, where patterns are more often based on features that can survive in translation, readers must deepen their appreciation of biblical narratives as continuous texts. For those whose primary encounter with biblical narrative is in the form of brief passages read in worship this is often a new and revealing experience. Attention to all the literary dimensions of a text—characterization, plot development, point of view, etc.—is an essential readerly task. In the case of biblical Hebrew narrative, structural arrangement is one of these dimensions.

4. There is a general correlation between the symmetrical pattern that organizes a text and the interpretive dynamic that is most suitable for the narrative. Reverse patterns (chiastic and concentric) point to dynamics of contrast and reversal; forward patterns (such as parallel symmetry) point to dynamics of linear development, and often of intensification; alternating repetition can point to the interweaving of two separate points of view. Asymmetry is often used to highlight a point of particular importance. The correlations are neither perfect nor inevitable, but they are consistent enough to serve as a guide to initial interpretive efforts.

5. Interpretation should not limit itself to a linear reading of the text. Intratextual comparisons of corresponding elements and sequences can offer fruitful additional avenues for discovering deeper or more complex levels of meaning. For a reader this implies that a single reading will not exhaust the riches of a profound text. Repeated probings, changed questions, varied viewpoints are necessary to explore the depth and breadth of a complex narrative.

6. The interpretive potential of symmetrical patterning argues that symmetry is not simply a mnemonic aid for the performer of an oral text, but is intended to affect an attentive audience, at least subconsciously, whether the text is received in oral or written form. Recognition of the response a text evokes in the reader, and of how the text evokes it, is the reader's surest way of coming to a critical and appreciative awareness of what shape the text is attempting to impose on his or her worldview.

7. Biblical Hebrew style also uses verbal, syntactic, and semantic clues to separate and conjoin adjacent literary units. These devices are all drawn from elements present in the aural fabric of the text; that is, they are perceptible to a hearer of oral performance. This points to their origin in oral literature.[1] They supply clues the audience needs to rec-

---

[1] See H. Van Dyke Parunak, "Oral Typesetting," *Bib* 62 (1981) 153–68. Whether the Masoretic cantillation marks are to be understood as aurally perceptible is uncertain. However, they are almost certainly centuries later than the verbal text.

ognize the structural organization of a text, which is, in turn, an essential indicator of thematic organization. By contrast, Western literatures depend heavily on visual and typographical marks of disjunction and conjunction: punctuation, paragraph indentations, blank lines, section and chapter divisions and headings, and the like. Translators ought to analyze the Hebrew text carefully to discern its inherent structure before choosing how to render the Hebrew conjunctive and disjunctive devices into Western typographical analogues.

SELECTED BIBLIOGRAPHY

Alter, Robert. *The Art of Biblical Narrative.* New York: Basic Books, 1981.

Auffret, Pierre. *La Sagesse a bâti sa maison.* Fribourg: Editions Universitaires, 1982.

Avishur, Yitshak. *Stylistic Studies of Word-Pairs in Biblical and Ancient Semitic Literatures.* Alter Orient und Altes Testament: Veröffentlichungen zur Kultur und Geschichte des Alten Orients und des Alten Testaments 210. Kevelaer: Butzon & Bercker; Neukirchen-Vluyn: Neukirchener Verlag, 1984.

Bar-Efrat, Shimon. *Narrative Art in the Bible.* JSOTSup 70; Bible and Literature 17. Sheffield: Almond, 1989.

_____. "Some Observations on the Analysis of Structure in Biblical Narrative," *VT* 30 (1980) 154–73.

Barré, Lloyd M. *The Rhetoric of Political Persuasion: The Narrative Artistry and Political Intentions of 2 Kings 9–11.* CBQMS 20. Washington, D.C.: Catholic Biblical Association of America, 1988.

Bengel, Johann Albrecht. *Gnomon Novi Testamenti: in quo ex natura verborum vi simplicitas, profunditas, concinnitas, salubritas sensuum coelestium indicatur.* Tübingen: Io. Henri Philippi Schranii, 1742. Cited in Nils W. Lund, "The Presence of Chiasmus in the Old Testament," *AJSL* 46 (1930) 104, and in Roland Meynet, *Rhetorical Analysis: An Introduction to Biblical Rhetoric.* JSOTSup 256. Sheffield: Sheffield Academic Press, 1998.

Bergen, Robert D., ed. *Biblical Hebrew and Discourse Linguistics.* Dallas: Summer Institute of Linguistics, 1994.

Berlin, Adele. *Poetics and Interpretation in Biblical Narrative.* Bible and Literature 9. Sheffield: Almond, 1983.

Bertman, Stephen. "Symmetrical Design in the Book of Ruth," *JBL* 84 (1965) 165–68.

Boda, Mark J. "Chiasmus in Ubiquity: Symmetrical Mirages in Nehemiah 9," *JSOT* 71 (1996) 55–70.

Boys, Thomas. *A Key to the Psalms.* London: L. B. Seely & Sons, 1825.

Bullinger, Ethelbert William. *Figures of Speech Used in the Bible Explained and Illustrated.* London: Eyre and Spottiswoode, 1898; reprint Grand Rapids: Baker Book House, 1975. Bullinger's work was incorporated into an edition of the Authorized Version known as "The Companion Bible." This edition was reissued by Kregel Publications (Grand Rapids) in 1990.

Butterworth, Mike. *Structure and the Book of Zechariah.* JSOTSup 130. Sheffield: JSOT Press, 1992.

Clark, David J. "Criteria for Identifying Chiasm," *LB* 35 (1975) 63–72.

Dahood, Mitchell. "Ugaritic-Hebrew Parallel Pairs," in Loren R. Fisher, ed., *Ras Shamra Parallels: The Texts from Ugarit and the Hebrew Bible.* 3 vols. AnOr 49–51. Rome: Pontifical Biblical Institute, 1972–1981. 1:71–382; 2:1–39; 3:1–206.

Davies, Gordon F. *Ezra and Nehemiah.* Berit Olam. Collegeville: The Liturgical Press, 1999.

Dawson, David Allan. *Text Linguistics and Biblical Hebrew.* JSOTSup 177. Sheffield: JSOT Press, 1994.

Dorsey, David A. *The Literary Structure of the Old Testament: A Commentary on Genesis–Malachi.* Grand Rapids: Baker Book House, 1999.

Emerton, John Adney. "An Examination of Some Attempts to Defend the Unity of the Flood Narrative in Genesis," *VT* 37 (1987) 401–20; 38 (1988) 1–21.

Fishbane, Michael. "Composition and Structure in the Jacob Cycle (Gen. 25:19–35:22)," *JJS* 26 (1975) 15–38.

_____. *Text and Texture: Close Readings of Selected Biblical Texts.* New York: Schocken, 1979.

Fokkelman, J. P. *Narrative Art and Poetry in the Books of Samuel: A Full Interpretation Based on Stylistic and Structural Analyses. Vol. 2: The Crossing Fates.* SSN 20. Assen: Van Gorcum, 1986.

_____. *Narrative Art and Poetry in the Books of Samuel: A Full Interpretation Based on Stylistic and Structural Analyses. Vol. 4: Vow and Desire.* SSN 31. Assen: Van Gorcum, 1993.

_____. *Narrative Art in Genesis: Specimens of Stylistic and Structural Analysis.* SSN 17. Assen: Van Gorcum, 1975; 2d ed.; Biblical Seminar 12. Sheffield: JSOT Press, 1991.

Forbes, John. *The Symmetrical Structure of Scripture, or, The Principles of Scripture Parallelism Exemplified in an Analysis of the Decalogue, the Sermon on the Mount, and Other Passages of the Sacred Writings.* Edinburgh: T & T Clark, 1854.

Funk, Robert W. *The Poetics of Biblical Narrative.* FF: Literary Facets. Sonoma: Polebridge, 1988.

García-Treto, Francisco O. "The Fall of the House: A Carnivalesque Reading of 2 Kings 9 and 10," *JSOT* 46 (1990) 47–65.

Graham, M. Patrick. "Aspects of the Structure and Rhetoric of 2 Chronicles 25," in idem, et al., eds., *History and Interpretation: Essays in Honour of John H. Hayes.* JSOTSup 173. Sheffield: JSOT Press, 1993.

Gray, John. *I & II Kings.* OTL. 2d ed. Philadelphia: Fortress, 1970.

Jebb, John. *Sacred Literature.* London: T. Caldwell and W. Davies, 1820.

Josipovici, Gabriel. *The Book of God: A Response to the Bible.* New Haven: Yale University Press, 1988.

Kikawada, Isaac M. "The Shape of Genesis 11:1–9," in Jared J. Jackson and Martin Kessler, eds., *Rhetorical Criticism: Essays in Honor of James Muilenburg.* PTMS 1. Pittsburgh: Pickwick, 1974, 18–32.

Licht, Jacob. *Storytelling in the Bible.* Jerusalem: Magnes, 1978.

Longacre, Robert E. *Joseph: A Story of Divine Providence: A Text Theoretical and Textlinguistic Analysis of Genesis 37 and 39–48.* Winona Lake: Eisenbrauns, 1989.

_____. "*Weqatal* Forms in Biblical Hebrew Prose: A Discourse-modular Approach," in Robert D. Bergen, ed., *Biblical Hebrew and Discourse Linguistics.* Dallas: Summer Institute of Linguistics, 1994, 50–98.

Long, V. Philips. *The Reign and Rejection of King Saul: A Case for Literary and Theological Coherence.* SBLDS 118. Atlanta: Scholars, 1989.

Lund, Nils W. *Chiasmus in the New Testament: A Study in Formgeschichte.* Chapel Hill: University of North Carolina Press, 1942; repr. Peabody, Mass.: Hendrickson, 1992.

_____. "Chiasmus in the Psalms," *AJSL* 49 (1933) 281–312.

_____. "The Presence of Chiasmus in the Old Testament," *AJSL* 46 (1930) 104.

Magonet, Jonathan. *Form and Meaning: Studies in Literary Techniques in the Book of Jonah.* 2d ed.; Bible and Literature 8. Sheffield: Almond, 1983.

McCarthy, Dennis J. "The Inauguration of Monarchy in Israel," *Int* 27 (1973) 401–12.

Mead, James K. "Kings and Prophets, Donkeys and Lions: Dramatic Shape and Deuteronomistic Rhetoric in 1 Kings xiii," *VT* 49 (1999) 191–205.

Meier, Samuel A. *Speaking of Speaking: Marking Direct Discourse in the Hebrew Bible.* VTSup 46. Leiden: E. J. Brill, 1992.

Meynet, Roland. *Rhetorical Analysis: An Introduction to Biblical Rhetoric.* JSOTSup 256. Sheffield: Sheffield Academic Press, 1998.

Milgrom, Jacob. *Numbers.* The JPS Torah Commentary. Philadelphia: Jewish Publication Society, 1990.

Muilenburg, James. "Form Criticism and Beyond," *JBL* 88 (1969) 1–18.

Niccacci, Alviero. *Lettura sintattica della prosa ebraico-biblica: Principi e applicazioni.* Studium Biblicum Franciscanum Analecta 31. Jerusalem: Franciscan Printing Press, 1991.

_____. *Sintassi del verbo ebraico nella prosa biblica classica.* Studium Biblicum Franciscanum Analecta 23. Jerusalem: Franciscan Printing Press, 1986. Revised English ed.: *The Syntax of the Verb in Classical Hebrew Prose.* Translated by W. G. E. Watson. JSOTSup 86. Sheffield: JSOT Press, 1990.

Parunak, H. Van Dyke. "Oral Typesetting," *Bib* 62 (1981) 153–68.

_____. "Some Axioms for Literary Architecture," *Semitics* 8 (1982) 1–16.

_____. "Transitional Techniques in the Bible," *JBL* 102 (1983) 525–48.

Pesch, Rudolf. "Zur konzentrischen Struktur von Jona 1," *Bib* 47 (1966) 577–81.

Porten, Bezalel. "The Structure and Theme of the Solomon Narrative (1 Kings 3–11)," *HUCA* 38 (1967) 93–128.

Radday, Yehuda T. "Chiasmus in Hebrew Biblical Narrative," in John W. Welch, ed., *Chiasmus in Antiquity: Structures, Analyses, Exegesis.* Hildesheim: Gerstenberg, 1981, 50–117.

Rendsburg, Gary A. "The Guilty Party in 1 Kings iii 16-28," *VT* 48 (1998) 534–41.

_____. *The Redaction of Genesis.* Winona Lake: Eisenbrauns, 1986.

Revell, Ernest John. "The Battle with Benjamin (Judges xx 29-48) and Hebrew Narrative Techniques," *VT* 35 (1985) 417–33.

_____. "The Repetition of Introductions to Speech as a Feature of Biblical Hebrew," *VT* 47 (1997) 91–110.

Savran, George W. "1 and 2 Kings," in Robert Alter and Frank Kermode, eds., *The Literary Guide to the Bible*. Cambridge, Mass.: Harvard University Press, 1987, 146–64.

_____. *Telling and Retelling: Quotation in Biblical Narrative*. Indiana Studies in Biblical Literature. Bloomington, Ind.: Indiana University Press, 1988.

Sternberg, Meir. *The Poetics of Biblical Narrative: Ideological Literature and the Drama of Reading*. Indiana Studies in Biblical Literature. Bloomington, Ind.: Indiana University Press, 1987.

Sutherland, Dixon. "The Organization of the Promise Narratives," *ZAW* 95 (1983) 337–43.

Trible, Phyllis. *Rhetorical Criticism: Context, Method, and the Book of Jonah*. GBS.OT. Minneapolis: Fortress, 1994.

Tsevat, Matitiahu. "The Biblical Account of the Foundation of the Monarchy in Israel," in idem, *The Meaning of the Book of Job and Other Biblical Studies: Essays on the Literature and Religion of the Hebrew Bible*. New York: Ktav; Dallas: IJS, 1980, 77–99.

Walsh, Jerome T. *1 Kings*. Berit Olam. Collegeville: The Liturgical Press, 1996.

_____. "The Contexts of 1 Kings xiii," *VT* 39 (1989) 355–70.

_____. "From Egypt to Moab: A Source Critical Analysis of the Wilderness Itinerary," *CBQ* 39 (1977) 20–33.

_____. "Genesis 2:4b–3:24: A Synchronic Approach," *JBL* 96 (1977) 161–77.

_____. "Methods and Meanings: Multiple Studies of 1 Kings 21," *JBL* 111 (1992) 193–211.

_____. "Symmetry and the Sin of Solomon," *Shofar* 12 (1993) 11–27.

Watson, W. G. E. "Chiastic Patterns in Biblical Hebrew Poetry," in John W. Welch, ed., *Chiasmus in Antiquity: Structures, Analyses, Exegesis*. Hildesheim: Gerstenberg, 1981, 118–68.

Welch, John W. "Chiasmus in the New Testament," in idem, ed., *Chiasmus in Antiquity: Structures, Analyses, Exegesis*. Hildesheim: Gerstenberg, 1981, 211–49.

Wenham, Gordon J. "Method in Pentateuchal Source Criticism," *VT* 41 (1991) 84–109.

Williamson, Hugh G. M. "'We are Yours, O David': The Setting and Purpose of 1 Chronicles xii 1-23," *OtSt* 21 (1981) 164–76.

Wilson, Victor M. *Divine Symmetries: The Art of Biblical Rhetoric*. Lanham, Md.: University Press of America, 1997.

Zevit, Ziony. *The Anterior Construction in Classical Hebrew*. SBLMS 50. Atlanta: Scholars, 1998.

AUTHOR INDEX

Alter, Robert, 7, 137
Auffret, Pierre, 21
Avishur, Yitshak, 9

Bar-Efrat, Shimon, 7, 146–47
Barré, Lloyd M., 44
Bengel, J. A., 8
Bergen, Robert D., 117
Berlin, Adele, 7
Bertman, Stephen, 88
Boys, Thomas, 8, 16, 27
Bullinger, E. W., 8

Cassuto, Umberto, 89

Dahood, Mitchell, 9
Davies, Gordon F., 183
Dawson, David Allan, 117
Dorsey, David A., 8

Fishbane, Michael, 31–32
Fokkelman, J. P., 16, 27–28, 50, 54, 65, 94
Forbes, John, 8, 16, 27

García-Treto, Francisco O., 44
Graham, M. Patrick, 20
Gray, John, 43

Jebb, John, 8
Josipovici, Gabriel, 37

Kikawada, Isaac M., 94

Licht, Jacob, 7
Long, V. Philips, 54

Longacre, Robert E., 117, 157
Lund, Nils W., 8, 16, 27

Magonet, Jonathan, 19
McCarthy, Dennis J., 54
Mead, James K., 179
Meier, Samuel A., 117, 147
Meynet, Roland, 8
Milgrom, Jacob, 15

Niccacci, Alviero, 117, 157

Parunak, H. Van Dyke, 2, 7, 58–60, 76, 175–77, 192
Pesch, Rudolf, 18
Porten, Bezalel, 84

Radday, Yehuda T., 16, 24
Rendsburg, Gary A., 32, 89, 111, 142
Revell, E. J., 117, 147, 157

Savran, George W., 23, 125
Sternberg, Meir, 7
Sutherland, Dixon, 89

Tishler, K., 105
Trible, Phyllis, 18
Tsevat, Matitiahu, 54

Walsh, Jerome T., 21, 24, 26, 84, 93, 113, 135, 141, 179, 182
Wenham, Gordon J., 181
Williamson, H. G. M., 30
Wilson, Victor, 8

Zevit, Ziony, 158

SUBJECT INDEX

Note: bold-face page numbers indicate more substantive treatments of the subject.

Acrostic psalms: 7, 36

Aside: *see* Breaking frame

Asymmetry: 8, 60, **101–03**, 191–92; examples: 52, 76–77, **103–14**
  non-correspondence, examples: 105–06, **107–10**, 132, 136
  transposition, examples: **110–14**
  unmatched subunit, examples: **103–07**, 109–10, 127, 132, 142, 153, 167

Breaking frame: 125, 166; examples: 125, 165, 168–69

Characters (change in): 120–21; examples: **125–31**, 133–38, 140, 149–51, 160–61, 182

Departure notice: 122; examples: 127–28, 130, 132–35, 137, 139, 160, 163–66
  See also Locale (change in)

Epitome: **59–60**
  concluding, examples: 54, **78–79**, 96
  introductory, examples: **76–78**, 171

Flashback: 123–24, 139; examples: 127, 140, 162, 165–66, 170–71
  See also Time (change in)

Foreshadowing: 124, 139, 162; examples: 163, 169, 171, 184, 186
  See also Time (change in)

Frame verses: *see* Inclusion, framing

Hinges: 177; examples: 126, 134, 152, **186–90**

Inclusion: 47, **57–59**
  complex, examples: **73–75**, 76, 79 188
  external, examples: **69–73**, 127, 133, 147
  framing: 47, 122; examples: 40–41, **64–69**, 76, 85–86, 88, 125, 132, 171, 179
  internal, examples: 39, **60–64**, 78, 82, 88–90, 95, 135–36, 172, 187

Interpretation: 2, 8, 11, 14, 36–37, 47–48, 59–60, 81–82, 102–03, 192

Length (of subunits): 11, 101; examples: 99, 108–10

Leprosy: 15

Links: 176; examples: 178, **182–84**

Linked threads: 176–77; examples: 178, **184–86**, 190

Locale (change in): 122; examples: 128, 130–31, **132–35**, 137–38, 149–51, 170
  See also Departure notice

Narrative sequence: 9, 118, 139, **155–59**
  breaks in: 157–59; examples: 97, 126–27, 129–30, 138, 140, **160–62**, **162–65**, **166–72**, 182

Narrative voice (change in): 119, 121, 124–25, 145; examples: 129–30, 136–37, **140–43**, 148, 168

Numerical psalms: 7

Paronomasia: 9, 191; examples: 33, 39, 61, 68, 91–92, 94–95, 103–04, 106, 163, 182, 186–87

Poetry, biblical: 7–8, 10, 36, 41, 105–06, 135, 137, 152, 187

Prolepsis: *see* Foreshadowing

Repetition: **7–10**, 118, 175–76
  alternating: 35, **47–48**, 192; examples: 41, **48–56**, 63–64, 82, 87, 95, 99, 149, 151–52, 161, 170–71
  conceptual: *see* Repetition, thematic
  immediate: 35–36; examples: 96–97, 99
  phonemic: 8, 10, 175; examples: 15, 26–27, 37, 49–50, 186–87
  resumptive: 59, 70, 84
  thematic: 9–10, 60, 175; examples: 16, 18, 21–24, 28–29, 43–45, 54–56, 66
  unnecessary: 145–47
    of information: examples: **147–50**
    of introductions to speech: examples: 136–37, 142, **152–53**
    of subject nouns: examples: 135, 138, **150–52**, 167, 172
  See also Word pairs; Paronomasia

Setting: *see* Locale (change of); Time (change of)

Structures, symmetrical (as conjunctive device): 175–77

Symmetry: 7–8, 191
  chiastic: **13–14**; examples: **26–34**, 40–41, 63, 66–68, 71–73, 76, 79, 82–83, 85–94, 96–97, 99, 106, 141–43, 161, 163, 166, 168–71, 179–80, 187–88
  complex: 81; examples: 84–85, 87, **88–93**, 168–69
  composite: 81; examples: **82–87**, 179–80
  compound: 36, 81; examples: **94–99**, 179–80
  concentric: **13–14**, 47; examples: **15–26**, 48–49, 72–73, 83–85, 98, 107–08, 128, 151, 190
  envelope: *see* Symmetry, reverse
  forward: 35–36, 192
  immediate repetition:
    see Repetition, immediate
  multiple: **81–82**
  parallel: **35–37**, 47; examples: **37–45**, 61–62, 65, 71–76, 84–85, 88–92, 95, 109, 111–12, 126–27, 132, 164, 167–69, 172, 179–80
  partial: *see* Inclusion; Epitome
  reverse: 13–14, 192
  See also Repetition, alternating; Repetition, immediate; Structures, symmetrical

Temporal construction: *see* Time (change of)

Tense, grammatical: 122–23, 155–57

Text linguistics: 117–18, 156–57

Threads: 176; examples: 98, **177–81**

Time (change in): 122–24; examples: 130, **135–40**, 161–62, 165
  See also Flashback; Foreshadowing

Translation: 1, 118, 123, 146, 156–59, 161, 191–93

Word pairs: 9–10; examples: 19, 39, 62, 65–66

Wordplay: *see* paronomasia

SCRIPTURE INDEX

Note: bold-face page numbers indicate more substantive treatments of the passage.

Genesis			6:7	145–46
1–11	**111–13**		6:11	28
1	**74, 162–63**		7:4	146
1:1-31	**37–38**		8:6	122
1:1	**37–38**		8:13	122
1:21-23	106		9:6a	**27–28**
1:25	178		10:1	**76**
1:26-28	37, **105–06**		10:21	76–77
2:1	**78**		11:1-9	**94–95**
2:18-25	**39–41**		11:27–22:24	58, **89–92**, 176
2:25; 3:1	**182**		12:1-9	50
2:25	**163**, 184		12:1	**49–50**
2:4	**187**		12:4	184
2:4b–3:24; 4:1-16	**177–78**		12:16b	**27**
2:4b–3:24	**21–23**		15:5	147
3:1	121, **160**		16:15-16	106
3:6-7	156–59		16:16; 17:1	**183–84**
3:7	163, 184		17:18-21	106
3:10-11	163		18–19	176, **180–81**
3:14-19	158–59		18	**133–34**
3:21	163		18:16, 22	**65**
3:22	133		18:17	**160**
4:1-2	123, 158, **161**		18:23-33	65
4:3	123, 158		19:1	133
4:8	122		19:4	65
4:17	158		21:1-7	**106–07**
4:25	178		21:6	92
5:1-5	178		21:10-11	106
5:29	178		21:25	**150**
5:32; 6:9-10	**147–48**		22	121

22:1-19	50		22:4	49
22:2	49		24	120
22:4	**139**			
23–25	138		*Judges*	
23:1–25:11	**187–88**		1:1	185
23:10a	**167–68**		8:33; 9:4	**183**
24	**135–38**		17–21	**179**
25:1	138		20:29-48	157
25:12–35:26	**31–34**, 58			
26:8	92		*Ruth*	
26:33-35; 27:1	**186–87**		1–4	**88–89**
27	137		1:1	185
29:1-12	137		1:14b	**166**
29:23	122		1:22	**184**
37–48	157		2:1–3:18	**129–31**
37:28	162		4:9-11a	**63–64**
37:36; 39:1	**70–71**			
37:36	162		*1 Samuel*	
39:1-6	**162**		1:12-13	**50**
41:46-57	120		7:15-17	54–55
41:47–42:5	**169–72**		8:1–12:25	**54–56**
49	120		12	120
			15:10-12, 34-35	**65–67**
Exodus			15:34	**163**
1:1-8	185		15:35	164
2:15-21	127		16:1-13	149
3:1	**160–61**		16:1	67
3:14-15	**78–79, 152–53**		16:14, 23	56
4:14-16	111		17:12a	**149–50**
5:4-5	**152**		21:10-15	103
6:10-13, 26-30	**71–73, 110–11**		22–23	30
20:5	98		25	120
			27:1–28:2	103
Leviticus			27	30
6:8-11 [Heb 6:1-4]	169			
24:13-23	**16–18**		*2 Samuel*	
36:13	185		2	30
			14:24, 28	**69–70**
Numbers			15:1-6	70
12:13	15		16:5	103
20:22–21:20	**135**		18:9	70
			18:18	**165**
Deuteronomy			18:33 [Heb 19:1]	145
32–33	120		22–23	120
			23:13-14	31
Joshua				
1:1	185		*1–2 Kings*	**23–25**, 185
7:26	125		regnal formulas	24, **74–75**, **184–85**
8:29	125			

1 Kings

1–11	**92–93, 178**
1–2	**186**
1:1–2:12a	**25–26**, 189
1	185
1:1-4	125
1:15-37	35–36, **128–29**
1:16, 23	189
1:24-27	**61**
1:28, 32-33	189
1:33-35	**15–16, 108**
1:38-40	16
1:44-46	16
1:53	189
2	120
2:1-10	**125–26**
2:12b, 46b	**64–65**
2:28-46	125
2:36-46a	**48–49**
2:38b, 41	**60**
2:39	**103, 138–39**
2:42	147
3:11-13	113
3:16–4:34;	
9:26–10:29	**113–14**
3:16-28	**141–43**
4:1-20, 21-25	**73–74**
4:32 [Heb 5:12]	13
5:1-12	
[Heb 5:15-26]	**82–84**
5:3-5	
[Heb 5:17-19]	69
6:1–9:10	**68–69**
6:9-36	**84–85**
9:25	69
11:1-8	**38–39**
11:11-13	41
11:26–14:20	190
11:26-43	**189–90**
11:31-39	**41–43, 108–10**
12:25	**184**
12:26	**150–51**
12:30-31; 13:33-34	**67–68**, 179
12:32-33	67
13	**179–80**
13:1-10	67, **168–69**
13:2	184

13:11-32	67
14:19, 29	75
17	**164–65**
17:3-6	145
18	107
18:1	**77**
18:3-4	**139–40**, 145
18:6-16	**134**
18:6b	**163–64**
18:9-14	**103–05**
18:12c-13	**140–41**, 145
18:20-29	121
18:21-40	**131**
19:14	**26–27**
19:15-16	30
20:12-15	51
20:16-21	**50–52**
20:34	124
20:43; 21:4	**182**
21	27
21:1-16	**28–29**
21:2-3, 6	145
21:20-26	**141**
21:22-24	45
22:6-12	121
22:28	146
22:28b	**153**

2 Kings

1	27, 108
2	24
2:1-25	107–08
2:15-24	121
2:15b	**188–89**
2:25; 3:1	**182–83**
2:25	**107–08**
3–9	29
3	108
4:38	107
6:1-7	121
7:3-11	**126–28**
8:7–9:13	**29–30**
8:18	44
8:26	44
8:28–9:2; 9:14-16	**148–49**
8:28-29	43
9:1-13	43–44

9:14–11:20	**43–45**		*Psalms*	
9:14–10:36	30, 43–44		119	7, 36
9:20	148			
10:12-17	**132**		*Proverbs*	
11:1-20	43		16:13, 21, 23	105
13:14-21	43		22:11	105
14:1-22	20		25:11	105
17:1	188		30:15-31	7
17:6-41	**52–54**			
17:6	**188**		*Song of Songs*	
17:24	188		2:10, 13	50
17:25-34a	**96–97**			
18:13	**139**		*Isaiah*	
18–20	**85–87**, **132–33**		6:5	111
21:19-26	**97–99**		39:1	87
22	184			
			Jeremiah	
1 Chronicles			35	132
10:14b	31			
11:1–12:41	**30–31**		*Lamentations*	
14:3b	**151–52**		1–4	7
			3	36
2 Chronicles				
25:1-28	**20–21**		*Jonah*	
			1	**18–20**
Ezra			1:4	**162**
3:13; 4:1	**183**		1:10b	**166–67**
Esther			*Micah*	
5:9-14	**61–62**		1:2	153